In Search of Reality

11/15/83

Bernard d'Espagnat

In Search
of Reality

Springer-Verlag
New York   Berlin   Heidelberg   Tokyo

Bernard d'Espagnat
Universite Paris XI
Laboratoire de Physique Theorique
  et Particules Elementaires
Centre d'Orsay
Batiment 211
F-91405 Orsay Cedex
France

Library of Congress Cataloging in Publication Data
Espagnat, Bernard d'.
  In search of reality.
  Translation of: A la recherche du réel.
  Bibliography: p.
  1. Science—Philosophy. I. Title.
Q175.E7313   1983   501   83-400

Typeset by Bi-Comp., Inc., York, PA.
Printed and bound by R. R. Donnelley & Sons, Harrisonburg, VA.

9 8 7 6 5 4 3 2 1

ISBN 0-387-**11399**-1 Springer-Verlag New York Berlin Heidelberg Tokyo
ISBN 3-540-**11399**-1 Springer-Verlag Berlin Heidelberg New York Tokyo

Preface

When I take up a new book I always read its conclusions first. For I have discovered that even difficult books have conclusions that are easy to read and that give a first idea of their content.

Of course, I expect my readers to do this also! Indeed, the present book offers them an opportunity for generalizing the method. After having gone over chapter 14 they should preferably look through chapters 5, 2, 13 and 10, or at least some of these (in this or in other orders), before engaging into any thorough reading. The point is that—at appropriate places in other chapters—the reader will find proofs; and, as we all know, all the proofs that are worth something are unavoidably ponderous. Of course, it is good to have them but, again, the most suitable procedure not to lose interest in their development is, I think, to first provisionally grant their conclusions, in order to see where they lead us to. Then, to study the proofs once we have been convinced that the goal is worth some effort. This is the reason why I suggest that at least chapters 4 and 11 should, on a first reading, be skipped, at any rate, by the "poets"!

The problem, a new approach of which is described in chapter 4, did not come to light, at least in its present form, before 1964. The first experimental investigations bearing on it date back from the seventies.

It was obviously quite impossible to do justice to the works of the many physicists who took an active interest in the subject. This is why they are not quoted in the text. Some extremely fragmentary bibliographical indications may be found at the end of the book. Their only purpose is to give the readers an opportunity of enlarging their information on the problem. Extensive reference to the relevant scientific papers may be found in reference 11.

Acknowledgments Professors J. S. Bell (CERN) and A. Shimony (Boston University) were kind enough to read preliminary drafts of chapters 4 and 12 of the first French edition. It is a pleasure to thank them here for their comments which proved extremely useful.

Contents

Contents

CHAPTER 1

Introduction

It is quite clear that experts in different disciplines of thought should communicate with each other more than they do. However, because human beings differ in their motivations, beliefs, and ways of thinking more than is apparent, it is always difficult to bridge the gaps between distinct fields. Incompatibilities between words and basic notions, differing conceptions of what strictness should consist of—these and other obstacles combine in making the task arduous indeed.

Above all, artificial associations of ideas must be banned. In this domain the only acceptable procedure is to patiently search for those sorts of links which naturally exist. After all, neither the mind nor the world is divided into compartments. Therefore, among the various fields of thinking, some relationships must exist. It suffices to discover them. Alas, even that is not an easy task! Brilliant general ideas are hardly useful for the purpose, owing to the fact that they are generally based on attractive *intuitions.* However, *science,* at least, develops its universality only by endlessly refining and generalizing its own principles, with the consequence that by now these principles are quite different from any *intuitive* idea. Such difficulties are presumably the origin of the fact that a strict partitioning, which is present neither in things nor in the mind, nevertheless governs our thought activities.

This book is the result of a long-term endeavor to overcome, as completely as possible, such obstacles in the path of thinking by making use of some factual knowledge. *Physics* and the *problem of reality* were taken as the starting point and as the central theme, respectively. These choices, of course, were not made arbitrarily. Beyond all practical, psychological, social, aesthetic, and moral questions, the problem of *what is* has always been considered by the author to be the central one, with which all the other questions must be linked in such a way that their answers depend on its solution. And, as regards physics, it seems quite clear that its present stage of development is sufficient to justify considering it to be the universal natural science—a science of that very "nature" that, apparently at least, it seems appropriate to identify with reality. Even though this latter view should be corrected to some extent—as will be seen—it is certainly quite a good working assumption.

To be sure, the problems of pure knowledge do not stand foremost in the *explicit* interests of present-day human beings. Those concerning practical life and, more generally, action, quite naturally gather the attention of the press and the mass media, which in turn take an ever growing part in shaping our explicit problematics. What is more, the properly philosophical idea that (human) Action is prior to Being has spread to such an extent, at least in an implicit vague form, that it underlies most written works. But in spite of that, it remains true that interest in the problems of pure knowledge and of pure understanding is still great. Indeed, its strength is increased by a certain disappointment that is now growing with regard to the many ideological or pragmatic variants of the philosophies centered on action. In this connection, many will consider as symptomatic the exclamation that Malraux, in one of his last books, attributed to an old revolutionary friend: "the so-often quoted words of Marx that 'the task is not just to understand the world but to change it' are beginning to plague me. Look here: what about giving up changing the world and trying just simply to understand it?"[1]

"Yes," some will say, "but it is still dubious that such an investigation should make use of physics; the argument that physics is the science of nature is far from convincing." It is quite true, of course, that people who are interested in the problem of understanding the nature of what *is* do not all worry about physics. In fact, some of them deny, right from the start, that physics, or indeed any other science, can ever get to know Being in itself. Others, for whom this is not the issue, conversely assert that physics only informs us about aspects of reality that are too elementary and too trivial to merit any attention: physics deals with the "plumbing of the universe," as stated by some who are mainly interested in qualitatively studying the most complex existing structures such as living beings and societies. And these are just examples of the very diverse standpoints that are taken on the subject.

Even if they are partly well grounded (and this still remains to be shown), such reservations are quite obviously insufficient to motivate a rejection of the present program. Some of them do, however, suggest that the study we intend to make, even though it is to be given an essentially scientific basis, cannot ignore the fundamental philosophical problems and pass over the solutions proposed by the philosophers—not of course that we need to make a tedious survey but rather that we should at least take into consideration those great philosophical intuitions on the problem of Being that are understandable to the scientist. This approach is in fact all the more necessary because such intuitions quite often resemble, contradict, or complement ideas which a study of the foundation of physics

---

[1] A. Malraux, *Hotes de Passage*, Gallimard. On the other hand, contemporary political events have proven to the intellectuals that principles for governing people that are explicitly based on *a priori* conceptions of reality easily lead to serious troubles!

leads to. In fact we should say even more, namely that the abilities and the imagination of the philosophers of the past enabled them to discover a considerable variety of possible conceptions. Consequently, what new material this book may contain should perhaps be less concerned with brand new ways of looking at things than with new and better ways of testing the validity of ideas already invented by great thinkers. In other words, it should essentially consist of new and more reliable procedures for making a choice between opposite philosophical views. With regard to the results, our undertaking should therefore not make the philosophers angry; indeed it should comfort them instead, even though the method employed—namely, the scientific method—may look peculiar to them in this domain. At any rate, it will give them the opportunity to moderate, if they choose, the harsh view that many of them have of science, which has been accused by philosophers of being exclusively prompted by an eagerness to dominate and to conquer, while philosophy would instead proceed from a pure longing for a candid understanding. Upon reading this book, it will perhaps become clearer that this is in no way the real difference between science and philosophy and that, on the contrary, the difference is to be found in the fact that science, while it is as eager as philosophy to understand, yields a more accurate knowledge of the difficulties of such a program, of the weakness of human reason applied to questions that go beyond usual practice, and of the slow pedestrian procedures that nevertheless make it possible to overcome all these obstacles, at least to an appreciable extent.

In truth, however, with regard to the knowledge of ultimate reality, one would be misguided to blindly trust the pure scientific method and to uncritically raise its results to the status of properties of Being. While physics is almost unerring in its *equations,* which scarcely meet with anything but successive improvements, making them suitable for the description of an ever-increasing diversity of phenomena, it must be granted that in its history, it has successively given rise to world views that have contradicted one another and that, therefore, can hardly be anything else than mere models. To be sure, such a criticism should not be taken as final, considering that science has arisen only in relatively recent times and that it has developed considerably during the past few decades. Nevertheless, it would be somewhat preposterous to unequivocally assert that any such model is a faithful description of what is. Here, therefore, such a procedure is not followed. To refine our naive ideas of reality, we shall test a certain set of apparently obvious assertions by deriving from them (*without* the help of any theory, hence *without* relying on any model) some consequences that in principle can be checked by measurements, and by ascertaining that some of the consequences contradict the experimental data. From this, we will conclude with certainty that at least one of the apparently obvious assertions in the set is false. (The set must of course include the assertion that a measurement result is real.) Then, but only then, will we take the liberty of extrapolating this result by reference to a universally accepted theory that predicts it and similar facts, and which in the field of the prediction of phenomena has proven beyond doubt its universal validity.

An objection of a general kind to this method which could be made *a priori* is that it starts from a very precise, and therefore extremely limited, set of facts while it results in highly general conclusions. This, it might be said, resembles a pyramid that rests on its point. On the other hand, it is unquestionably true that *one* counterexample, selected from *one* precise factual domain, suffices to ruin a general hypothesis if this counterexample is firmly based upon the data and if it is really contrary to the prediction that can be derived from the hypothesis. This is indeed one of the most valuable features of the scientific method. In the past, even quite wonderful intellectual constructions, which bore witness to the brilliant abstracting powers of their authors, frequently crumbled under the pressure of quite limited and quite unimpressive (but cleverly chosen) sets of facts that turned out to be inconsistent with the constructions. Moreover, the experimental facts alluded to here, while contrary to some intuitive assumptions about reality (and therefore forcing us to modify our views), are nevertheless correctly accounted for by *quantum mechanics,* that is, by a theory—or, more correctly, by a set of rules for calculation—which seems universal, which undoubtedly is extremely fruitful, and which is at the root of our present understanding of natural phenomena.

Under such conditions, it would have been admittedly possible to ground a description of the proposed changes concerning our conception of reality directly on the theory in question. This method was not chosen, in part because it turns out to be less strict in the long run than the one used here, and in part for so-called "pedagogic" reasons. Its use would have required an introductory description of some technical aspects of quantum mechanics; that is, it would have meant writing down long formulae and introducing a vast mathematical apparatus. The direct use of the facts alluded to above makes it possible to avoid this. As a matter of fact, the gain in simplicity here is great enough to open up the possibility of an argumentation understandable to the layman, since it calls for no prior knowledge, and that nevertheless constitutes a genuine *proof.* To be sure, this implies, as its unavoidable counterpart, the presence in the text of somewhat arduous passages and therefore of an unevenness in the general level of difficulty of this book. Thus, in spite of the vividness of the examples used in Chapter 4, which contains the proof in question, to be understood correctly, they must be read somewhat in the way in which, for example, a mathematician would read the works of one of his colleagues; that is, slowly and occasionally reviewing previous pages. But some chapters, on the other hand, can be read quite easily and quickly. This is due to the fortunate fact that not everything is esoteric! Things exist that are really quite essential but whose study can nevertheless be tackled without prerequisites because they concern problems with which everybody is familiar.

The formal drawback due to the unevenness just alluded to is—as one would expect—more than compensated for by the advantage that any *proof* gives to the reader, and which consists of course of the fact that the latter can pass a reasonable judgment on it. In other words, to know whether it is correct or faulty, the reader need only make use of his own intellect. Here, at least in the first stages, the reader must therefore rely on the author's assertions *only* with regard to *a few experimental data* unanimously considered to be correct by the community of physicists, whence the proof derives some interesting consequences. In a time like ours, in which so many conflicting doctrines are put forward to which our adherence is in most cases requested through purely emotional arguments (when it does not simply appeal to some deep-seated group orthodoxy), the advantage just mentioned is considerable. This advantage is worth seeking, even though the mass media as they now exist in Western societies tend to generate indifference toward it. Incidentally, it can also be noted that the approach thus summarized is in no way a return to the Cartesian method, since some measurement results play an essential role in it.

But—sober minds may ask—are you not luring us with unattainable prospects? Are you not overlooking the fact that this highly cumulative knowledge of physics is now far removed from its beginnings, that its reasonings are difficult, that they must necessarily make use of complex mathematical techniques, the description of which fills up many heavy books, that, at the university, at least five years are necessary in order to learn such methods? You, who apparently intend to tackle very basic— that is, very intricate—matters, are you not forgetting that "in physics practically no difficult problem remains whose statement would be simple," as Valéry wrote a long time ago? And are you not disregarding an extremely well-known fact, namely, that the problems you intend to tackle by means of your deductive method, allegedly within the comprehension of the ignorant intellect are nevertheless among those which the greatest scientists have been discussing for fifty years without being able to reach an agreement?

To be sure, this objection looks formidable. Its discussion calls for a short historical review. It is quite true that, about fifty years ago, a vast reexamination of the foundations of physics had to be undertaken by the physicists themselves. This need was due in part to the discovery of the theory of relativity, but even more to that of the new theory of the atom. Contrary to the old mechanics, this new theory—quantum mechanics, to call it by its proper name—was found to be capable of accounting for all the practically infinitely numerous facts concerning atoms and molecules. However, it had to give up the use of some seemingly basic notions, such as determinism, on which classical mechanics was grounded. It was also forced to give up the idea—elementary as it looks—that atoms and their constituent particles—electrons, protons, and neutrons (or quarks)— possess a reality that is completely independent of our means of observing it.

In the opinion of most physicists, the uselessness of such concepts (determinism, "intrinsic" reality of localized particles) and their continued fruitlessness, obviously mean that these allegedly basic concepts must finally be discarded. But in the minds of other physicists, the fact that these concepts are presently of no practical use does not entail such a radical conclusion. Hence, the latter physicists have strived to build up theories that would include the concepts in question and that, at the same time, could account at least as well as the presently accepted theory for the basic facts concerning atoms and molecules. Until quite recent times it looked as if—at least when questions of simplicity and practical efficiency were disregarded—such an undertaking was workable, at least in principle, without any substantial breach of the basic content—determinism, locality—of the conception whose reintroduction was being attempted. The theory would simply have had much added ponderousness and less generality. Admittedly such a situation generated controversies that could not help making use of highly technical arguments. Incidentally, at this stage it may be noted that many contemporary philosophical textbooks argue (with some apparent justification!) from such intricacies that physics seems hardly useful for clarifying the basic problems and that the wiser attitude is therefore to discard the scientific approach altogether and to tackle such problems with only the help of pure philosophy.

In the following chapters we shall do our best to disprove such an objection, in particular by providing clear-cut information on the advances that can be attributed, in this field, to the discussions between members of the two groups of physicists, and to the theoretical investigations they gave rise to. However, a systematic historical survey is out of the question. Many ideas that were studied failed to lead to any interesting results. Of course, such ideas are not described here. As a matter of fact, it is only during the last fifteen years that a substantial advance could be made in this difficult domain so far removed from the usual scientific problems. Now, strangely enough—and *this* is the answer to the objection described above—the advance in question, though originally made with the help of the mathematical apparatus normally pertaining to the field in question, turns out to be describable without any mathematical formalism whatsoever.

Is this merely a stroke of good luck? Maybe not. It could well be asserted that such a nontechnical nature was bound to be characteristic of a discovery whose bearing is, in fact, philosophical. At any rate, it is a fact. Here special attention is therefore given to that advance, the nature of which is described in Chapter 4. And this, of course, is done using a language that takes advantage of the possibility of a nontechnical description.

A last general remark is in order here. This simple and formula-free book is intended to be an introduction to the basic problems of physics. But that it should constitute an appropriate introduction to *research* in physics is out of the question. It is quite easy to understand why this is so.

As everybody knows, to teach any subject matter adequately it is neces- sary to possess a knowledge of the subject far exceeding what is actually to be conveyed. With regard to research, a very similar condition holds; in fact, it is even stronger. In other words, concerning in particular the physical and sometimes highly specialized problems alluded to in this book, it unfortunately seems quite impossible that any reader, bright as he may be, could conceivably contribute to their solutions unless he has previously made long, serious studies in modern theoretical physics that have brought him at least to the level of university post graduate courses. While it is unfortunate that such a limitation should exist, some degree of comfort may be found in its universality. ''To have to play the violin ten years to become not too bad a violinist, what a miserable being man is!'' The wisdom of such an exclamation (Musset, Fantasio) is unquestionably still very relevant. In compensation, it may be hoped that a perusal of this little book may be of help to readers who are considering the possibility of exploring more deeply the general problematics.

Finally, it should be pointed out that to the extent that such an investi- gation finally arrives at some definite conclusion, in the eyes of the author, it is essentially the conception of *veiled reality* introduced in Chapter 9 (page 94). The first portion of this book can be considered a detailed description of the maze of constraints that directs the mind toward that solution; the last portion investigates the content as well as the implica- tions of such a thesis.

CHAPTER 2

From Democritus to Pythagoras

The child and the man-in-the-street both believe that reality is as we see it. To them the notion of the existence of a given pebble or of a given chair is clear and obvious and they can hardly imagine questions being raised about them, even if they believe in fairy tales.

Quite early—as everybody knows—philosophers challenged that view. From the fact that objects decay, they inferred that objects do not possess an intrinsic reality. Reality, they said, is the opposite of dream, and is that which is permanent. What degree of reality can we attribute to things that arise and then die, that are made and that come undone? Underlying, within, or above them, *something* must exist, some absolute reality not immediately perceptible to man and the approach to which is therefore difficult.

Later, more elaborate arguments, such as, for example, Cartesian doubt, appeared to support this view, which, it must be added, is not the private property of philosophers. At such a level of generality ("knowledge of Being is difficult"), the view in question is also that of most religions. Moreover, it meets with an inborn poetical intuition of the existence of a deeper Reality hidden behind or beyond things; an intuition that the beholding of beauty may well induce in the minds of more people than might be guessed at first sight.

To assert that knowledge of independent reality (or of Being) is difficult obviously implies accepting—contrary to the views of some thinkers—the postulate according to which the very notion of reality has a meaning that in some way surpasses the knowledge of man. It does not yet imply a specification of the ways in which we can hope to approach it. To associate, in one way or another, this approach with the apprehension of beauty is already more definite, but still not completely so. Even if—explicitly or not—we choose the approach in question, two directions remain possible that conceivably supplement one another but that nevertheless are quite distinct. We can search for a better understanding of Being either through mathematics—pure or applied—or through perceptible beauty.

For a long time, the approach of Being through perceptible beauty was the avowed purpose of the poets. Nowadays this is no longer the case. The poets of today would never dare to candidly display a yearning that we intellectuals taught them to consider as too naive. This is regrettable, for we shall see that, after all, the naiveté of the old-time poets is less considerable than that of the modern literary rhetoricians, as well as that of the many scientists who—on the opposite side—presently labor under extremely naive delusions as to the meaning and the bearing of the concept of objectivity.

Nevertheless, the rejection of the old poetic vision is today unquestionable, so that we are left with the mathematical approach. We think at first of pure mathematics. Offhand indeed this science seems to constitute a set of noncontingent, universal, and eternal truths. It is not surprising that many thinkers saw, and still see, in it a manifestation of what is thoroughly permanent; or, in other words, of Being itself. However, discoveries made in this century have made such a conception seem somewhat naive; for they have brought out the fact that mathematics seems to mirror the operational abilities of human beings. I write "seems to" only because I think the possibility should not be ignored that some parallelism might exist between Being itself and the structure of human beings, a parallelism that might then be viewed as justifying, to some extent at least, the transcendency that has been attributed to mathematics for so long. But without entering into the details of questions whose analysis would necessitate extensive developments, I must at least point out that recent mathematical investigations have brought to a more reasonable level the exaggerated glamor that the notion of universal mathematical certainty enjoyed in the past.

If the beauty of pure mathematics does not by itself constitute an assured avenue towards Being, the mathematicians can still transfer their hopes to mathematical physics. Indeed, this is the conception that many of them immediately consider more natural. In the view of many contemporary scientists, mathematical physics (or theoretical physics, though a distinction between the two is unnecessary here) essentially aims at systematizing our knowledge of reality. The reason that led men to choose for that purpose the mathematical apparatus over any other was just that they progressively ascertained that it was, by far, the most appropriate for such a synthesis. Since the physicist who makes use of it must necessarily comply with the corresponding canons of mathematical wisdom, it is clear that the use of theoretical physics is indeed a way—and an *a priori* reasonable one—to approach reality under the guidance of beauty.

The fact that mathematical methods are more effective than any other with regard to the synthesis of the various aspects of reality has important consequences for the ways in which reality can be envisioned. For mathematics does not simply play the part of a kind of stenography, or, in other words, of a shorthand writing of relationships that, if more space and time were available, could just as well be formulated in usual everyday language. To be sure, it has such a role, but this role is secondary. Much more basic is the role played by the process of defining new entities. Let us think of the appearance of the concept of energy. At first we had a law of conservation internal to point mechanics; in other words, a purely abstract law, "the sum of the product of such and such quantities and of a function of such other quantities does not change with time." But today energy is a commodity that is bought and sold at high prices! In many cases, what happens is that, even without becoming concepts in common use, as was the case for energy, the abstract concepts elaborated by the theoretical physicists progressively take the place of the former ones—which sprung from ancestral experience—in the description of the world that physics sets forth. Such a process is simply due to the fact that the new concepts have a wider range than the old ones ("mass" is more general than "weight"; "energy" is more general still than "mass"). One of its consequences is a phenomenon that was sometimes somewhat improperly called a "derealization" of the physical world. The word is not free of ambiguity: "deobjectization" would be more accurate. For, in fact, at this stage it is not yet a matter of questioning the validity of the concept of a reality independent of human beings, but it *is* a matter of denying any validity to the concept of reality that is entertained by the man-in-the-street having some nodding acquaintance with science. We are here referring to the conception in which the familiar notions that in our eyes are obvious, such as those of particle (speck of dust) and of contact force, are *a priori* taken as being absolutely appropriate (and as being *the* only appropriate) elements of any description of ultimate reality.

Along these lines, a view of the world seems progressively to emerge, according to which the materiality of things is seen to dissolve into equations; a view in which materialism is forced more and more to conform to a kind of "mathematicism" and in which, if one may say so, Democritus must finally take refuge with Pythagoras. For, indeed, what is matter? "That which is conserved" was the old answer. Hence, matter is not mass, unless the latter is identified with energy. But, in, turn, energy is nothing other than the pure "immateriality" of a four-vector component defined in a space which, moreover, has a "curvature"! Or shall I identify the "matter" of an object with the set of all its "Democritian atoms"? The permanence of matter will then be that of these atoms; that is, of the particles that compose it. But things cannot be as simple as this, since particles can annihilate—together with "antiparticles"—and thereby transform into a mere acceleration of other particles already existing. Hence, the particles themselves are not conserved in all cases. To be sure, some numbers, some differences between numbers of particles and numbers of antiparticles, remain unchanged. But, again, these are merely abstract quantities. Conceived, at first, in order to describe a mere *property* of a set, that is, an entity distinct from the set (a collection of balls is something else, one used to think, than just the number of balls present in the collection), the *number* now appears in physics as the only entity with sufficient permanence to be taken seriously by the physicist.

It is a short step from this to the assertion of the Pythagoreans that numbers are the very substance of things. And it should be stressed that there can be no question here of an extenuated Pythagorism. Rather, an essential Pythagorism is called for, one that is definitely irreconcilable with the Democritian concept which asserts the stability of the ultimate particles. In other words, it is no longer possible to borrow from Democritus his basic conception of reality and to merely add to it that the "atoms" interact by means of forces obeying given equations and that the criterion of mathematical beauty is useful when we search for these equations. Such an attempt at reconciling Democritus and Pythagoras would not provide a solution, since, again, it seems that no localized indestructible "atom" exists, and since the only entities stable enough to allow physicists to regard them as basic are numbers, functions, or other even more abstract mathematical entities. "All is geometry," some experts readily shout.

It does not seem necessary to describe in more detail a conceptual development that took place some time ago and that is therefore rather well known. The discovery of antiprotons, and hence the certainty that annihilation and creation processes are completely general aspects of nature, dates back to the 1950s. These facts had been predicted long before by theorists, and everyone knows that it was in the elegance of the mathematical formalism that they found the most reliable guide to success. Therefore it is just as a reminder that I mentioned here a stage of physical thought that was quite essential but which, however, is not final: the stage that could be labelled the *emergence of Pythagorism* (provided, of course, any mystical or magical implication of the term is duly discarded). Having completed these essential preliminaries, we should now consider developments that are more recent and less well known, and that therefore are worthy of a detailed description.

CHAPTER 3

Philosophy of Experience

While materialism dates back to Democritus, positivism is much more recent. Still, even now there are some people who confuse the two or who, at least, consider materialism and positivism to be closely related. Such a misinterpretation must be corrected right away, for it would conceal the problems that we are about to study. To be sure, many scientists embraced materialism and many took up positivist standpoints. But a closer look at the matter shows that very few of them adopted both concepts, and the number of those who did grew smaller and smaller during the course of history.

The existence of several kinds of materialism makes that doctrine difficult to define. However, as a first approximation, we may link it with a more easily definable stream of thought that shall henceforth be called *realism* and that also includes nonmaterialistic systems such as Platonism (also called "realism of the essences"). According to realism, it is meaningful and correct to assert that a reality exists and that it is independent of the human mind. (In what follows, such a reality will be called "independent" or "intrinsic.") Moreover, according to this concept, the human mind can steadily increase its knowledge of reality. If realism is accepted, then it is natural to assume that the purpose of science is simply to contribute to that increase; and, indeed, in the opinion of the realist, and in particular of the materialist scientists, this is just what science aims at.

Positivism is an entirely different view, particularly in its modern forms which, to avoid rambling off into subtleties, I shall designate here by the generic name "philosophy of experience." Not that the philosophy of experience definitely denies the existence of independent reality, but, with more subtlety, it attributes to such a notion only a minor importance. According to positivism, most important is the obvious fact that what we can know is but the set of our observations and/or our actions.

As a rule, we tend to attribute a cause to our perceptions and, consequently, we have a natural tendency to conceive of an independent reality that would play the role of such a cause. The philosophy of experience does not claim that this standpoint is always necessarily erroneous, but it points out that such a conception is not a requirement of pure logic,[1] that it increases the risks of errors, and that the errors are difficult to predict beforehand. The history of science, and in particular that of physics, justifies in part such reservations, for it shows that much too often the ideas of permanence, of localization, and so on—which are quite difficult to separate from the very concept of physical reality—have led to unjustified extrapolations and that the latter were later found to be erroneous. For this reason the philosophy of experience asserts that systematically attributing the phenomena to an independent reality is a procedure that should not be viewed as a strictly scientific one. According to this philosophy, such an attribution is in many cases just an adornment of speech, an adornment which most often turns out to be harmless and which is even sometimes useful as an image—that is, for guiding imagination—but which, in the long run, may become harmful if it is raised to the level of an absolute prerequisite and which, anyhow, has nothing to do with the real purpose of science. As a matter of fact, this purpose is, in this conception, to systematize observations and to yield rules (most often mathematical ones) that on the basis of past observations make it possible to predict some of the results of experiments yet to be performed. Clearly, it is a long way from the basic ideas of the philosophy of experience to those of materialism, or even, more generally, of realism.

The philosophy of experience is, of course, closely linked with science. It is at the origin of a methodology whose considerable efficiency is due to the care with which it defines its basic concepts. In it the definitions always refer either to an equivalence class of possible operations or to other concepts whose meanings are defined in that way. However, the superiority of this methodology is manifest only in some fields of a particularly basic nature. In other fields of research it is quicker, and therefore more effective, to borrow the basic concepts of theory directly from common experience or, in other words, from everyday life. Therefore, the scientists who work in these fields—and they are by far the more numerous—naturally tend not to worry about the deep meaning of some basic concepts such as that of *object*. However, neglecting to call into question the meanings of a number of basic concepts necessarily amounts to implicitly accepting the uncritical realism that pervades everyday life. This is why these scientists usually consider the philosophy of experience to be merely a *method*. And this is also why these scientists feel there is no reason for this philosophy to reflect upon their basic conception, which remains a kind of objectivism, extending down to the microscopic scale and thus raising atoms, molecules, and so on to the level of absolute entities existing all by themselves. To reiterate, such is frequently the case

---

[1] It should be noted that for anyone who considers Kant's philosophy to be self-consistent, the mere existence of it suffices to create an alternative, for in that philosophy, causality is an *a priori* element of human understanding, which we *erroneously* attribute to things.

in fields of research that do not directly deal with phenomena on the atomic scale and in which, therefore, the liberty of viewing atoms and the smaller molecules as if they were just "black boxes" can be taken.

But, in fact, even among the experts in those basic sciences that are most directly concerned with such problems—theoretical physics in particular—the philosophy of experience is seldom unconditionally accepted. Again, many of these experts (and, to clear up any possible misunderstanding, let me say here that I share their views on this) are realists at heart. They are unwilling to consider science, as Paul Valéry did, as merely "the set of recipes that never fail." They believe that the everlasting success of a recipe must have a cause, and they attribute this success to the existence of a structured independent reality, whose very structure entails the success of the recipe. In the realist's view, the main interest of the discovery of a successful recipe lies, of course, in the fact that it informs us—or at least we hope it does—about the structures of independent reality.

However, a basic difficulty which is well-known to the philosophers appears at this stage. As long as I decide to remain within the realm of facts and to discard any hypothesis of any kind, I must admit that the information in question is *not* conveyed. The everlasting success of a recipe in fact merely apprises me of the validity of the recipe. To infer from it some indications as to the structures of reality, it seems necessary to introduce some additional postulates stipulating that "such a symbol, or such an operation, which is an element of the recipe, corresponds to an element of reality."

When I deal with *simple* recipes, such as "to observe a uniformly accelerated motion in the vicinity of the Earth, it is sufficient to drop a ponderous object in a vacuum," this is precisely what I implicitly do. I say, for example, "the object is real," it would exist at any time, it is in a well-defined position which it would be in even if it were not observed. Or, more correctly, I envision these propositions without making them explicit, since I feel so strongly that they are matters of course. But if I become aware of the fact that I make such assumptions, then I discover both a lesson and a warning, for I cannot help but notice that almost unavoidably the concepts that I tend to bring to the level of "elements of reality" are the most *familiar* concepts (object, position, time). Again, this is the weakness of realism. It is at this point that it may give way. As a matter of fact, modern physics provides us with spectacular examples of mistakes that were due to the tendency in question; mistakes that constitute so many arguments in favor of the philosophy of experience.

As everybody knows, the advent of relativity theory is one of these remarkable examples. In fact the basic equations of relativistic mechanics were already available before Einstein entered the scene. The works of Poincaré and Lorentz had been quite conclusive in that respect. But both of these authors remained captive to the concepts of absolute space and of universal time, which are concepts borrowed from everyday life (and, of

course, suitably refined). It was by proving that it is impossible to operationally define in a unique way the simultaneity of distant events that Einstein carried through the crucial step. More precisely still, final success
was achieved only when Einstein dared to say "such an operational definition is impossible, *hence* the very notion of distant simultaneity can be
merely a relative one."

But quantum mechanics—which was discovered soon after relativity—provides the upholders of the philosophy of experience with
arguments of still greater weight. There are two reasons for this. One is
quite elementary: it is that the quantum principles are even more basic
than those of relativity.[2] They control not only the physics of atoms but
all of chemistry—and thus, in principle, at least a good part of biology—
solid state physics, contemporary optics, nuclear physics, and so on; in
short, the bulk of the exact empirical sciences.

The second reason is that the ordering "experimental data rank first,
elements of reality rank second" plays, in quantum physics, a role that is
even more decisive than the one it plays in relativity.

Such an assertion can be justified on the basis of actual facts. Let us,
for example, consider a photoelectric cell, or better still, a "track
chamber," that is, a kind of photoelectric cell filled with a transparent
medium.[3] If a low-intensity plane ultraviolet electromagnetic wave
traverses such a chamber, we observe that the existence of that wave—
the energy of which we could have thought was *distributed* uniformly in
the entire volume of the chamber—becomes apparent only at one point in
that volume. It does so just by stripping off one electron from one atom of
the medium, and, in appropriate cases, that electron takes up all the
energy of the wave contained in the chamber.

In view of such a fact, an attractive hypothesis is of course to assume
that within any electromagnetic wave some particles of light (photons)
exist at any time and are all, at any time, well-localized, and that, as a
rule, these particles are guided by the wave (this would account for the
interference phenomena), but that they may also undergo individual colli-
sions with the electrons of the medium. It would then seem natural to
extend such a view to the so-called "matter waves," which then would
also be assumed to guide some permanently localized particles.[4]

Unfortunately, such a scheme is most certainly too naive, for it entails
some consequences that turn out to be contrary to facts. It is then possible

---

[2] It is ludicrous to consider that a knowledge of the *existence* of relativity theory should be
a part of our general culture (at more or less the same level as the knowledge of the existence
of the pyramids!) and that a knowledge of the existence of quantum mechanics should not be
a part of the same general culture. It is absurd that on the part of, say, a banker, it should be
shameful not to have heard of the former, but good form to be unaware of the latter. This fact
alone would suffice to discredit the selection processes that govern the elaboration of modern
general culture.

[3] Track chambers are used for many purposes. Here we consider only one of them, with
respect to which these chambers are comparable to photoelectric cells.

[4] This is the starting point of Louis de Broglie's "theory of pilot waves."

either to discard it altogether or to make the theory more elaborate while
retaining its main idea, which is that a knowledge of the wave does not by
itself yield a complete description of the whole system (for example,
within the foregoing model, one and the same wave could guide a particle
whose trajectory could be any straight line parallel to the direction of
travel). The second possibility is often referred to as the conception according to which there exists "hidden parameters"[5], namely, the parameters whose values must be specified, in addition to the wave, in order to
describe the state of motion of the system. An appreciable number of
physicists—including famous ones such as Einstein and Louis de
Broglie—chose the second possibility,[6] whose main advantage is that it is
both realistic and conceptually very clear. However, one fact must be
pointed out: when that possibility is worked out, the resulting equations
are of an extreme complexity, and, moreover, the theories thus built up
have never yielded—in more than fifty years—any observable prediction
beyond those that had already been furnished by the mathematically much
simpler theories that involve no hidden parameters.

   The present day fruitlessness of the hidden-parameters theories is undeniable. This is an argument in favor of the philosophy of experience that
is put forward by physicists most often. Again, an unconditional supporter
of that philosophy merely expects from science that it yield the best
recipes for calculating predictions about phenomena. Since he does not
even try to imagine any underlying reality, he is at liberty to deny that
hidden parameters exist. Nay, he *should* even deny this, since the parameters contribute nothing to his technical predictive procedures.[7] It then
turns out that by means of a purely mathematical description of the
wave—conceived of as being just an element in a prediction program—he
can calculate relatively easily many physical and chemical properties of
atoms and molecules that no other theory can yield.

   Does this mean that "the wave is real"? It can rather easily be shown
that to assume the validity of such a statement (taking the word real in its
naive sense) would again lead to difficulties with regard to the interpretation of the observed phenomena. But, in the eyes of an unconditional
upholder of the philosophy of experience, it would also amount to reintroducing "through the back door" that very concept of reality that,
according to him, is unclear and of which science can make no use. Finally
what exclusively matters to him is that a mathematical description of the
wave makes it possible to predict (statistically at least) the results of

---

[5] The theory thus obtained incorporates, in a subtle way, some action at a distance;
therefore, it is said that the hidden parameters are *nonlocal*.

[6] But without noting the nonlocality of the hidden parameters, which is implied by the
nonseparability property, on which more is said below.

[7] For instance, in the example described above, it was never possible to predict beforehand in what part of the track the stripping of the electron would take place. For such a
purpose, the hidden-parameters theories are just as ineffective as the conventional theory.
This is the reason why it is said that these parameters are either "hidden" or nonexistent.

future measurements on the basis of a knowledge of the results of previously made measurements. And conventional quantum theory—without any hidden parameters—is remarkably effective for this purpose.

3.1 The Copenhagen Interpretation

This, very briefly sketched, is the justification of the support that, mainly throughout the last fifty years or so, the theoretical physicists have constantly given to the philosophy of experience. Moreover, it has been more than passive support. What I mean is that the theorists did not just learn the philosophy in the appropriate textbooks and apply it to their problems. Some of the most prominent among them took part themselves in its elaboration and appreciably remodelled, modified, and refined it so as to adapt it as well as possible to the needs of contemporary physics. This was essentially the case with Niels Bohr, one of the main authors of what is conventionally called "the Copenhagen interpretation." The bearing of this author's ideas has been so considerable that it is necessary to give at least a broad view of them here. Indeed, the fundamentals of the Copenhagen interpretation were, until quite recently, accepted unreservedly by almost all physicists.

Bohr's starting point is a conception of science which—as may easily be guessed—does not define it in terms of a given intrinsic reality that it would purport to describe. In fact, in Bohr's writings, science appears to be essentially a collective endeavor at unambiguous communication among men, a communication concerning "what we did and what we have learned." In other words, science to him seems to be a synthesis of *that* part of human experience that is communicable to any human being. In his view the concept of reality is secondary to such an objective, and I believe that he perhaps would have preferred not to have to make use of that concept. When a discussion forces him to introduce that word, reality, in his writings, it always appears as a mere construct, as a general label that covers a great many *phenomena*. And in the attempts to bring it to the level of an absolute entity, he undoubtedly beheld serious dangers of unjustified extrapolation.

But then, some will say, Bohr was philosophically an idealist.

Such a view is too simplistic and Bohr would undoubtedly have rejected it. The reason why it is too expeditious is the existence of an intermediate level that Bohr introduces between atom and man that I have not mentioned yet. This is in fact simply the measuring instrument. Bohr considers, it seems, as clear and distinct the notion of the reality of instruments. At any rate, with regard to them, he takes for granted a view that he does *not* accept with regard to electrons or atoms. He takes it for granted that an instrument, even when it is *not observed*, always is in a well-defined state, occupying a well-defined portion of space. In the eyes of his numerous nonidealist followers, this would suffice to clear him of the sin of idealism. Let us not enter into such a debate here, except to observe that a word such as "idealism" would presumably have been criticized by Bohr as an imprecise and unjustified generalization. Nevertheless, it remains true that according to this author (this is quite clear in some of his writings),[8] the measuring instrument is mainly defined *as such*. In other words, it is defined not just with reference to its composition and structure, but also with reference to the fact that it is *used as an instrument* by members of the community of human beings. Hence, since Bohr defines reality with reference to the phenomena, the phenomena with reference to instruments, and the instruments with reference to their use by the community of human beings, it is quite clear that ultimately his notion of reality refers to human beings.

A consequence of the importance ascribed by Bohr to the instruments is that, according to him, no phenomenon can be described in a nonambiguous way except when a description is given of the complete experimental arrangement used for its study. Indeed, it should even be said that the experimental set-up is part of the phenomenon. For example, the travelling of a particle in free space is not, by itself, a phenomenon. The system composed of the emitting device, the particle, the medium, and a measuring device (the localization and, if necessary, the direction of which is specified), *that*, according to Bohr, defines the type of *phenomena* on which physics can make nonambiguous assertions. As L. Rosenfeld wrote, "it is now the indivisible whole constituted by the system and the instruments of observation that defines the phenomenon."[9]

A straightforward consequence of these views is that, quite properly speaking (and contrary to intuition), a particle does not by itself have any such property as position, velocity, and so on (it still can possess generic properties, such as mass, that are common to all those of a given type, but that is quite another matter). Such an absence of intrinsic properties is quite basic to the theory studied here, for with its help Bohr can account for the well-known apparent "paradoxes" of quantum mechanics (e.g., Young's two-slit experiment).[10] Indeed, these "paradoxes" are really

---

[8] And less clear in some other writings of his! Bohr's ideas are not always easy to grasp, with the consequence that his exegetes do not always agree with one another.

[9] In *Louis de Broglie, Physicien et Penseur*, Albin Michel, Paris, 1953.

[10] In Young's two-slit experiment, a beam of particles—of photons, for example—impinges on a diaphragm in which two slits are cut. A "diffraction pattern," that is, an alternation of light and dark areas, then appears on a screen placed beyond the diaphragm. This diffraction pattern disappears when either of the slits is shut. This fact is quite difficult to explain when it is assumed that each particle has, at any time, a well-defined position, for each particle then necessarily passes through only one slit, and the pattern observed on the screen when the two slits are open should therefore be a mere superposition of those that are observed when either one is open. This holds unless the assumption is made that the trajectory of a particle that goes through one open slit is in some way influenced by the fact that the other slit is open or shut, an assumption that seems extremely unlikely in the realm of conventional physics.

such only when it is claimed that a particle must at any time have at least *some* properties (position, velocity, etc.) that are its own.

"Man is the measure of all things," Protagoras said a long time ago. Like many other lapidary sayings of philosophers of the past, this one is somewhat ambiguous. It can be understood as an expression of radical idealism: man *is*, and things are just inventions of his. If the philosophy of experience finally reduces to such a concept, then there is no reality outside and above phenomena, each one of the latter being defined by means of a set of observation devices which, incidentally, can in some cases (and we shall return to such a strange *indivisibility*) be extended over vast distances in space. Protagoras' statement can also be understood to mean that things and their "measures" (in particular, their relative positions in space) are the only schemes that (because of the structure of our brain and mind) we can form of an intrinsic reality whose existence is unquestioned but which is in fact composed differently. We would then somewhat resemble a man forced to wear blue spectacles all the time, and who therefore would enjoy only monochromatic sights, while the world, in fact, is multicolored. If the philosophy of experience is understood this way, then the indivisibility mentioned above could be interpreted to mean that the reality we here call "intrinsic" is structured otherwise than in space–time.

The difficulty of making a choice between these two points of view is quite well known. The second of the two is subject to the objections of the radical positivists, who stress that the notion of intrinsic reality cannot be defined in any way that they could consider acceptable (in particular, to define it in any "operational" way is out of the question). The first one seems to enhance the mystery that regularities should be observed within the phenomena, and even more, perhaps, the mystery that the existence of several human beings endowed with the power of percieving and comparing their perceptions should be possible.

3.2 Discussion

The philosophy of experience was a great help to modern scientists, to such an extent that it even became an element of their conditioning, so to speak. This was a consequence of the necessity to reject, one after another, most of the "clear and distinct" notions that, up until then, had proved so reliable that their use was considered a matter of course. Such was, for example, the case of the notion of a universal time, or the notions of a position and a speed pertaining, at any given time, to the center of gravity of any object. Faced with such a conceptual revolution, the scientists came to doubt the universal validity of even quite trivial-looking concepts. Such doubts can be communicated only with some difficulty to "outsiders." (Indeed the dialogue between scientists and "thinkers" is often hindered by the latter's natural tendency to consider as logical truths some ideas whose contingency has already been acknowledged by the former).[11] These doubts are, nevertheless, both justified and quite necessary. But they create a gap. Bridging this gap was possible, it seemed, only by referring very explicitly to experience when defining basic notions. Every concept may turn out to be inadequate. Every one is doubtful. But a reproducible experiment, *that,* at least, does not lie! Or, if it does, it always does so along the same pattern in all cases. Consequently, science is sound, useful, and interesting even if it is, in the last resort, merely a study of the regularities of these lies. And the philosopher of experience will go so far as to ask: according to what criterion does a set of appearances, whose regularities are steadily reproduced and are the same for everybody, qualify as a lie?

Were they just simpletons running after a chimera, these old philosophers who aimed at discovering reality below appearances? Alas, with regard to the details of their query, the answer, on the whole, is affirmative. The wider our knowledge expands, the greater grows the part of it which bears on ourselves—on our structures as human beings—at least as much as on some hypothetical "external world" or "eternal truth." Thus, for example, the thinkers who could not content themselves with "unrefined" sensory data, those who taxed them with imposture and who aimed at rising above all this too-man-centered material, have often ideally referred in the past to pure mathematics, assuming that, by contrast, *this* field attained the realm of absolute realities. Spinoza's thought exemplifies such a noble belief, such a wonderful hope and—for we *must* characterize it this way—such a rash surmise.

Again, indeed, the following is now well known: the basic concepts of mathematics, and even those of logic, are gradually built up by children on the basis of what they do with objects and by "abstracting knowledge from action," as Jean Piaget stresses. Or, perhaps, as Jacques Monod suggests, these concepts are inherited from our prehominid ancestors, who had similarly constructed them. Under either assumption, what they immediately convey is but a set of possibilities with regard to human actions. The question as to whether or not they also indirectly mirror some eternal reality is debatable. It is a difficult question to answer. Therefore, it has become clear nowadays that this attitude, held in the past, of intuitively and hastily giving a positive answer to this question—as if it were obvious!—is rather naive indeed.

Having become aware of such truths, one should not be too surprised

---

[11] Such as, for example, the idea that no object can, at a given time, occupy the same location as another object.

that, in Bohr's philosophy, the whole reality of atoms, molecules, and so on is in the last resort rooted in that of the instruments, which, again, are apparently defined simply by the fact that they are used as such by men. But, on the other hand, one must also acknowledge the fact that, to some extent, Bohr thereby undid what Copernicus had accomplished: he reinstated man at the center of his own description of the world, wherefrom Copernicus had expelled him.

Moreover, in this comeback, the pendulum has now moved quite far beyond its point of departure, for the pre-Copernican view of the world was considerably more realistic than the one that would be taught by the vast majority of scientists, if only the latter were fully consistent with regard to their general views. The scientists considered here are all those who assume that all the exact sciences ultimately reduce to atomic and molecular physics and who, at the same time, go on to say that the problem of the physical interpretation of quantum mechanics does not come up, for it has been solved by Bohr. Assuredly, it has been solved. But the solution was achieved within the realm of a conception in which the notion of a *reality* of the properties of objects seems to be very much subordinated to the notion of human experience, and seems to derive its meaning exclusively through the latter. With regard to the subordination in question and the possible reasons for accepting it, it is interesting to note the opinion of Wolfgang Pauli, who was one of the pioneers of atomic theory.[12] While discussing and questioning Einstein's "realist" conception (and the criticism of the Copenhagen interpretation that Einstein derived from it), Pauli first specified that he, Pauli, considered *untrue* the idea that a body—*even a macroscopic one*—has, at any given time, a well-determined or even an almost determined position. He added that, in his opinion, diffraction experiments[13] on macroscopic objects of any dimensions whatsoever are quite conceivable in principle,[14] that in such cases we must grant that the position of the center of gravity of these objects is not defined—not even approximately—and finally that, in such cases, the emergence of a well-defined position (when the position is measured) and the discovery that "the object is there" should be thought of as "creations" escaping the natural laws. This last point does not

---

[12] In Einstein–Born correspondence, Gustav V. R. Born, London, 1969.

[13] On photons, such experiments are well known. See any elementary physics textbook.

[14] In fact, arguments have been put forward indicating that solids of a mass larger than about 10^{-14} g might not diffract, not even in principle. These arguments rest on the observation that the probability distribution of the center of gravity of any object with a finite mass suffers quantum fluctuations due to the existence of the uncertainty relations. Now, general relativity theory shows that the curvature of space—and more generally, its "metric"— depends on the mass distribution, so that these entities also suffer fluctuations. Between two terms in a linear superposition of matter waves, this can create appreciable random phase differences that can destroy the coherence. Such ideas were developed in particular by F. Karolyhasi. See, e.g., A. Frenkel in *Quantum Mechanics a Half Century Later*, edited by Lopes and Paty, Reidel, Dordrecht, 1977.

worry him, for, according to him, under the circumstances just described, the very fact that one imagines that *relevant* elements of reality already existed before observation (and specified in advance the place where the object was to be found) is tantamount to imagining that realities exist that not only are unknown but are also unknowable in principle (since the observation in question directly informs us only of what takes place at the time at which it is done). With regard to this attitude, Pauli wrote that "the question as to whether an unknowable thing exists or not should bother us as little as the old question of knowing how many angels can stand on the head of a pin."

Was the center of gravity of Jupiter on its present orbit even before *that* night during which, for the first time, a human being lifted his eyes towards the star-studded sky? "This question is stupid," the average scientist will say, "since the answer 'yes' is obvious." "This question is absurd," Pauli would presumably have remarked, "for it bears on something that, by definition, cannot be known and it is therefore meaningless."[15]

Although the conclusions from these two judgments coincide, their motivations obviously do not. If I adopt the judgment of the "average" scientist, I lose my right to assume that the investigations of the Copenhagen group have definitively solved the interpretation problems of the atomic theory and that, therefore, I need not worry about these problems. If I adopt Pauli's motivation, I should have no qualms concerning this. But, in that case, what should I think of the scientific descriptions of, say, the origin of the solar system? Presumably this: that they are, in the final analysis, merely metaphors or, otherwise stated, myths; that they are essentially similar in nature to those myths which the primitive tribes used to help them classify and rationalize their views about the world, even though, to be sure, they are more extensive; that they are also similar in nature to the "myth" of the ecliptic, that is, to the model (which remains useful even today) according to which the earth is motionless and the sun travels on the sphere of the fixed stars. Both the extension and the coherence of the "model of the ecliptic" are admittedly less substantial than those of our present day theory of the planetary system. But it would contradict the basic conceptions of the philosophy of experience to assert that the model in question is completely false and that, on the contrary, the theory just alluded to "describes what really is."

---

[15] Meaningless at least in its literal sense. To be sure, the philosophy of experience does impart a meaning to *some* statements bearing on past events: these are the statements that are an element of a hypothetico-deductive sequence of assertions making it possible to formulate predictions about future observations. But, according to that philosophy, the meaning of such statements is exhausted by such predictions: in other words, the meaning lies exclusively in the coherence that these statements impart to the set of perceptions of living human beings.

As we see, in view of our present day turn of mind, the philosophy of experience has much difficulty in getting us to accept some of the very radical consequences of the centering of reality on man that it implies. Not all endowed with Pauli's lucidity, many of the scientists who are the most enthusiastic in applying this philosophy to scientific research hesitate, in fact, due to these consequences. Frequently, they entertain the naive hope that they will succeed in *avoiding* these consequences just by taking what we here call the "philosophy of experience" to be a mere *methodology* and by clinging to the principle that "any philosophical consideration should be banned." But conceptual problems cannot be solved by mere rules of behavior! So that the realist (and, *a fortiori,* the materialist) or the individual who takes paleological or astrophysical descriptions at face value should be haunted by the problems of the foundations of physics. He should not be content until finding—elsewhere than in Bohr's work!—a solution to these problems. Actually, the only definition of a *state* of a physical system that is accepted by those theorists who are authorities on such matters is one that identifies the "state" with a procedure of "preparation by some human being." (It may be shown that identifying the state with a natural preparation, free from any human interference, has the effect of reintroducing at some higher level all the difficulties that realism meets within quantum mechanics.) If *that* identification is viewed as scandalous, can we abolish the scandal solely by the maxim that philosophy should be banned?

However, for a realist, what is most extraordinary in this domain is the fact that application of the philosophy of experience to atoms was a great success, to the extent that it has led to a hitherto unequalled harvest of scientific and technological results, which no other method can reproduce. If we now consider the present stage of the material sciences—among which biology itself is now looked upon as a member by a majority of biologists—we must grant that, on the other hand, at least in some respects, their foundations are to be found in atomic and molecular theory. We must then admit that they are based on a science which, as Heisenberg puts it in a well-known statement, "is but a link in the infinite chain of dialogues between man and nature and can no longer refer simply to nature-in-itself."

Up to the time when experimental methods of proving nonseparability were discovered (more about this below), it remained possible to hope that all the apparently paradoxical features of quantum mechanics as interpreted by the Copenhagen group would disappear when the mechanics in question (or its interpretation) would be replaced by another subtler one. We now know that this is not the case, since nonseparability (which is one of these apparently paradoxical features) can be experimentally proven (as will be shown) quite independently of quantum theory. We therefore know with certainty that some of the old philosophical foundations (such as the intrinsic reality of space–time, causality, or locality) of the scientific description of the universe must be modified, and that they should be changed in a manner identical, more or less, to that suggested by quantum mechanics. But still, this does not imply that everything suggested by quantum mechanics in this field should be taken at face value. In particular, the anti-Copernican revolution, the return of the pendulum in the direction of an idealism thinly veiled with positivism, are matters that remain open for discussion. Such a discussion is undertaken in the next chapter.

CHAPTER 4

Nonseparability

The scientific method for testing an assumption entails the derivation of consequences and an attempt to observe them experimentally. If the experimental results are identical to prediction, this is a good indication in favor of the original assumption. It is not, however, a final corroboration. Other assumptions might conceivably entail the same consequences. On the other hand, if the experimental results turn out to be incompatible with the predictions derived from the assumption, this, in principle, is enough to establish the falsity of the latter. Hence, the scientific method is never more interesting than when it necessitates the rejection of some ideas that were hitherto taken for granted. It then bewilders us by compelling us to acknowledge the truth that indeed "there are more things in heaven and earth" than common sense is able to grasp.

A proof of just this kind has been taking shape over the last few years within a branch of atomic and corpuscular physics. It is a proof that does not rest in any way on arguments of plausibility, of simplicity, or of maximal efficiency (all three types of arguments are frequently used, even in physics, but they are nevertheless extremely questionable from a philosophical point of view). Quite on the contrary, it is a proof that partakes of the mathematical exactness of the *reductio ad absurdum* method. It aims at proving beyond doubt the following proposition: "If the notion of a reality both independent of and knowable by man is considered meaningful, then such a reality is necessarily *nonseparable*." Roughly, "nonseparable" means that if we want to conceive of reality as having spatially localizable parts, then, if some of these parts have interacted in some specified ways in the past, they will somehow continue to "interact," regardless of how far apart they may be (see pp. 43, 174).

Obviously, to a considerable extent, such a property damages the plausibility of any assumption to the effect that, somehow, independent reality is imbedded in space or in space–time. The bearing of such a proposition upon our conceptions of the world is therefore quite considerable. I shall attempt to describe this bearing in the subsequent chapters.

Unavoidably, any proof has difficult elements, and the present one is no exception. Indeed, this should not be surprising, considering the importance of the result. But these difficulties are of a somewhat unusual kind in this case, for they consist neither of the use of a technical vocabulary nor of a resort to a mathematical formalism known only to a few. In fact, they are simply a matter of the patience the reader must draw upon in order to keep in mind the thread of the argument throughout the successive stages needed to arrive at any significant conclusions. As a matter of fact, right from the start the reader should be informed that the really significant conclusions of the present chapter are to be found neither in the lemma below nor even in the theorem of page 34 (all of which are but preliminaries), but in the fact that the conclusions—and hence, of course, the premises!—of the theorem in question turn out to be *false* in some cases (see below: *nonseparability*).

4.1 The Lemmas

The proof rests first of all on a very simple lemma, called "Lemma A" here, and which will be formulated by using a special example (see Fig. 1).

Lemma A (Stated on an Example). *Within any given population of human beings, the number of women who are less than forty years old is smaller than or equal to the sum of the number of female smokers and the number of nonsmokers who are less than forty years old.*

PROOF. Let us consider a woman who is less than forty (henceforth termed "young" for short). We can think of a great variety of *classes* to which she belongs (such as the class of the *young* people or that of the

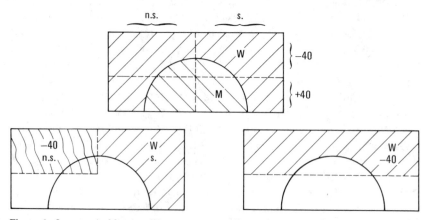

Figure 1. Lemma A. M, men; W, women; s, smokers; n.s., nonsmokers; +40 (−40), more (less) than forty years old.

women or that of the *featherless bipeds,* and so on). In particular, it is quite clear that she necessarily belongs *either* to the class of the female smokers *or* to that of the young nonsmokers (if she is a smoker, she belongs to the first class; if she is not, she belongs to the second one). Hence, in any population, the number of young women is necessarily smaller than, or at most equal to, the total number of all the female smokers *plus* that of the young nonsmokers (since these two classes do not overlap!). The lemma is thereby proved.   □

Statistical methods make it possible to generalize this lemma. Public opinion poll agencies, insurance companies, and the like all know quite well that within a sufficiently large population, unbiased samples may be selected. The law of large numbers has the effect that the proportions of individuals who, in these samples, have certain properties approximate the corresponding proportions considered within the whole population. More precisely, they approach the latter within a margin of error that—in relative value—can be made arbitrarily small simply by increasing the size of the sample. In the given population, let me therefore select three such samples of the same size (that is, having the same number of elements) and let me label them by the numbers 1, 2, and 3. With these I can then formulate Lemma B (which, with regard to statistics, I deliberately state here in a somewhat simplified form so as not to overload it with details that are irrelevant here[1]). The proof of Lemma B follows from that of Lemma A.

Lemma B.   *When the samples are large enough, the number of women who are less than forty years old in sample 1 is smaller than or equal to the sum of the number of female smokers of sample 2 and of the number of less-than-forty-year-old nonsmokers of sample 3.*

On the other hand, it is clear that the proof of this lemma does not involve the specific nature of the properties that serve to formulate them. Just like Lemma A, Lemma B is a theorem of pure mathematics. Therefore, it can obviously be extended to any properties whatsoever. The only requisite is that these properties be *dichotomic.* This means it is necessary that for any one of them there should exist only two possibilities: male or female, smoker or nonsmoker, etc. These two possibilities can then always be conventionally represented by the symbols + and −.

Lemma B constitutes an important element of the argumentation developed here. The relationship it states is connected with a general type of inequality called "Bell inequalities."[2]

---

[1] Strictly speaking, the statement of Lemma B should begin "With a probability that approaches unity. . . ."

[2] Reference 1.

4.2 The Case of Measurements

One of the simplest—but also one of the most unquestionable and most important—contributions of philosophy is the observation that we never have a direct knowledge of the world external to us. We have to observe and, when preciseness is required, we have to measure. What we then know is merely the set of results of the measurements in question.

Concerning macroscopic quantities in general, it seems possible for all practical purposes to measure them without modifying them. On the contrary, with regard to microscopic quantities, such as quantities pertaining to an atom, it often happens that they are disturbed—or even, in some cases, that they are made definite—by the instrument used for measuring them. The very existence of such a possibility should obviously prompt us to take great care in the formulation of our statements. Instead of asserting that I know a certain property of a given physical system because I have measured it, I should instead state that I obtained a certain result when I did what is appropriate to "measure" the quantity in question on this system.

But then, if I consider directly applying Lemmas A and B to atoms or to any microscopic systems, the first question that I should ask is the following one: Are these lemmas—which were stated with regard to *properties possessed* by systems (to *be* a female, to *be* a smoker, etc.)—generalizable to measurement results? In particular, are they generalizable in the case in which the result might conceivably be disturbed, or even somehow induced, by the interaction with the measuring instrument?

The lemmas involve three properties possessed by every "system." One manner of generalizing them is to consider cases in which all three properties are measured one after the other, on *each* system, in a sequence defined once and for all and the same for every system. It is easily verified that, with a mere change in the wording (replacing the "properties" by the corresponding "measurement results"), the proof of the lemma can then be reproduced and, for example, the validity of this proof is not spoiled by the fact that the result of the second measurement may be influenced by the performance of the first measurement. However, I shall not expand upon this way of generalizing the lemma, for up until now it has failed to lend to applications opening any new vistas.

More significant in this respect is the problem of generalizing Lemma B to the case in which each individual system actually undergoes two measurements instead of three. Unfortunately, the generalization in question cannot be achieved directly. For example, let us consider three equally large unbiased samples of students who have all taken the same courses and to whom three examinations are proposed: one in Latin, one in Greek, and one in Chinese. Moreover, we assume that each student takes two distinct examinations, and that these are the same for all the students within a given sample. The generalization of Lemma B, if it were true, would read "the number of students who pass both the Latin and the Greek examinations is smaller than or equal to the sum of the number of students who pass both the Latin and the Chinese examinations and the number of students who pass the Greek examination and fail the Chinese one." However, there are situations in which such a statement is false. For example, it may be the case that the Chinese examination takes place first and is especially tiresome. In an extreme case, it may even be that the mere practice of writing in that language exhausts the candidate to the point that he unavoidably fails the next examination; whereas, on the contrary, a normal fraction of the students who take the Latin and Greek examinations succeed in both. In such a case, the statement in quotation marks above turns out to be false.

Of course, such difficulties are simply due to the fact that, in the example, the registered results do not accurately reflect the real aptitudes of the students. A statement similar to the foregoing one, but bearing on the real aptitudes of the candidates—instead of on the registered aptitudes— would be correct. Hence, I should ask myself the following question: May I conceive of special situations insuring that, in the case in which the entities under study undergo only two measurements, these measurements faithfully reveal the measured properties? May I conceive of situations such that—in the example concerning examinations—neither the effect of fatigue nor any other source of disturbance can operate?

Indeed, such situations may be imagined. But they *are* special, for they involve populations that are no longer composed of isolated individuals but are instead composed of pairs, the elements of which are correlated. The process of the argumentation based on this idea is explained in the following section.

4.3 Considering Pairs

I have just noted that I cannot directly generalize the inequality stated in Lemma B to the case in which two (or more) measurements are made on the same individuals. How should I then manage to determine situations in which I would be able, with some reasonable-looking assumptions, to assert with certainty the truth of such an inequality which I demand should bear on measurement results?

It is obvious that to answer this question I need a new idea and that when I have found it, I shall have to reconstruct the entire argumentation.

The new idea that will allow such an advance to be made is the following one: instead of considering measurements or tests made on a population composed of individuals, I shall consider measurements made on a population whose elements are pairs of individuals. For instance, if I again seek an example concerning examinations, I can imagine a university that would only accept pairs of identical twins for registration. To avoid the possibility that the exhaustion created by one examination may disturb the outcome of the ensuing one, I shall assume that every student takes only one examination, during which he is isolated from his comrades. To be able to make use of this idea, let me imagine that, in addition, in the university in question, the records show that within a period of time extending over a great many years, for every pair of twins who took the same examination, either both succeeded or both failed (this is an instance of what is called a "strict positive correlation"; the correlation would be strict and negative if, on the contrary, one twin succeeded and the other failed in every pair).

For the time being, let us put aside our intention of finding a counterpart to Lemma B and let us first study the possible assumptions regarding the circumstances just described.[3] To simplify the argument, let us, for the time being, discard any notion of fraud or any disturbance whatsoever. Here, then, are concrete statistics, proving that in our university no twin ever succeeded without his brother succeeding as well. What conclusions can I draw from this? Many, to be sure, most of which will appeal mainly to either the sociologist or the specialist in human psychology. But, in particular, there is a conclusion that a completely elementary *reductio ad absurdum* argumentation makes possible with absolute certainty. This is that for every candidate, preexisting aptitudes, not chance, decide success or failure. For indeed, if all the students, or even some of them, had answered the test questions haphazardly rather than according to their aptitudes, then it is obvious that within the huge number of twin pairs that had been tested, there would have been at least a few in which one of the twins would have given the right answer and his brother the wrong one. Since, by assumption, this never occurs, I am obviously forced to infer that chance played no significant role in these tests. In other words, exclusively with reference to preexisting aptitudes correlated within every pair and faithfully[4] disclosed by the "measurements" (the examination re-

---

[3] When, as is the case in this chapter, the reasoning takes place in several successive stages, it is often useful to summarize some of these stages by somewhat intuitive but simple argumentations in order to keep in mind the thread of the argument. With regard to the stage described in this section, its conclusions can be intuitively but easily reached as follows: after the first twin has taken his examination, his examiner knows in advance the result the other will achieve. Hence, this result is predetermined. This shows that the second candidate possesses a quite definite aptitude beforehand and that this aptitude will be (faithfully) disclosed by the test. In the case where the absence of fraud is assumed, he must obviously have possessed this aptitude even before his brother passed *his* test. Since the time ordering of the tests taken by the two brothers can be decided at the last moment, this clearly shows that the two twins have definite aptitudes in common that the examinations will simply disclose rather than induce. This is the main point asserted in this section. Readers who find complex argumentations discouraging can, on a first reading, keep this footnote in mind and proceed immediately to the next section in which the main theorem is proved as a consequence of this result.

[4] The word "faithfully" should be understood as follows: It is conceivable that in the university in question, some courses may be poor and that, consequently, success in, say, the Latin examination does not guarantee that the candidate has an aptitude for speaking Latin. Even in this case, however, some precise aptitudes are *faithfully* disclosed by the results; these are the aptitudes for passing or failing Latin examinations as they are—and will continue to be—organized in the university in question. Needless to say, our reasoning deals exclusively with such aptitudes.

sults) can I account for the results. With regard to the very existence of such a correlation between the aptitudes of any two brothers, there is nothing intrinsically mysterious about it. On the one hand, the twins have the same chromosomes and, on the other hand, they received the same education, they attended the same courses, and so on. This is more than is necessary for "explaining" that their aptitudes are the same!

Thus, I have been able to infer with certainty from the observed facts that I can discard the assumption according to which chance played a role in the results of the preceding years. At any rate, I could reach such certainty with regard to all the pairs in which both brothers passed the same examination (regardless of the nature of the test). This can be rephrased by saying "all the students belonging to pairs both of whose members took the Latin examination either possessed, prior to the test, the aptitude for passing the examination in question or the "aptitude" for failing it with certainty; and this (positive or negative) aptitude was faithfully disclosed by the results." Similarly, all the students belonging to pairs both of whose members took the Greek examination either possessed the aptitude for passing the Greek examination or possessed the lack of aptitude, etc.

But now let us assume that, in our university, the number of students is enormous, that they all attend the same lectures, and that it is only at the last moment that each one *draws by lot* the subject matter of the examination he will take, without being allowed to inform anyone—not even his brother—of the result of this draw. Up until that moment, the university population is homogeneous. I would therefore be unable to justify my assumption if, observing (as above) a strict correlation between the (extremely many) results achieved by the pairs both of whose members drew the same subject, I were to suppose that, before the tests, only *those* students whose brothers are about to draw the same subject as they, happened to possess precise aptitudes strictly controlling their success or failure. Such a coincidence is very unlikely. In other words, with regard to the previously reached certainty that some students possess, before the draw, precise aptitudes strictly controlling their success or failure, say, in Latin, I now see that as a matter of fact I must extend this certainty to *all* students, including those whose brothers will *not* draw the subject "Latin" in the ballot and including also those who themselves will not draw that subject. And of course the same is true with respect to Greek, Chinese, and all other subjects in which the students are examined in this manner.

Moreover, on this point a very elementary *reductio ad absurdum* argument could, if necessary, reinforce our conclusion. Indeed, if in a given subject, a statistically significant number of students had no precise aptitude whatsoever (so that they could merely answer questions haphazardly), in all likelihood it would often happen at the time of drawing that two twins, one of whom at least would be in such a situation, would both draw that very subject. Within a densely populated university, this would happen to many pairs, with, as we have previously seen, the statistically unavoidable consequence that, at best, a mere *partial* correlation would be observed between the results of these pairs.[5] By assumption, however, this is not the case. We must therefore conclude that even before the determination of the nature of the test, all the students *do* have precise aptitudes in all subjects on which they took courses. Of course, in view of the observed strict correlations, these aptitudes must be the same for both members of every pair.

4.4 The Basic Theorem

The premises of the following reasoning are the very conclusions we have just reached. Hence, in no way do these premises constitute independent hypotheses. Below, if at any stage it happens that, for some reason or another, we need to question their validity, we shall be logically permitted to do so only if we also question the validity of the argumentation that has led to them. We shall then have to show, for example, that this argumentation is erroneous, or that it is itself based on premises that are not necessarily true. In short, the bearing of this section cannot be fully understood independent of the content of the foregoing one.

This being so, what then are these previously reached conclusions? Essentially they are as follows (under the assumption that the candidates cannot communicate with one another): In the university in question (a) at the end of each year term (but even before drawing lots) the students always[6] have definite aptitudes either for success or failure in each of the subjects taught; (b) the measurements actually made (with the same examination taken by each individual) faithfully reveal the aptitudes in question; and (c) the two twins in any given pair have, at the time considered here, exactly the same aptitudes.

---

[5] It should be noted that, strictly speaking, this result holds true only because of the condition stated above, that the students are forbidden to let even their brothers know of the result they drew with regard to the nature of the examination they are required to take. For, indeed, it is possible to imagine a population of students who, on the one hand, would be endowed with an intense brotherly love and who, on the other hand, would have a poor knowledge of Chinese, so that for them neither success nor failure in that subject would be certain. By assumption, such students have no precise aptitude for either success or failure, but, if the condition just referred to were not satisfied, it could nevertheless happen that every student would be informed of the nature of the test drawn by his brother and that all of those who learned that their brothers drew the (difficult) subject *Chinese* would be so painfully moved by such sad news that they would fail at their own examinations. The results would then show a "strict correlation" (a general failure) within the set of pairs both of whose members drew the subject *Chinese*; but obviously it would be erroneous to interpret this as disclosing the existence, before the examinations, of a precise (negative) aptitude of the students. The condition that the students are forbidden to inform their brothers of the result of their drawing eliminates that loophole in the argument: If nobody passes, it is because, either for emotional reasons or for any other reason, nobody has the *aptitude* to pass. (Such critical analyses, which look ridiculous within the present analogy, must not be omitted when dealing with the real physical problem, which is described at length below.)

[6] "Always" refers here to the fact that this was true for the entire (long) time during which records were compiled.

However, up to this point we have considered mainly those pairs of twins both of whose members happen to draw the same subject matter. To be more definite, let us again assume that the subjects taught are Latin, Greek, and Chinese and let us retain the assumption that at the last moment each student draws by lot the subject matter on which he will be examined. In addition to the three sets of pairs both of whose members are examined on the same subject (Latin, Greek, and Chinese), there are then three other sets of pairs, statistically[7] equal in numbers: among them, one is the set of pairs one of whose members is examined in Latin and the other in Greek, another is the set of pairs one of whose members is examined in Latin and the other in Chinese, and the last is the set of pairs one of whose members is examined in Greek and the other in Chinese. We can then note that, if we take into account what has been established above, the results of the examinations in question accurately inform us of the aptitudes of each pair with regard to *two* different subjects, for again we know that the results faithfully reveal the aptitudes and we also know that each student has the same aptitudes as his brother (see the foregoing paragraph). For example, let us consider a pair one of whose members was examined in Latin and the other in Greek. If the first member succeeded and the second one failed, this tells us that "the pair" (i.e., each twin) had, just before drawing lots, the aptitude for success in Latin and the "aptitude" for failure in Greek.

These aptitudes, as we have seen, are "possessed" by the students even before they draw lots. We could even prove that each student then possessed definite aptitudes either for success or failure in Latin, Greek, *and* Chinese simultaneously. Hence, we can apply to these aptitudes the argument we used above for proving Lemma B:

Before drawing lots, any student who possesses the aptitudes for success both in Latin and Greek belongs either to the class of those who have the aptitudes for success both in Latin and Chinese or to the class of those who have the aptitude for success in Greek and the aptitude for failure in Chinese. These two classes are quite separate. Hence, in our university, *the number of students who have aptitudes for success both in Latin and Greek is necessarily smaller than or equal to the sum of the number of students who have aptitudes for success both in Latin and in Chinese* plus *the number of students who have both an aptitude for success in Greek and an aptitude for failure in Chinese.*

But, it might be asked, can such a statement be experimentally verified? In other words, are we sure that the "numbers of students" considered here are faithfully revealed by the examinations?

Essentially the answer is "yes." For indeed, if we again take into account what has been proven in the foregoing paragraph (and, of course, unless the examina-

---

[7] "Statistically" means "except for fluctuations." It is a well-known fact that it is always possible to make these fluctuations as small in relative value as desired by increasing the total number of elements under consideration.

tion grade given to one twin is somehow influenced by the drawing or by the result of the other one; but we have discarded such possibilities), we know that the answers actually given by the candidates do *faithfully* disclose the aptitudes of the pair that issued them. Within the set of the pairs whose members drew Latin and Greek, for example, I therefore know, by analyzing the results, the exact proportion of those who before the drawing possessed the aptitude for success in these two subjects. For the very reason that these subjects were drawn by lots, the proportion in question cannot differ very much from the proportion of pairs possessing these same aptitudes within the total population of student pairs. The laws of statistics also inform us that, in all probability, the difference between these two proportions can be made as small as desired by increasing the total number of students. With precision that can be improved, in principle, as much as necessary, the examinations thus *faithfully* inform us about the proportion of pairs possessing aptitudes for success both in Latin and Greek within the total population of the university. Similarly, the results of the examinations yield information on the proportions—within the total population—on the one hand of the pairs having aptitudes for success both in Latin and Chinese and, on the other hand, of the pairs having both an aptitude for success in Greek and an aptitude for failure in Chinese. These proportions are simply equal, to within a common factor (and also to within negligible statistical fluctuations), to the corresponding numbers of successes and failures that can actually be obtained by scanning the records of the examinations that took place. (Of course, within these records we must now select only the results of the pairs whose two members were examined on two different subjects.)

If we turn back to the italicized statement above, we now observe, on the one hand, that this statement obviously remains true if the words "number of students" are systematically replaced by the words "proportion of pairs within the total population" (for indeed the second quantity is obtained by dividing the first one by the total number of students) and, on the other hand, that these proportions are equal (again within a common factor and within negligible fluctuations) to quantities that are genuine measurement results, namely the number of pairs both of whose members succeed or one of whose members succeeds and the other fails, as the case may be. Again, these numbers may be discovered in the records of results of examinations actually taken.

To summarize, we have just proven that in our university the results of the examinations faithfully reveal the aptitudes of the candidates (aptitudes which preexist, as we have shown). We see that we can reformulate the italicized statement in terms of measurements results. And this leads to a theorem that, considering its importance, I shall simply call below "the Theorem." Its precise formulation is as follows.

Theorem. *In the university described above (and under the assumption that at the time at which the candidates draw by lot the subject matter on which they are to be examined the candidates are isolated from other people), it can be asserted that, with a probability that approaches unity when the number of students is large enough, the number of pairs one of whose members succeed in Latin and the other succeeds in Greek is smaller* *than or at most equal to the sum of the number of pairs one of whose members succeeds in Latin and the other succeeds in Chinese, plus the number of pairs one of whose member succeeds in Greek and the other one fails in Chinese.*

The assumption that the candidates are isolated is of course quite essential to the validity of the theorem. It must therefore be assumed that the president of the university in question will take all conceivable measures for ensuring this condition. In the following, we shall assume that, to this effect, he has ordered that the candidates be examined in separate rooms, that every candidate draws the subject matter of his examination *after* entering the room, and that he is examined immediately afterwards.

4.5 Coming Back to Physics

In physics, the cases of strict correlation, that is, situations in which two objects (usually called "systems") initially possess some identical properties (or some properties that are in a one-to-one correspondence between the two systems) are not infrequent. If these two systems get separated from one another later, while retaining their original properties, it is then possible to measure (as above) a property a on one of them and a property b on the other. This will then be equivalent to measuring both a and b on any one of them. Moreover, under weak conditions stipulating the absence of some influences at a distance, this procedure guarantees that the first of these two measurements will not modify the property that is measured in the second. If under such conditions we manage to produce a great number of such pairs of systems, if a and b are measured on a large number of such pairs, if a and c are measured on an equal number of other pairs, and if, finally, b and c are measured on an equal number of still other pairs, then we would expect that the equivalent of the theorem be verified for the results of the measurements in question.

In the foregoing paragraph we had to introduce the phrase "under weak conditions stipulating the nonexistence of some influences at a distance." These conditions are essential. Let me make them more precise.

For this purpose I must first recall their most obvious motivation. It is to prevent a candidate who is already in the room in which he will take the Latin examination from being worried by the fact that his unlucky brother is undergoing a test in Chinese. This might conceivably occur if, after they parted, the two brothers still remained somehow linked by means of a walkie-talkie or even by means of a mere thread (which could transmit to one the shivering of the other!). However, with respect to this possibility, two remarks must be made.

The first is that any signal—even a pull on a thread!—takes some time to travel.[8] If the examinations taken by the two brothers take place at essentially the same time, at separate distant locations, I have every reason to believe that neither one of the two brothers can be influenced by the test that the other one is taking. The same type of assumption can be made in physics, with regard to measurements made on two correlated systems in the cases in which the two measurements are performed at essentially the same time and at places that are very distant from one another. Hence, these conditions are among those under which, if they are realized, I should expect the conclusion of the theorem to be verified by experiment.

The second remark bears on situations in which such restrictive conditions are not fully verified. It consists of observing that, even then, the idea that no appreciable influence at a distance takes place between the systems seems—at first sight—quite likely to be true in many cases, as shown by the example of the two students taking examinations in two different rooms. In fact, it is the very notion of separation that is at stake here. The reason why such a notion appears to be meaningful is simply that we believe that two objects once separated do not influence one another as strongly as when they were united. In other words, the non-existence or at least the weakening of such reciprocal influences-at-a-distance is an essential element in our intuitive definition of the very concept of separation. Insofar as we do indeed consider that such a concept is meaningful and actually applies to existing realities, and insofar as we consider that it applies to certain precisely defined cases of objects or beings that did in fact "separate," we shall *a priori* expect the theorem to hold for such cases. Or, at least, we shall *a priori* expect that its predictions should be increasingly verifiable in proportion to the increasing distance between two components of each pair in the system being studied.

These considerations are enough for understanding what follows. However, a few remarks still need to be made.

Remark I. The Role of Chance and the Role of Necessity

It has been shown above that from the strict correlation observed between certain results (those of two twins who were examined on the same subject), it can be inferred with certainty that the students already possess definite aptitudes before they are examined. In the university under consideration, the students do *not* answer questions haphazardly. With respect to this fact, two points should be noted. One of them is that—as already stressed—this piece of information is not a supplementary assumption in the proof. On the contrary, it is a consequence of it, or, more

---

[8] No signal can travel faster than light. This is a principle of relativity theory that experiment fully confirms.

precisely, of its premises (and, in particular, of the hypothesis that no interaction takes place between the candidates either at the time of the examination or at the time immediately before it). Hence, it would be utterly erroneous to assert that, in this chapter, *the hypothesis of determinism* is made. The second point is that, of course, we have not proven determinism *in general* but exclusively with regard to the strict correlation phenomena described here.

With regard to the proof itself, it is perhaps not irrelevant to stress that it assumes the examiners behave in an impartial fashion. In particular, it would not be valid if the examiners graded each candidate not on the basis of his actual answers but according to his serial number or according to the answers given by his predecessors or, again, according to the nature of the subject drawn by his brother. With regard to the applications of the theorem to physics, I shall henceforth assume that the measuring instruments have been devised so as not to exhibit such erratic behavior.

Remark II

It may be noted that in the physical case (pairs of particles, see below), the proof of the theorem admittedly postulates that somehow, just like the twins, the particles can be viewed as separated from one another. But the opposite assumption—which, to be sure, is suggested to some extent by the most elementary interpretation of quantum mechanics—would be tantamount to taking for granted that very *nonseparability* whose proof is the essential aim of this chapter.

Remark III

At the basis of the proof of the theorem, are there some assumptions other that those already mentioned (postulated *existence* of an external reality in which the regularities of the phenomena are rooted and weak conditions stipulating the absence of some influences at a distance)? A thorough analysis leads to an affirmative answer to this question. Over and above the use of induction, it is possible to discover in the argument carried through above an implicit assumption that can be formulated in several distinct ways. One of them is to assert, as Einstein did (see Chapter 7), that if it is possible to accurately predict beforehand the result of a measurement of a physical quantity pertaining to a system, without disturbing the system, then there exists an element of reality corresponding to this physical quantity. Other formulations fulfill the same function without explicitly introducing the notion of reality. But these points are subtleties into which it is unnecessary to enter right now (see Chapter 12). Here it should be enough to point out that if there is any implicit assumption, it is one whose validity is, at any rate, very difficult to question.

Remark IV

If in our university—just as in any "normal" one—the students were informed in advance of the subjects on which they would be requested to take their examinations, it would presumably happen that, for example, the students for whom these subjects are Latin and Greek would neglect Chinese and that, as a result, on the day of the examinations the Latin–Greek group, the Latin–Chinese group, and the Greek–Chinese group would no longer be three unbiased samples of the total population, even in the cases in which at the beginning of the year they were composed of students having the same aptitudes on the average. In such a situation, the proof of Lemma B obviously does not apply. But we have eliminated this possibility by stipulating that each student draw by lots, just before the examination, the subject matter on which he will be examined.

In physics, such an impediment to proving Lemma B is much less likely to occur. For this impediment to appear, it would be necessary that the choice of the physical quantities to be measured—or the setting up of the corresponding instruments—should be able to act at a distance on the measured physical systems or on their sources before the measurements take place. Care will of course be taken to design an experimental set-up that will exclude any such influence due to known forces. As for the unknown influences, if they exist, we can, at any rate, hope to render them negligible by placing the source far from the detecting devices. A small loophole in the proof nevertheless remains, at least in principle, because of the possibility that such effects may exist, however unlikely. The elimination of this loophole will be accomplished only when methods are applied that will somehow be equivalent to setting up the instruments *after* the particles leave the source, that is, in practice, within a time interval of the order of a billionth of a second. Incredible as it may seem, bringing such methods into play is not an utterly unattainable objective. Efforts are currently being made along these lines.

Remark V

The theorem bears on the number of pairs of students who *actually* succeeded in Latin and Greek, succeeded in Latin and Chinese, and succeeded in Greek and failed in Chinese. Quite obviously, its proof holds for the corresponding *recorded* numbers only if the secretary in charge of recording the examination grades was careful enough not to omit registering those of any of the students; or if, at least, his inattentiveness was unbiased. In this latter case, indeed, the numbers of recorded grades are proportional to the real numbers, and if the inequality holds for the latter this entails it holds also for the former (and conversely). This, in short, is the case that is realized when "what is not seen" (the marks overlooked by the secretary) does not behave differently from "what is seen."

Unfortunately, for several technical reasons, the instruments used in the experiments described below are not perfectly efficient. They fail to detect all the events, and a number of pairs of particles escape detection. However, we have reason to believe that this phenomenon is unbiased. The lack of detection is uniform, so that in these experiments as well, it is very unlikely that what is not seen should behave differently from what *is* seen. It is therefore possible to apply the theorem to the results of the experiments that have been carried out up until now, in spite of the defectiveness of the instruments that are presently available.

4.6 The Experimental Test

As we have already pointed out, it is in physics that the theorem has its most significant applications. The "table of correspondence" between the concepts used in the example and those relating to any physical experiment is clear and has already been used. The candidates represent the physical systems under investigation (atoms, particles, etc.); the examiners represent the measuring instruments; the examination tests represent the interactions taking place between the systems and the instruments; the examination results represent the results of the measurements of dichotomic variables[9] that are thought of as describing some properties of the systems; and finally the aptitudes of the students represent these properties.

So long as physics is not conceived of as being a mere set of recipes—in other words, so long as the concept of reality existing independent of our consciousness (without, however, being utterly outside its reach) is considered meaningful—the previously developed proof of the theorem is a general proof. This means it applies to any physical system, be it classical or quantal. (In the latter case, however, some conceptual problems must first be solved; these questions are studied in Chapter 12.)

The physical examples of strict correlations in which the inequality predicted by the theorem is verified are extremely numerous. Let us describe just one. Initially, some small bar magnets are arranged in pairs. Within each pair the two magnets are parallel but have opposite magnetic moments: the south-north direction of one of them coincides with the north-south direction of the other. Let us say they are "anti-parallel." But the common direction of a pair in space differs from one pair to another and is stochastically distributed. In a second stage, the elements of each pair are separated from one another by some external force. As seen by the experimenter, one of them travels towards the right and the other towards the left, without the common direction of their axes suffering any change thereby. The experimenter passes all the magnets that travel to-

---

[9] See page 27.

Figure 2. A schematic representation of a measurement bearing on a pair of bar magnets.

wards his right through a device whose direction is labelled by a vector[10] **a** and that automatically records, for every magnet, whether the angle between **a** and the north-south direction of the magnet is acute (it then registers +) or obtuse (it then registers −). He also passes all the magnets that travel towards his left through another device identical to the former except that its direction in space is **b** instead of **a**, and again the device registers, with the same symbols + and −, whether the angle between **b** and the north-south direction of the magnet is acute or obtuse (Fig. 2).

Having completed such measurements on a set composed of a large number N of pairs of bar magnets, the experimenter performs the same operations again, with the same number N of magnet pairs, but with devices whose directions in space are **a** and **c**, **c** being a vector different

---

[10] Here and in the remaining part of this chapter, the use of a few expressions pertaining to the scientific language cannot, unfortunately, be avoided. These expressions are the word "vector," the word "spin," and the expression "spin component along a direction **a**."

To the physicist, the notion of a *vector* is extremely simple. It is merely an arrow that can, if so desired, be imagined to be a material object having a specified direction in space. Generally speaking, a vector is also characterized by its length, but quite often the vectors used here will merely serve to label a direction, and their lengths are then irrelevant. As for the *component* of a vector along a given direction, it is a *number* equal in magnitude to the length of the projection of the vector along that direction (and is given an appropriate sign). For example, the component of the (directed) hypotenuse of a right triangle along the direction of one of the sides is (disregarding the sign) simply equal to the length of the side in question.

The concept of *spin* is more difficult. It can be introduced with the help of the concept of *intrinsic angular moment*. When a body spins around some axis, like, for example, the earth which spins around the axis of the poles with a twenty-four-hour period, it is convenient to characterize its motion by means of a vector lying along the axis in question, the direction of which is determined by the direction of the rotation and the length of which depends on the angular velocity. Such a vector is called an *intrinsic angular momentum*.

Many types of elementary particles exhibit remarkable properties that make them resemble, in some respects (but in some respects only!), macroscopic objects possessing an intrinsic angular momentum. Such particles are said to *have a spin*. A spin is conveniently represented as a vector attached to the particle. But the comparison with the intrinsic angular momentum of a macroscopic object must not be carried too far. For example, measuring devices, called Stern–Gerlach instruments, exist which can be given arbitrary directions in space: any such device makes it possible to measure a quantity that—for theoretical reasons too long to explain—is interpreted to be the *spin component* of the particle along the direction defined by the device in question. However (and it is in this respect that the identification of a spin with a classical vector would be faulty), in any case, the numbers thus measured are no more than integral multiples of a given quantity which depends solely on the type of particle under study, and this is true for any choice of the direction of the instrument in space.

from **b**. Finally, he performs the same operation a third time, using devices whose directions are **b** and **c**.

The conditions necessary for the theorem to apply are obviously satisfied here. However, its formulation must be rather trivially modified in order to take into account the fact that the strict correlation introduced here is negative[11] (see p. 30 for the definition of negative correlations). By means, for example, of the method described above, the following assertion can easily be proved. If, in such an experiment, only *those* pairs of magnets are counted that lead to measurement results recorded as two + signs, then the sum of the number of such pairs corresponding to the two last operations is necessarily larger than, or at least equal to, the number corresponding to the first one.[12] Of course, experiment will eventually corroborate these predictions, just as it will corroborate those of the theorem relative to any macroscopic experiment to which the theorem can be applied.

The set-up we have just imagined was intended to be a qualitative model for an experiment in the field of microphysics. Why, therefore, should we not also consider the actual microphysical experiment of which the set-up in question is a model? In fact it is the actual experiment, not the macroscopic set-up, that was first conceived. Theoretical considerations made it interesting, and in fact it *was*. For here I must underline the fact that, unlike the thought experiments previously described—the one on students and the one on bar magnets—the experiment described below *was* actually performed. In fact it was performed several times. These experimental investigations were taken up in several physics laboratories in Europe and in the United States at the beginning of the 1970s, on the basis of theoretical ideas that took shape during the 1960s. My present purpose is not, of course, to enter into their technical aspects (see Ref 2–9, 11, 14). It is merely to show their principle and results. These results are indeed very far reaching.

In some cases, the experiment that I am about to describe was made with pairs of photons (these are the particles that compose light). In some other cases, it was made with pairs of protons (these are merely hydrogen nuclei). Let me describe more particularly the guiding idea of this second

---

[11] And, to be quite explicit, also by taking into account rather trivial symmetries. In fact the procedures used in the actual experiments (on particles) are tantamount to supplementing the simplified description given above with the following condition: within a given pair, the question of *which* magnet travels toward the right and which one travels toward the left is independent of the initial direction in space of the (common) axis of the two magnets. (Note, however, that a slightly more elaborate formulation of the theorem would make this condition unnecessary even here.)

[12] The proof is quite similar to the one described above concerning the cases of strict positive correlations. The reader may easily reconstruct it. If he chooses to do so, he will have to take into account the fact that here a positive result relative to one magnet corresponds to a negative "aptitude" of the other one in the pair, and he will argue by using two "aptitudes" of the same magnet and by taking the symmetries into account. See also Appendix I.

method. Essentially it consists of first bringing two protons together in a manner that brings the pair into what is called a "spin-zero state."[13] In some aspects, the protons resemble tiny bar magnets and, by definition, what is called a spin-zero state is a state in which the magnetizations of the two protons cancel one another, just as those of the two bar magnets of the foregoing example cancelled one another when these magnets were set in opposite directions.[14] After colliding and achieving the spin state just described, the two protons travel farther and farther away from one another, without modification of their spin state. Finally, each proton runs through a Stern–Gerlach (or an equivalent) device, whose direction in space is fixed by the experimenter and is not necessarily the same on the two sides. Each device is connected with a counter that registers whether the corresponding protons escape in the "north beam" or in the "south beam" of the device, where these phrases denote the beam that upon emerging from the device is bent towards the north (south) pole of the magnet that constitutes the essential part of the latter. The registering in the north beam is indicated by + and in the south beam by −. Within the registering device composed of the two counters, every proton pair thus gives rise to the appearance of either two plus signs, or two minus signs, or one + and one −. This last case occurs in two distinct ways, differing with regard to which one of the two devices registers, say, the +. This first stage of the experiment is repeated with N pairs of protons. Afterwards the direction in space of one of the Stern–Gerlach devices is changed and the experiment continues with N other pairs of protons. Finally, the direction in space of the other device is changed also (as described on p. 41) and the experiment continues with, again, N proton pairs. In each of these three stages, the number of cases in which a pair induces the emergence of two plus signs (let us call this "the number of + + cases") is registered (see Fig. 3).

Similar experiments are made, each time varying the angles that define the relative directions of the instruments in space.

For some such relative directions, it is observed that the sum of the numbers of + + cases in the second stage and in the third stage is larger than the number of + + cases in the first case. This is not surprising since, as already pointed out (p. 41), it is just what should be expected on the basis of the (suitably transposed) theorem.

But now comes the essential point. For some other choices of the relative directions of the instruments, just the opposite is observed. The sum

---

[13] It can easily be shown that this result can be obtained simply by shooting a beam of low-velocity protons—produced, for example, in a van de Graaf accelerator—onto a target containing a sufficiently large amount of hydrogen.

[14] The reason why it is then said that the pair is in a "spin-zero state" is that each proton is considered to have a spin parallel to the vector representing its magnetization, and that, in the state in question, the vector sum of these two spins is zero. However, the protons are microscopic particles; they do not obey the laws of ordinary mechanics, and, as we saw, the notion of a tiny spin vector belonging to every proton must not be taken too literally, especially when the components of such vectors are considered, as is the case below.

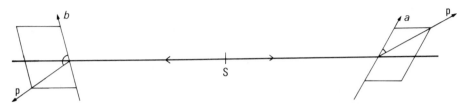

Figure 3. Schematic diagram of a measurement on a pair of protons (p,p) emitted from a source S.

of the numbers of $++$ cases corresponding to the two last stages is *smaller* than the number of $++$ cases corresponding to the first stage.[15] This is a reproducible phenomenon, and the difference between the two members of the inequality is much too large to be accounted for by mere statistical fluctuations.

4.7 Nonseparability

Such an experimental result contradicts the predictions of the theorem. This is quite an important fact, and indeed it is the very purpose of this chapter to make it known. Let us therefore comment upon the interest it presents. Any theorem can in a way be compared to a slot machine. When a given hypothesis is introduced the theorem provides us with a conclusion. "If the hypothesis is true, then the conclusion is also true": such is the content of any theorem. So if the conclusion is disproved by the facts the theorem informs us that the hypothesis is false.

In the case under consideration, the conclusion of the theorem is of the nature of an experimentally testable prediction. If the hypothesis were true, this prediction would be correct with regard to *any* relative directions of the instruments. However, for some of these directions, it is not. Hence, the hypothesis is false.

What, then, exactly is the false hypothesis? In Remarks IV and V, it was pointed out that, after examination, the few reservations that are described there do not appear to be significant. Under such conditions, the only hypothesis that is introduced as a premise to the theorem is—apart from the assumption of *realism*; see Chapters 3 and 12[16]—the assumption that influences due to bodies that lie far enough away must somehow be

---

[15] Taken literally, the result stated here is what would be obtained with an ideal set-up and with absolutely efficient detectors. In order to suitably take into account the existing defects and inefficiencies of these instruments, the physicist had to replace the inequality stated in the theorem by a somewhat more complicated one, the origin of which, however, is essentially the same; and it is the violation of this new inequality that is observed for some choices of the relative directions of the instruments. (See Ref. 2).

[16] And apart, also, from the assumption that unbiased samples can be selected. But this latter assumption is a very general one which pervades all fields of scientific and technical research.

negligible [this constitutes the physical equivalent of the assumption, made in the proof of the theorem, that the candidates are not allowed to communicate (see pages 30 and 32)]. Hence, there can hardly be any doubt: in the eyes of a realist, there must be something wrong with the ideas we have in mind when we speak of "negligible influences."

This is a far-reaching idea. Making its true meaning quite clear and explicit is not, for this reason, a completely easy task. If we want to tackle it, we must guard against trying to use any incisive sweeping formula similar to those through which attempts at summarizing long discussions are often made, and which actually, as a rule, misinterpret them.

Hence, we must very carefully recall the assumptions we made before we knew these experimental results. We must try to remember why we considered extremely unlikely the existence of distant influences capable of preventing the proof of the theorem from succeeding. We must find out what types of influences at a distance could conceivably have such effects.

Fortunately, such an exercise turns out to be rather easy. Indeed, we have already noted (see page 36) that if the measurements are made almost simultaneously and at very great distances from one another, then the predictions of the theorem can be violated only if influences exist that are conveyed extremely rapidly, for these influences must obviously travel with a speed equal to or greater than the ratio between the distance in question and the time interval between the measurements. If, in some given experiments, this ratio were larger than the velocity of light, "influences" whose effects propagate faster than light would have to exist, and this would clash with a conception quite generally held as true concerning one of the main principles of relativity theory. This would appear as being remarkable indeed. Unfortunately, such a ratio is quite difficult to obtain experimentally, so that (account also being taken of the content of Remark IV) present-day experiments are not yet entirely conclusive with regard to this. It should nevertheless be stressed that they actualize conditions which are such that the tentative explanations explicitly constructed so as to avoid any kind of direct or indirect[17] faster-than-light "influences" have become very unlikely. Any other attempt unavoidably introduces extremely artificial assumptions, and there is strong evidence that technical improvements of the experimental procedure will sooner or later render them inoperative.

But to this we can still add one point. Again, indeed (see page 36), the very concept of separation, the notion of objects that having once been

---

[17] Indirect, that is, bringing into play both a normal kind of causality and another one, *directed towards the past*. Arguments exist both for and against such an idea. It should moreover be noted that it is possible to replace the very concept of influences at a distance by the idea that the two measured physical systems constitute but *one* system, which, contrary to all the extended physical systems that we know of, is "nonseparable", not even separable by thought.

united later were separated, or spontaneously separated, is a concept that somehow implies a weakening of the influences that each of them can exert upon the other. Thus, it is a concept that, as soon as we consider it to be applicable to a given pair of objects, implies that for these objects the predictions of the theorem more closely approximate the results as the distance is increased between the different locations where the quantities are measured on the objects. Now the experiments described above involve very different distances and no such effects were ever disclosed, not even in the cases in which these distances were a great many orders of magnitude larger than the dimensions of the objects themselves. Moreover, there exist arguments, which are not experimental but theoretical, that strongly favor the idea that the predictions from the theorem should remain valid however great the distance between the objects happens to be. Under such conditions, we are forced to admit that these objects—even if they occupy regions of space that are extremely far from one another—are not truly *separated*. It is this idea that, for short, I shall henceforth call "nonseparability" (see also Glossary).

Two additional remarks must be made. One of them bears on the fact that these experiments testify to the existence of nonseparability, but merely with regard to rather special physical systems: particles with spin paired within spin-zero states (or within states corresponding to some definite total spin). To what extent is it admissible to extrapolate this notion to the cases of arbitrary systems having interacted in the past? The answer to such a question—and this is the essence of my first remark—can be obtained only by means of a reference to theory. As has already been stressed, a general theory of microsystems (particles, atoms, molecules, etc.) has existed for quite a long time now. It is called "elementary quantum mechanics." With regard to the pairs of particles with spin lying in a state of zero (or of precisely defined) total spin, this theory already foretold that the theorem would be violated. In other words, it predicted nonseparability. As a matter of fact, if we could have taken all its predictions for granted, we would not even have found it necessary to perform the experiment: we would have known its result in advance.[18] But, on the other hand, nonseparability runs contrary to so many "obvious," or at least apparently obvious, facts that it would not have been appropriate to rely exclusively on theory in this domain. It is therefore much more satisfactory that the experiment was performed.

However, now it has been! At present we have therefore no choice but to assume that nonseparability does indeed hold true at least in *some* cases, so that we have no good reason for not believing in its existence in the other cases as well, in which quantum mechanics tells us it should exist. Again, since quantum mechanics is the general theory of atoms, and

---

[18] This is why nonseparability was a theoretical discovery before being an experimental one.

since the whole world is "made of atoms," we are led to consider that nonseparability is a most general feature.[19]

The next remark is more of the nature of a warning. Although intuitively the notion of "influence" is clear, in particle physics it turns out to be a delicate one (see Ref. 13). In particular it should not be thought that the appearance of strange faster-than-light "influences" entails the possibility of sending utilizable signals that travel faster than light. It does not. And it can even be shown that the experiments described above open no such possibility. Hence, nonseparability should catch the attention of those who are, first of all, anxious to *know*; but those who are exclusively keen on *doing* should take no special interest in it.

To end this chapter, it may perhaps be useful to qualitatively summarize the mode of reasoning that has been used here, in order to make it quite clear that this reasoning is indeed compelling. For this purpose, the simplest procedure seems to entail returning to an idealized case and again take up the example of the examinations. And since the physical experiment has shown us that the predictions of the theorem are violated in some cases, it is appropriate, for our purpose, to imagine an extreme case of violation of some corresponding predictions bearing on examination results. Let us consider a situation in which some pairs of twins succeed both in Latin and Greek but in which no pair is successful in both Latin and Chinese and in which no pair is composed of one student successful in Greek and one having failed in Chinese. This, again, is imagined to take place in a university in which a strict correlation is constantly observed with regard to those twins who take the same examination. It is needless to add that, in order for this university to resemble the experimental devices relating to subatomic particles, it is necessary for its population to be immensely numerous and that the examinations should be as frequent and repetitive as we like. We thus assume that it is not in just one given term but in all similarly organized terms that the theorem is violated and is so in many of them, as specified above.

How then shall we manage to account in the most reasonable way for these results? If no drawing of lots had taken place, an outline of a possible solution would, for example, consist of speculating that "Chinese is a difficult subject, so that seeing their brothers on the verge of being examined on Chinese demoralized the students whose brothers were in such a situation to the extent that they lost all their abilities in other fields." But such an argument is not valid since all the students learned all three subjects and since it was only at the very last moment, when each twin was already well separated from his brother, that he drew the subject

---

[19] Incidentally, it should be noted that the experiments in question constitute a most valuable test of the validity of quantum mechanics at macroscopic distances. This shows how extremely erroneous it would be to state—as was sometimes suggested—that quantum mechanics applies only to phenomena involving lengths of the order of atomic distances, that "the *scale* determines the law."

on which he was to be examined. Another attempt at a solution would consist of trying to attribute the facts to a queer fancy of the examiners, who would have decided in advance that the brothers of all the students taking Chinese would be failed. But this explanation is faulty as well, since the examiners of a candidate cannot know which subject the brother of this candidate has drawn. And as for attempting to solve the problem by considering solely the aptitudes of the students, the theorem clearly shows that this idea entails a contradiction. Here, the proof is even simpler than in the general case. It can be summarized as follows: The notion of "aptitudes of a given pair" is meaningful (since, as the strict correlations have shown, the twins within a given pair have identical aptitudes). By assumption, no pair has both the aptitudes for success in Latin and Chinese, regardless of the size of the sample. This shows that there are none whatsoever (apart from possible but negligible fluctuations). A fortiori there are no pairs having aptitudes for success in all three subjects—Latin, Greek, and Chinese. Similarly, the nonexistence (which follows from the assumption) of pairs having both an aptitude for success in Greek and an aptitude for failure in Chinese entails (and hence proves) the nonexistence of pairs having aptitudes for success in both Latin and Greek and having, at the same time, an aptitude for failure in Chinese. Therefore, on the whole, there should be no pair whatsoever having aptitudes for success in Latin and Greek (since any such pair would obviously either be able or be unable to pass in Chinese!).

How can we then explain the results that we have assumed were obtained (and which run counter to the foregoing conclusion)? Apart from imagining some strict "pre-established harmony" (which, here, would look artificial to the extent of being unthinkable!), no solution will be found that does not somehow bring into play some influence at a distance, either between the twins or between the examiners (or, what amounts to the same, some hypothetical "nonseparation" of the two twins or of the corresponding particles). On the other hand, as soon as the possibility of such distant influences is introduced, solutions become available. One of them, for example, would be to assume that drawing the subject "Chinese" fills any student with an uneasiness which, by telepathy, makes his brother feel uneasy as well, so much so that the latter is unable to succeed in any subject whatsoever.[20]

The physical experiments we alluded to are actual experiments. They suffer from all the usual instrumental defects which are easily eliminated only through *thought* experiments! We therefore should not be surprized that they are not cases as pure as the model just examined. But they point in the same direction, and the idealization described by the

---

[20] Of course, this is merely an analogy. In physics, there is *a priori* no reason that the corresponding distant "influences" (between instrument and system) should have anything to do with telepathy.

model therefore makes it possible to grasp the essential point of the argument by which, for some experiments, nonseparability is inferred.[21,22]

4.8 Indivisibility

Finally, it should be noted that in this chapter nonseparability was unquestionably proven but only in the realm—made explicit at the

---

[21] Each one of the measurements performed in these experiments takes place—as, in principle, every measurement does—at a given location and at a given time. Therefore, they are of the type of entity called an "event" in physics. This clearly shows how incorrect it would be to assert that somehow nonseparability can be eliminated by simply "switching from a statistical to a dynamic viewpoint" or, in other words, by simply transferring from the "objects" to the "events" the exalted ontological status that the old physics attributed to the former. In fact, it must be that the events themselves, or at least some of them, are governed by nonseparability in such a way that the concept of "an event" should in fact be refined and made less absolute.

Similarly, it would be quite hopeless to try to eliminate nonseparability by simply giving up the concept of "particle" (that is, by trying to exclusively use the wave or the field concepts). A pure wave theory of *classical* physics, such as the Maxwell electromagnetic theory, is one in which the strict correlation phenomena of the type investigated in this chapter *do*, if they exist, obey the conditions of the theorem. Essentially, this is due to the fact that in any *classical* wave (or field) theory, it is meaningful to speak of the value of a given field at a given space–time point. The facts reported here therefore constitute an experimental indication, free from any dependence on any particular theoretical interpretation, in favor of giving up all attempts at building a general theory whose ultimate constitutive elements (in the sense of truly existing entities) would be such fields. (In *quantum* field theory, this is not the case, as is well known; see Chapter 9.)

[22] The following question is sometimes asked. "Is this nonseparability—which quantum mechanics formally introduces and which is shown actually to exist by the experiments described above—really such a new concept as asserted here? Is it not possible that a few of its aspects existed within old physics? For example, is it not the case that the total (i.e., kinetic plus potential) energy of an extended complex system is already a nonseparable entity?"

To that question the answer is as follows. Let us, for example, consider a double-star system. It is quite true that whereas the kinetic energy of such a system is separable, its potential energy is not. It is jointly possessed by the two components. However, let us imagine that the system explodes. The two component stars then travel farther and farther from one another, the distance between them increasing steadily but without limit. In this process, their interaction energy decreases and approaches zero. However small a preselected number ϵ may be, a distance L can always be found such that as soon as the distance between the two stars grows larger than L, the interaction energy becomes smaller than ϵ. After this time, we can (at least) say that the two stars constitute a system that is "separable to within ϵ." On the contrary, in the case of the two protons considered in the text, the distance, as we know, does not play any basic role. The inequality stated in the theorem is violated as strongly in the case in which the measurements are done on mutually faraway protons as when they are performed on protons that are still rather close to one another. Hence, as we see, the situation here is altogether different from that in the classical case just described. So a reasonable thing to do is to use the word "nonseparability" exclusively for describing nonclassical situations, such as those described in the text, in which increases in the distances settles nothing. And under these conditions, the answer to the question asked above is that nonseparability is indeed a new concept, that the possibility that it should correspond to something real arose when quantum mechanics first appeared, and that its actual correspondence to an objective feature of reality was experimentally proven only by the recent experiments alluded to in this text.

beginning—of a "realistic" philosophy. An interesting last question would be to ask whether or not something similar to nonseparability appears within the conceptions of Bohr and the Copenhagen School which, in a way, pass beyond such a realm. A thorough analysis of this problem turns out to be quite complex. Some starting points that seem appropriate to this effect are developed in the following chapters. But, fortunately, the leading guideline to the correct answer is rather clear nevertheless. To find out what it is, it suffices to again consider the already quoted statement of L. Rosenfeld—"it is now the indivisible whole constituted by the system and the measuring instruments that defines the phenomenon"—and to remember that in the experiment described above there are two measuring instruments arbitrarily far from one another. Nevertheless, they constitute—according to Rosenfeld's phrase—an "indivisible whole" of which the system is also a part. If such an "indivisibility" of a "whole" which is obviously extended in space has any meaning, it can only be a notion very closely related to that of nonseparability, if not identical to it.

Such a judgement is confirmed by a detailed study of Bohr's analysis of the experiments described above.[23] Substantially, Bohr mentions the phenomena constituted by the recording of the measurement results by two instruments that lie far away from one another. He points out that the very conditions which define the possible types of predictions regarding the future behavior of (here) the proton travelling towards one of the instruments depend on the entire experimental set-up (including, therefore, the other distant instrument), and he asserts that "these conditions constitute an inherent element of the description of any phenomena to which the term *physical reality* can be properly attached."

Conditions that relate to an instrument lying far from the considered location and that nevertheless constitute an inherent element—irreplaceable by any other—of the description of the physical reality as it *is* at that location at that moment: indeed, this is unquestionably the mark of a basic indivisibility. This indivisibility is not exactly identical to the nonseparability defined above, since it involves instruments instead of microscopic systems alone. It also differs, to some extent, from the latter because of the fact that somehow it links together even objects that have not, or have not yet, interacted. However, when we ponder this, we observe that these two features make the indivisibility (*à la* Bohr) something even more remote from common sense than nonseparability. Apart from these details, the two notions are quite similar, since both of them can hardly be interpreted otherwise than by considering the notion of physical distance as relative to, and dependent upon, the notion of *human* abilities: a dis-

---

[23] Bohr could not know the results of these experiments, but he could discuss some rather similar "thought experiments" that had been previously imagined by Einstein, Podolsky, and Rosen. And he knew the results the quantum theory predicted for the latter. Therefore, his discussion remains well grounded experimentally since, again, the results of the actual experiments corroborated these predictions (N. Bohr, *Phys. Rev.* **48**, 696 (1935).

tance does not intrinsically *exist* between certain elements of independent reality. We ourselves put it, so to speak, between the elements of *empirical reality,* or, otherwise stated, in the *picture* of reality that we devise for communication and other uses.

The systematic investigation of these problems will be taken up again, but only after some "interludes" will have underlined as forcefully as deemed necessary the substance of what is philosophically at stake here.

CHAPTER 5

Unkind Artless Interlude

5.1 Matter

The physical sciences are quite often termed "sciences of matter," which implies that matter is their basic concept. And one of the facts that it seems to me scientists try to persuade us of is that indeed everything narrows down to the notion of matter; that, in the Absolute, only matter exists, with innumerable properties.

The least we can demand from such diehard materialists is that they should tell us what the notion of matter means to them. To make this clear, a friend of mine once visited some professors, my dear colleagues. The first one he met was an extremely old chemist. He said, "young man, this is easy: matter is conserved whereas form is lost. See Lavoisier for supplementary details." But in the meantime, an elementary-particle physicist mentioned mass defects and the discovery of anti-particles. To save the notion of conservation, he suggested that the number of baryons minus the number of anti-baryons (or one-third the number of quarks minus that of the anti-quarks) be called "matter." Before he could define these terms, though, one of his colleagues stepped in. To this number he proposed the addition of the number of leptons minus that of anti-leptons. They finally agreed that the choice between these proposals—and between others as well—was entirely arbitrary. And as somebody said, "but then Number is the Idea of Things," the two fellows unobtrusively slipped away, afraid of being labelled Platonists!

5.2 Objectivity

Atomistic, or mechanistic, materialism is a set of three assumptions. An ontologic one: independent of us, the world is made like a clock. Tiny bodies, fields, and forces constitute its parts and its springs. An epistemological assumption: we are all able to know better and better, and finally quite well, the world just as it is, with all its composite wheelworks. Of course, these two propositions cannot be *derived* from any obvious truth. Under the incentive of various views, both philosophers and mystics can therefore quite well discard them without inspection. But their upholder (who, at present, is, as a rule, the biologist) then has a ready-made reply: a conception, he will answer, can only be justified by considering its consequences. Now what are those of the philosopher's standpoint? Or of the mystical standpoint? Objectively, there are none whatsoever. Whereas, look at my own: it is verified by the totality of classical physics, by quite a large part of astrophysics, and by the whole of contemporary biology. Even in fields such as those of life and thought, in which, naively, we could have believed in finality and in an active role of mind, our present day discoveries show the reign of pure chance and necessity. Think of the model of the twin helix!

Thus, this scientist proceeds, would it not be foolish or, at any rate, infantile to go on talking about final causes? Or, again, foolish to consider mind (and the consciousness we may have of things) to be *entities* on the same level as matter, that is, on the same level as the tiny bodies or fields which, taken alone, account for the whole universe including man and including man's mind and consciousness? These are all childish views, or, better to say, secondary effects, bewitching and luring semblances from which every strong lucid adult should free himself. A multitude of tiny bodies bound together by forces described by quantum physics, sometimes subject to determinism and sometimes to objective chance—such indeed is the ultimate stuff of the world. Everything comes down to physics, to the pure and icy objectivity of physics!

Overawed by such a triumphalism and such a bulky self-reliance, idealists and thinkers have to hang their heads. They all confess that they, up until now, gave themselves up to trifles instead of beholding the very essence of mankind, which is, of course, molecular biology. But, by the way, is it actually molecular biology? No indeed. If it is true that (as our scientist was just saying) biology reduces to physics, at least in principle, then physics, not biology is at the heart of the matter. The most inquiring minds within their troop (but these are not many, this track being more uphill than the former!) therefore turn to the physicists, to learn what *they* have to say on this point.

These sing another tune, and their triumphalism is different. Less youthful to be sure, but no less powerful. For some thirty years now, basic physics, laboring in the field of artificially produced phenomena, has been digesting—painfully a times!—its pre-World War II conquests. Indeed, what does the physicist assert? Just one short simple but true proposition: "In principle, I can account for the totality of the phenomena that you see around you—All of them really!" We reply with astonishment, "Yes indeed, really all—How then?—Basically by means of the Maxwell and Schrödinger equations."

At this point, we divines and thinkers are overawed even more. "This indeed corroborates what our mechanist interlocutor was saying a moment ago!" we exclaim together. But "Hush!" the physicist whispers, "the word *mechanist* is not in our good books here." "But why?" we ask. "Don't you agree with, say, the biologists, that science, and science alone, is objective?" "Yes, to be sure," our man exclaims with determination. "But, then, why do you brush aside this qualification of *mechanist?*" "Oh, well, the point is just that these biologists and us do not agree entirely on the meaning of the word *objective,* so that the term *mechanist* somewhat offends our ears. However, please believe me, this is but a minor irrelevant detail; its explicitation would just bore you." "But, look here, we must know what we divines and thinkers should tell our flock. What should we say to them about the nature of science?" "Well, just that it is objective. Isn't that extremely easy?"

These words bring about a general hush that the physicist takes to be skepticism. To try to convince us, he stresses the point: "You see, he says, between religious orders—and conceptually the scientists are such ascetics that, in a way, they are our modern monks!—between religious orders, as I was saying, this is not the first time that such—oh so minor!—difficulties have arisen. But, drawing our inspiration from what the shrewd author of the *Provinciales*[1] reports, we and these biologists did in fact succeed in making peace on this subject. For that, we just had to agree to say in unison that the basic principles on which science is based *are objective ones,* full stop. As a matter of fact, we, the physicists, do not understand that statement as most people do: in our interpretation, the principles in question *can refer in an essential way to the abilities or to the inabilities of the observers,* provided they should be common to *all* potential human observers instead of being particular to one of them. Indeed, we are tied down to such a careful formulation; otherwise, conventional atomic physics would be inconsistent. Crumbling down, it would sweep away molecular physics in its fall, and molecular biology as well! On the contrary, when biologists say that a given statement is objective, the idea they are trying to convey is that it bears on Reality itself, of which men are merely an accident, so that it should obviously not refer in an essential way to them. *That* is why we, quite appropriately, call them *mechanists,* which is among us a disparaging epithet. But these differences remain secret, for, as you may well grasp, it would be unseemly to display such discordances! The laymen would not understand! Thus, to those who ask, you should just answer that science is *objective,* and you must be very careful not to try to define that word."

"But, Reverend Father—oh, sorry, we meant Professor—we then reply, still, this *does* make some difference. For after all, if it is true that the basic principles of physics cannot even be formulated without some essen-

---

[1] *Note for English-speaking readers:* Blaise Pascal (1623–1662), one of the best French classical writers, was one of the main pioneers of the experimental method in science. In particular, he proposed and closely directed the experiment that established the existence of atmospheric pressure. Later he became a Jansenist. In his witty criticism of the Sorbonne prosecutors of the Jansenius followers (*Lettres Provinciales,* 1665), he ruined the ponderous argument of the former by showing that they were united only in words.

tial reference to the abilities of human observers, or even merely to the limitations of their general faculties, then is it not sheer nonsense to go on speaking of *naked apes* and of all the other leitmotivs of a materialist world view which fancies itself to be in the vanguard? Man, then, would *not* just be a negligible physical system. He would *not* come out of Nature, as a mere adventitious petty excrescence, in but a tiny portion of the Universe that his science describes and that his senses grasp. On the contrary, he would be the very measure—and even, finally, the co-author—of all this empirical World that he perceives and that he believes exists all by itself. Protagoras, not Lucretius, would have been right!''

"Please excluse me,'' the scientist replies, "specialization is binding: I simply may not listen to nonscientific remarks!''

CHAPTER 6

Comments on Scientism

Irony has some advantages. It brings out the gist of a question. It reveals in what way that question concerns us. Used after some tedious argument, it emphasizes the possible significance of the results obtained and it makes even the most heedless readers aware of their novelty.

This is why I feel no remorse with respect to the content of the foregoing chapter. Too many of our contemporaries derive, from the very vague scientific notions they hold, a world view that has definitely been rendered obsolete by recent advances in physical research. I refer to the discovery of experimental procedures that tend to clarify and prove some esoteric postulates that had for some time been known to be lurking in the depths of contemporary theoretical physics. This discovery is of more than academic interest. And it would be a pity if such new insights and questions were only perceived on a technical level. They deserve a better fate. However, in order to clearly depict their significance and scope to more than a small group of theorists, well-defined colors must be used. Moreover, the use of irony as a mere revealer clearly has nothing to do with the intellectual fallacy of trying to really *solve* problems by irony. It is clear that irony must necessarily confine itself to casual talk. Hence, with regard to difficult concepts and conclusions that defy outward common sense, the ironist, as a rule, simply avoids taking them into account! On the other hand, if a result is already established, then why not be ironical—now without fear of being simplistic!—toward those people who continue to ignore the result?

Still, I agree that the risks of a "boomerang effect" that this procedure presents, even if used with caution, are appreciable. There are a good number of people who are at the same time superficial and dogmatic and who readily claim innate universal knowledge. Many among them simply scorn the results arrived at by the scientists. Many even try to reverse the roles. They tax with dogmatism those very scientists who (at the price of an occasionally disheartening intellectual asceticism) strive to conquer some nonillusory knowledge. The criticism of science is quite definitely healthy, and so is that of philosophy, but under the explicit condition that neither one nor the other be undermined by the charlatans of mere denial! If Chapter 5 were to be understood to bring grist—be it a mere

speck!—to the mill of the latter, this would constitute a total misunderstanding: the professors envisioned in the preceding chapter do not resemble real scientists any more than Pascal's monks resemble St. John of
the Cross. They are mere puppets, invented only for the purpose of
explicating a *problem*.

This problem, for its part, is far from imaginary. It proceeds from the
existence of a kind of diffuse scientism. Admittedly scientistic thought is
hardly attractive in itself, especially at a time such as ours, when the
pernicious consequences of some scientific technologies are so very much
emphasized. Even with regard to pure knowledge, this thought is far from
being attractive *a priori*. In the eyes of many, it is, on the contrary, des-
perately barren. But, nevertheless, many serious thinkers have defended it
with perseverance. Why is this so? The answer is simple. They fought for
it just because they considered it to be objectively *true*. And because of
the obvious, though often overlooked, fact that an idea can be at the same
time both unpleasant and true! As has been said pertinently, "there is no
proof by awfulness." And no refutation either. Even though, for reasons I
shall elucidate, I do not share the scientistic view of the world, I cannot
but approve of its supporters for having firmly upheld such a truth.

It is not by mere hand-waving nor by vague references to "human
values," "hope," etc. that I, for my part, prefer to see scientism disproved. For again it is built on truly serious foundations. It is trivial—and
beyond question!—that the Newtonian force accounts for the motion of
the planets more satisfactorily than Kepler's hypothesis involving angels,
that, in a sense, matter is composed of atoms obeying the same laws
everywhere, on Earth as well as in the most remote galaxies; that the great
forests, which astonish us with their beauty, are, in the same sense, built
of myriads of molecules reproducing themselves mechanically like so
many tiny machines; that the moon illuminating the night is a conglomer-
ate of rocks and not a haven for forsaken love! As tedious or laborious as
it may be to recall these very plain facts, do we have the right to forget
them? To forget that they are facts?

I, for my part, think that it would be dishonest to act, under the pre-
tence of their banality, as if they did not exist—a weakness succumbed to
so readily by mystics. I understand very well that many physicists of the
classical age of physics—that of the discovery of molecules, atoms, electrons, etc.—could have been convinced of the truth of a "plain" scientific
vision of the world. I understand very well, too, that many biologists of
our time, sometimes in spite of the feelings in their hearts, think the same
way. Is it not true, by the way, that "reductionist" thinking strongly
inspired by scientism has subtly taken hold of the diffuse mentality in each
of us, compelling even, for example, nonmaterialists to think somehow of
their own mind using concepts borrowed from the technique of electronic
computers? If scientism were correct, or more precisely, if the view of the
world it proposes so forcefully, that of a world ultimately consisting of
myriads of small localized objects merely endowed with quasilocal prop-

erties were correct, then such an evolution of our mentality would admittedly be excellent. It is always good for man to know the truth! But on the other hand, if the ultimate vision of the world which scientism proposes is false, if its conceptual bases are mistaken, then this development is, on the contrary, quite unfortunate. As the philosophy of enlightenment quite rightfully proclaimed, a general widespread sociological mental habit grounded on false ideas is dangerous in any case!

Now my thesis regarding this, as could be seen in Chapter 5, is that the second of the two possibilities is in fact realized, or in other words, that common "scientism" is false. On this I agree with prominent philosophers, whose reasoning will be made explicit below. But, contrary to their argument, mine is founded on scientific, that is, on specific, facts. We could imagine a world to which it could not be applied; it is applicable to the world that experimentation reveals to us.

We already know the elements of this argument. But it must now be made precise, and this requires a discussion of three postulates, that of *physical realism*, that of *strong objectivity*, and that of *multitudinism*. Here it is no longer a question of irony and even less of a search for some striking formula suitable for reviving the attention of the reader. It is therefore appropriate to introduce these concepts one after another, taking care, each time, that the definition is unambiguous and consistent.

6.1 Postulate of Physical Realism

I know of no recourse better than to borrow from A. Messiah his definition of this postulate. In his classic reference work, *Mécanique Quantique* (Dunod, Paris), we read:

> The first thing to demand from a theory is of course that its predictions should agree with experimental observations. It is quite certain that quantum mechanics fulfills this condition, at least in the domain of atomic and molecular physics. But a physical theory can not claim completeness if it restricts itself to predicting what can be observed in this or that experiment. At the start of every scientific enterprise a fundamental postulate is made that nature possesses an objective reality, independent of our sensory perception and of our means of investigation; the object of a theory is to give an account of this objective reality.[1]

I will call the postulate stated here by Messiah, the "postulate of physical realism." Contrary to what the text seems to indicate, the postulate of physical realism is not universally accepted. In this respect, empiricists

---

[1] The author goes on to remark that the statements of quantum theory as they are taught take, on the contrary, a form that refers to our perception or to our instruments. Yet, like other authors of textbooks in microphysics, he refrains from discussing the problems that this observation presents.

have adopted an attitude of reserve, as we have seen, and many theoretical physicists have followed suit. But the majority of scientists do not share this view. On the contrary, the postulate in question constitutes, in effect, the point of departure of their entire enterprise. This is particularly true with regard to those among them who could be regarded as upholders of scientism. But it is also true of others. Finally, one could note that physical realism is obviously a particular case of the realism defined at the beginning of Chapter 3, and which also encompasses the philosophies of *nonphysical* realism, those that deny that any theory founded on experience could ever reach the Real (for example, the philosophy of Plato).

6.2 Postulate of Strong Objectivity

The postulate of physical realism has a consequence of considerable importance as far as the definition of one of the most essential words in the scientific vocabulary is concerned, namely the word *objectivity*. To show this, let us consider a scientist who does not accept physical realism. How can he define this key word? Not, of course, by referring to some intrinsic reality, since for him such a concept is not scientific. Since, for him, the concept of observation is essential, it is of course with the help of this concept that he will build up his definition. And indeed this is what he does. For example, it is apparent from the works of Niels Bohr, as we have seen, that for this author a statement is objective as soon as it is *valid for any observer*. Thus, for such scientists, a statement or a definition that makes reference, even in an essential way, to the concept of the human observer can very well be *objective*: it suffices that it be invariant with respect to a change of observers. Let me call objectivity defined this way *weak objectivity*. It differs from subjectivity fundamentally through this invariance. It could also be called "intersubjectivity." Even a die-hard realist could not deny that weak objectivity is sufficient for the development of science, at least so long as it refrains from any claim of describing what lies beyond human experience.

Yet it is obvious that the realist—or, more precisely, he who accepts the postulate of physical realism—cannot be content with such a definition of objectivity. If, as in the statement of Messiah, the object of a physical theory is to give an intelligible account of a reality independent of our sensory perceptions or of our means of investigation, then it is clear that whatever the role of observation with regard to establishing a theory, the objective conclusions of the latter must exclusively bear upon this reality. This means that it must certainly not make *any* essential reference to the community of human observers.[2] Let me say that *strong objectivity* is

---

[2] Here the use of the word "essential" should perhaps be explained. Its presence in the text is an intentional schematic allusion to the unquestionable fact—well known to

objectivity understood in this way, and let me define the *postulate* or *principle* of *strong objectivity* to be the postulate according to which all statements and definitions that a science calls objective should be expressed—or should at least be expressible—in the language of strong objectivity. In particular, the upholders of scientism assert, as we have

---

philosophers—that any statement is composed of words, that these words express concepts, and that these concepts unavoidably map the human experience from which they stem. Such an observation might lead some readers to believe that, after all, no statement exists which, strictly speaking, would not be objective merely in the sense called "weak" here. Strong objectivity either would reduce to weak objectivity or would just be a delusion.

Personally, I do not think that this conclusion is correct. More precisely, I consider that *to a* (conscious or unconscious) *supporter of physical realism*, it does not follow from the premises. For, indeed, by definition such a realist believes in the real existence of the entities to which at least a few of the words he uses refer. For example, let us consider the statement of Newtonian mechanics expressed by the sentence "two massive objects isolated in space from one another both suffer an acceleration which is inversely proportional to the square of the distance between them." It is quite true that, in this statement (which is intentionally simplified with respect to irrelevant details), words such as "distance" and "acceleration" express concepts that we human beings recognize solely through human experience and human thinking. In other words, they are what we call "constructs" (and the second one is even quite an elaborate one and, in fact, arose rather recently). Nevertheless, the supporter of physical realism—like most supporters of realism—does believe, according to the very definition of his philosophical standpoint, that it is meaningful to speak of entities that "really exist," quite independent of the existence or nonexistence of any actual or potential observer. Therefore, with regard to the above statement from Newtonian mechanics, he has only two choices. Either he assumes that the distance and acceleration mentioned are indeed such entities (i.e., at every time the two massive objects are actually at different locations and *do* possess the accelerated motion in question) and thus the statement is truly strongly objective and not merely weakly objective, or he assumes that either the distance, or the acceleration, or both are not entities that exist independent of any observer (and that presumably the same is true of the objects to which they relate). Admittedly, in the second case, the statement in question is, to the realist, objective merely in the weak sense. But concomitantly, if he wants to be consistent with regard to his physical realism, this realist is forced to seriously investigate the problem that then arises for him. Since, by assumption, Nature has a reality independent of any observer, and since the ultimate purpose of science is to describe that reality, he must try to discover that deeper level of reality and describe it by means of statements bearing upon it effectively, hence, strongly objectively. If he does not succeed he must hope others will. To be content with statements whose objectivity is merely weak amounts, *for him,* to being deceived by fine words (see, also, Chapter 11, "the philosopher's beeline").

Conversely, could weak objectivity be reduced to strong objectivity? The answer is that it depends on the statements considered. To be sure, any strongly objective statement can be replaced by a weakly objective one; for it is enough to replace such phrases like "the physical quantity A has value a" by an expression of the type "if A is measured, a is found." But the converse is false. In particular, with regard to quantum-mechanical statements, there is at least one of them, the one that concerns the probability of obtaining a certain result if a certain measurement is made (this, for the benefit of the experts!) for which it is quite difficult to substitute a strongly objective statement. For indeed, in order not to lead to erroneous results, such a statement would have to refer either to the universe in its totality or to the measuring instruments. Now, the attempts that have been made at reducing the latter notion (with regard to those of its features that are relevant to the present problem) to the notion of macroscopic systems are admittedly quite interesting. But their complexity is so tremendous that, all by itself, it nevertheless suffices to cast doubts on their actual relevance; for it would be—to say the least—disconcerting that the most basic laws of the universe should hide such inextricable intricacies beneath their apparent simplicity (in this connection, see, also, *the macroscopic diversion* in Chapter 11).

seen, that man, including the human mind, is a mere accident of an independent reality that can be described by science. Would it not be inconsistent with such a conception to make the very laws of the universe dependent on the abilities of human beings, especially when it is observed that the latter occupy but an insignificant portion of the universe and seem to exist there only by mere chance? The upholders of scientism therefore necessarily agree with the principle of strong objectivity. In fact most of them regard it as so obvious that the idea that it might be questioned does not even occur to them. And, parenthetically, the compartmentalization of the various branches of science, which an increase in knowledge has unfortunately made unavoidable, has the consequence that the upholders in question are unaware of a basic fact: this fact is that the theory of atoms and molecules taught by their physicist colleagues is built upon a definition of objectivity that itself is *not* based on the principles of strong objectivity.

6.3 Postulate of Multitudinism

In ancient times, the doctrine of Democritus and his followers, such as Epicurus and Lucretius, contrasted with that of most other philosophers in that it identified Being with a huge *multiplicity* of extremely simple objects, all well localized in space. For a long time the majority of thinkers considered such a view a drastic oversimplification. How could a cloud, a star, or a bird be a mere aggregate of atoms? But by degrees the situation changed. The theory, which at first had seemed childishly elementary, proved more and more fruitful as time went on, so that near the end of the last century, what had at first been just a provocative thesis became an accepted idea. It is the idea in question that the term *multitudinism* is meant to express. In other words, I shall call *multitudinism* any view of the world in which the universe is seen as composed of a huge number of extremely simple components (of merely a few different kinds), each occupying only one region of space at any given time and exerting only very small influences on the behavior of remote components, so that a "Laplace demon," a being endowed with exquisite sensitivity and with perfect intelligence, would be able to account for everything happening in a finite region of space during a given time interval, without having to consider events taking place in remote regions during that same time interval.[3] Democritian atomism is an example of multitudinism. But a

---

[3] A little thinking will show that such a "locality postulate" is indeed a part of "multitudinism"; for denying its validity would be tantamount to believing in some manifestations of a globality. The denial of such a globality is the very essence of multitudinism.

classical relativistic theory of fields constitutes another example since, according to this theory, at any place and time the fields possess definite values that can be locally modified without changing the values the fields have at that *same* time at different locations. Contrary to the tendency of many persons lacking scientific education, it should not be believed that multitudinism is a concept that is easy to ignore.

Is it possible to conceive of a scientism that would do without multitudinism? Our answer to this question must obviously depend on the range we are prepared to attribute to the very notion of "scientism." However, it is clear that all the world-views that have hitherto been put forward and that can properly be classified under that heading are multitudinisms. Moreover, any view of the world that discards multitudinism calls for conceptual movement along lines that widely differ from the elementary reductionistic attitude specific to traditional scientism.

Considering this, it is very easy to show that scientism is false. Indeed, the proof is obvious, in view of the fact that, in any description of the world based on physical realism and on the strong objectivity requirement, the nonseparability concept definitely has a meaning: either there are phenomena in nature that exhibit nonseparability or there are no such phenomena. At present, the experimental and theoretical evidence is strongly in favor of the former alternative, as shown in Chapter 4. Hence, there are cases in which even the Laplace demon described above could *not* account for what takes place during a given time interval in a given region R of space—containing an object S—without taking into account that which takes place during that same time interval within another region R' which may be far from R. Specifically, R' is a region of space containing an instrument that interacts with a physical system that itself interacted in the past with object S. It is quite clear that the distance between the two regions R and R' can be arbitrarily large. Hence, the postulate of multitudinism is violated. And since it is, as we have seen, one of the components of traditional scientism, the latter must be discarded for its disagreement with experimental data. This is the conclusion we must keep in mind.

Of course, there is no novelty in the idea that scientism is a view of the world that does not really fit the structures of contemporary theoretical physics. Even in scientific circles, this idea has been considered for quite a long time, especially among theoretical physicists. Some of the writings of Werner Heisenberg are particularly enlightening in this respect. Two facts should be noted however. One is that the alternative conception that is put forward by the scientists in question is based on the philosophy of experience, a philosophy already described in Chapter 3, but one which actually also suffers from some defects that make it highly questionable, as will be shown. The second fact is that, until nonseparability was proven, the thesis that scientism is false could only be *made likely* through simplicity arguments that appealed more to pragmatists than to realists.[4] The discovery of experimental checks of nonseparability has changed this and has made the thesis a certainty, even for the realists.

---

[4] In this regard, the value of the indications that have been given for a long time by the study of the problem of irreversibility should not be minimized. Indeed the definition of entropy is definitely not objective in the strong sense, since it refers to our ignorance of details. It is true that contemporary physicists have tried to eliminate at least the most visible aspects of this "defect"; and, to some extent their efforts have been successful. Models of "infinite" macroscopic systems have been introduced (see Chapter 11) for which proofs of the existence of an "entropy" definable without reference to our ignorance of details have been provided. But in all these cases we are dealing with a rather formal entropy and with models which, in the frame of scientific realism, cannot be considered to be approximations of reality (see the discussion on page 125).

CHAPTER 7

Einstein's Objections to the Philosophy of Experience

To be sure, the conclusion that scientism is false can easily prod those scientists who reach it into leaning towards a positivist viewpoint or, in other words, towards "the philosophy of experience." They would then give up the idea of describing reality as it is; they would even have reservations with regard to the possibility of giving a meaning to such a concept and would lower their ambitions to the description of appearances. They would henceforth be content with finding general rules that make it possible to predict observations under given circumstances. If they feel that such a purpose is somewhat too unimpressive they can—in a very standard way!—find comfort in modifying the usual meaning of the words. They would call "reality" the set of all appearances and give the name "thing-in-itself" to the independent reality, that is, to the kind of reality that they gave up all hope of describing. They may then lift their heads and again claim that the subject matter of their investigation is indeed—as the man-in-the-street believes it to be!—objective reality.

The history of twentieth century physics shows—as already mentioned—that to a great extent such a moderate attitude is both wise and successful.

Deep down, though, the philosophy of experience lays itself open to objections. Not all of these, to be sure, have equal weight. Thus, for example, such a philosophy tends, as we have seen, to set aside any notion of a reality that would be completely independent of man (on the grounds that such a notion is useless, the reality in question being unknowable and that, moreover, it cannot be operationally defined). The rather obvious observation that this point of view bears some relationship to Berkeley's idealism is not *in itself* a significant criticism. It does not become one until some objective criticism of idealism is put into words and made explicit, for, obviously, it would be absurd to base a rejection on a simple question of labelling.

But, in my opinion, other objections against the philosophy of experience carry great weight. One of these is that I do not, and cannot, directly know the sensory data of other people. Hence, strictly speaking, all references to communicability—on which, in this philosophy, the very concept of objectivity is based, as previously noted—are references to something rather mysterious that positivism does not explain (Bohr's reference to an instrument conceals this defect to some extent, but it does not fully succeed in correcting it). If you take this philosophy seriously, then, as Einstein wrote, "avoiding solipsism becomes quite an undertaking."

Another objection is that we are not able to directly apprehend the events of the past. If it is granted that a statement can be given a meaning only when the possibility of its verification exists (which is ultimately provided by our sensory data), then a question arises as to the possibility of giving a meaning to statements which bear upon past events. A first answer could be that such a meaning is nonexistent. In fact, when such statements involve microscopic systems, such a meaning is often ill defined or ambiguous, as quantum mechanics shows. But what if the systems under consideration are of our own order of magnitude? According to the philosophy of experience, the usual answer is to assert that the statements in question are in fact statements about the future. Thus, the description of forests and lakes in the Mesozoic period would *exclusively* be a convenient procedure for summarizing indications helpful to anybody interested in finding oil or in discovering some skeletons of great reptiles! Very few scientists would readily support such a thesis. All, or at least most of them, would insist that the statements formally bearing on the past *do* in fact concern it and have clear, obvious, and unambiguous meanings as soon as they bear on macroscopic systems. But then, strictly speaking, this meaning cannot be purely operational. And, furthermore, a question then arises "between the microscopic and the macroscopic realms, where is the dividing line?"

Finally, how can induction be justified if it cannot be based on the regularities of a reality presumed external to our senses and independent of our abilities? I know quite well that such a justification is difficult in any case, even when external reality is granted. But then it is only a question of rigor, whereas in the philosophy of experience, when it is taken literally, all justifications, even intuitive ones, seem to be missing. If the sun does not exist as a reality in itself—if it exists only as a convention of language to account for the set of our past experiences—what justifies my belief that there will be daylight tomorrow? If it is nothing but habit, upon what is my confidence in this habit based? This objection to pure positivism constitutes an argument in favor of realism which, assuredly, is not rigorous (thus, for example, it is in *our* structure, not in an independent reality, that Kant sees the origin of the regularities we observe). Nevertheless such an argument is so simple that we use it all the time without noticing. In fact it leads us to believe in the existence of an external reality independent of all observations or measurements, and, with all due respect to Kant, the argument is credible. If we abandon the realm of general ideas, if we consider the details of the regularities we wish to explain, and if we think of the multitude of observers and the unanimity of their judgements in the case of simple questions, then we realize that the belief in an independent and structured reality remains the most plausible way to account for the regularities in our observations. This is without doubt what Einstein wanted to express when, criticizing Bohr, he wrote: "All men, quantum physicists included, firmly believe in this thesis about (the existence of) reality whenever they are not engaged in discussing the foundations of quantum mechanics."[1]

7.1 Einstein's View

We have reviewed the most serious general objections to the philosophy of experience. But there are other, more specific ones, which have been formulated against the way in which the philosophy of experience has been used to set up the foundations of the quantum theory of atoms and molecules. Again it was Einstein who led the attack. According to a prevailing opinion, if he found quantum theory unsatisfactory, it was because of its indeterministic nature. To be sure, his well-known quip "God does not play dice" might easily lead to this belief. But, considering available texts, it seems probable that such a condensation of a view which on the whole is rather classically Spinozan was in the end considered to be only a secondary objection by its author. The primary one, again, was based on the lack of strong objectivity[2] in the theory in question. This, in any case, was the conclusion arrived at by Wolfgang Pauli in the course of his conversation with Einstein himself—as he explained to Born in the letters already alluded to (see the end of Chapter 3).

In short, Einstein's reasoning developed through the following stages. Consider a macroscopic body moving freely through space—a little lead ball, for example. According to quantum theory, its wave function[3] depends on all of the coordinates, and on time as well. The partial differential equation obeyed by such a function ("the Schrödinger equation" of this system) is of a well-known type. From it, by an appropriate change of variables, a simple equation E can easily be obtained, which controls only the wave function of the center of gravity of the body under consideration. It can be shown that E is the "Schrödinger equation" of a free particle. Incidentally, all these mathematical developments are well grounded and undisputed.

Einstein then draws attention to the fact, equally well known, that E has an infinite number of acceptable solutions, the majority of which are "extended" wave functions, which means that these functions are appreciably different from zero in an extended region of space. By means of

---

[1] A. Einstein, in *Louis de Broglie, Physicien et Penseur*, Albin Michel, Paris, 1953.

[2] For a definition, see page 58.

[3] The wave function is the basic mathematical entity of elementary quantum mechanics. The square of its modulus represents the probability of finding the constituents of the physical system in question in specified positions.

arguments rarely questioned (few, even among his adversaries, criticized them), this author shows that the theory should then actually retain such solutions. In other words, he shows that for the sake of consistency, it must be conceded that in some cases the motion of the center of gravity of a physical object should be describable by *extended* wave functions.

He then notes that quantum theory claims to be capable of giving a *complete* description of physical reality. But if such an expression is to make sense, then *every* element of physical reality must be determined by the information provided by the theory, at least if that information is the maximum that the theory can provide.[4] Now, in conventional quantum theory, the wave function is simply the entity *that is supposed to supply maximal information.* But, on the other hand, if this wave function is extended, it does not specify the position of the center of gravity in space. If the theory is complete, the apparently absurd consequence then follows that the center of gravity of the body in question does not occupy any definite position, in spite of the fact that the body is macroscopic. As Einstein observes, if quantum theory were complete, "we would have to be astonished that a star, or a fly, that we see for the first time, should appear to be practically localized." He concludes that the description given by the wave function is an *incomplete* description which omits some elements of reality.

I have already explained (see Chapter 3) how the supporters of the philosophy of experience—and Wolfgang Pauli in particular—responded to Einstein's objections. Their argument consisted, as will be remembered, of maintaining that to talk about the structures of a given reality at a given moment is meaningless if, by assumption, this structure cannot be known at that moment. Within the epistomological framework of empiricism, such a refutation is justified. But that framework must first be accepted. Hence, Einstein's objection should admittedly not be used as an objection to the philosophy of experience, but, rather, as a contribution to forcefully illustrate the rather radical manner in which the philosophy in question is being used in contemporary physics. Here, there is no middle ground. There can be no question of a declaration in favor of empiricism that would remain purely verbal or that would more or less reduce to the mere statement that it is better to believe in facts than in theories, or the like. To be sure, if the maxim is put forward that we should only speak of what we know, I shall applaud. If it is added that all of our knowledge about reality ultimately comes from our senses and that theory is ancillary to experiment, I may applaud again (less loudly, though, because I shall remember the objections to pure positivism of philosophers such as J. Piaget). But if I am told that such general ideas embody *the whole* of the

---

[4] If I want to describe a rectangle, but mention only its length, then my description is incomplete. In the same way, thermodynamics, which provides only macroscopic entities and densities of relative distributions of molecules, but not the position or velocity of each of the latter, is an incomplete description, as any physicist would acknowledge.

philosophy of experience, I shall point out that, if this is so, then the philosophy in question is of no use in removing Einstein's difficulty concerning quantum theory. If the purpose is to somehow ground this theory—and, thereby, modern physics—on the philosophy of experience, then the analysis that centers on Einstein's objection makes it possible to estimate something like a "minimal price" that a realist must "pay" (by giving up some cherished beliefs) in order to obtain this result. That price consists of believing that reality is nothing more than the set of all phenomena and that these phenomena essentially refer to the means of investigation that man has at his disposal, so that, indirectly, reality itself refers to man.

But—it will be said—is it not true that the necessity of accepting a statement such as this has been known to philosophers for a long time? Do they not know that, as, for example, Bergson wrote, "that which is visible and tangible in things represents our possible action on them?" Admittedly, a great many of philosophers have expressed such views. But their usual practice of confining their arguments to rather general formulations does not always make it possible to discover their exact ideas. Here, for example, there exists a way of understanding Bergson's sentence that would make it look acceptable even to a realist (and I wonder whether this author himself did not intend just that); it consists of observing that the various living species are endowed with sense organs that differ very much from one species to another with regard to the kinds of contrasts they are able to perceive. A garden as seen by a human being and that same garden as seen by a frog are undoubtedly extremely different structures. These two living beings perceive different contrasts. Thus, each one "carves up," so to speak, reality in his own way. And since the senses are largely tools for action, tools endowed to these beings by natural selection, it is true to say that ultimately this "carving up" takes place according to the possible actions of each species.

Once again, even the most convinced realist (in the sense in which I have defined "realism") could not object to this interpretation of Bergson's sentence. But, on the other hand, it is essential to understand that such an unobstrusive interpretation of the statement that reality refers to man—to his abilities as an observer—is definitely *not* sufficient to disprove Einstein's objection. In the preceding example, the garden is—to the realist at any rate!—a structure of its own, and one that is extraordinarily complex, considering all the tiny parts of its composition. Hence, its correct complete description involves a huge number of parameters, and the individuals of each species are sensitive to only *some* of these parameters. In other words, the descriptions their sensory data provide them make up an *incomplete* description of the garden. Of course, we then have no difficulty in conceiving that these descriptions differ from one another and that therefore the phenomena—or "appearances"—ultimately depend on the possibilities of action. But, in contrast to this, the description of reality that quantum theory provides is, according to its founders, supposed to be a *complete* description. For example, whoever knows the wave function of a system is thereby supposed to know *all* the parameters relating to the system. If this view is accepted, then the assertion that the description in question should still somehow be relative to the possibilities of investigation of mankind takes on a new dimension. Philosophically it becomes deeper—much closer, in a way, to Berkeley's ideas or at least to a very radical interpretation of Protagoras' already quoted statement that "man is the measure of all things."

7.2 A New Criticism from Einstein

If a realist may legitimately criticize the hidden idealism that he detects among upholders of the Copenhagen interpretation, could they not, on their part, charge him with dogmatism for his interpretation of the concept of reality? Could they not blame him for attempting to force physical theory into the mould of a preconceived vision of the form it should have? The history of science shows how great such a danger is. And the theorists of the generations that followed Einstein's were in fact almost unanimous in blaming him for having given up—in these matters—the open-mindedness of his younger years, which had led him to the discovery that universal Newtonian time does not exist. More precisely, the criticism may be stated like this: "Einstein formed an idea *a priori,* a philosophical one, and *consequently* (at this point, any professional philosopher among the readers should cover his face!) an ill-defined one, of the concept of reality."

The most basic concepts are also, of course, the most difficult ones to define. Nevertheless, Einstein accepted the challenge. He tried to operationally specify what should be meant by the expression "element of reality." Of course he was quite aware of the fact that we do not have a direct knowledge of things themselves but only of our perceptions and actions. He therefore aimed at defining elements of reality by relating them to observable physical quantities.

In order to understand Einstein's definition—which is reproduced below—it is appropriate to argue in terms of an example similar to that studied in Chapter 4. Let us therefore consider a test of a certain type A. We assume that we have made the observation that any individual who once passed (or failed) the test, passes (or fails) it whenever he takes it again, this being true at least in the cases in which he did not take a test of another type in between. I inquire as to the degree of reality that, in view of this, it is legitimate to assign at any given time to an *aptitude* of a given individual to pass a test of type A.

The answer, in such a case, seems quite obvious. It is clear that *after* an individual has passed a test of type A, his aptitude for passing a test of the same type is very real (at least until he takes another kind of test). On the other hand, nothing can be said about the reality of that same aptitude of his *before* he takes the very first test. In fact the "type A tests" might be of such a nature that most people, when they first take one, answer haphazardly and at random and that these answers are imprinted in their minds, so that they repeat it upon any uninterrupted sequence of such tests. In such a case, it would obviously be unjustified to speak of the aptitude of an individual for passing a test of type A if he has never taken one. Such a notion corresponds, in most cases, to nothing real.

If we now ponder this argument, if we inquire why it is a convincing one, we discover that it is based on the notion of predicting with certainty. Knowing what we know, when an individual has once passed a type A test, we can, with the help of induction, predict with certainty that he will also pass the following ones, whereas before the first test we can make no sure prediction.

As we see, the criterion spontaneously used above in a simple case in order to specify what should be called a *real* aptitude (or property) is now made explicit and general. It is thus appropriate to consider it a definition and to say that if the result of a measurement of a given physical entity can be predicted with certainty, then to that physical quantity there corresponds an element of reality. This is exactly what Einstein did. However, he also took a supplementary measure motivated by the need to discard an ambiguity still present in the phrase "if the result . . . can be predicted with certainty." This measure is as follows. In the preceding example, could it not be claimed that such a possibility exists before the first type A test is taken, due to the fact that the aptitude in question can be measured at will at any time (with, if necessary, the help of a preliminary test)? To dispose of this ambiguity—which, in other examples, could be less apparent and hence more serious than it is here—Einstein and his collaborators, Podolsky and Rosen, finally put forward the following, now quite well-known, definition.

Elements of Reality (Einstein, Podolsky, and Rosen). *If, without in any way disturbing a system, we can predict with certainty the value of a physical quantity, then there exists an element of physical reality corresponding to that quantity.*

Here the phrase "without in any way . . ." eliminates the aforementioned ambiguity, since, in our example, the possibility of a preliminary measurement entails the possibility of a disturbance of the individual by that very measurement (and, in turn, the disturbance could create a non-pre-existing aptitude).

Given such an operational definition—due to Einstein himself—of what may be called real, it is natural that we should return to this author's argument, as described above, concerning macroscopic objects. Can it be that before any measurements the center of gravity of a macroscopic object should not be localized better than within the limits of the domain in which the wave function is nonzero (i.e., quite poorly in some cases)? In other words, can it be that under such circumstances the position of the center of gravity is not an element of reality?

Here the realist may well be surprised. For the answer is "yes it can." This, at any rate, is true if the Einstein–Podolsky–Rosen definition is used. In fact, before any measurement of the position in question (or of quantities related to it), it is quite clear that we cannot predict with certainty the result that will be provided by the observation. This should reinforce, if necessary, the opinion that an operational definition of the concept of reality is not easily found, since even Einstein, when urged to exhibit one, could only arrive at a formulation that did not inforce his first intuition.

However, this is not to say that the definition of Einstein, Podolsky, and Rosen remained unused. Indeed, these authors simply applied it to another case by which they thought they could disprove the thesis that quantum theory constitutes a complete description of reality. The case is that of the correlations at a distance studied in Chapter 4.

In order to understand the principle of their argument, we need only recall the substance of some developments of that chapter. Let us imagine that in a sufficiently large sample of a population of couples, each male submits to a test A at a given location and each female submits to the same test at a different location. Moreover, let us assume that the outcome of the test is not always the same, but that all previous observations made on other couples of the same population have shown that if the outcome is favorable for the male, then it is also favorable for the female, and conversely. If, knowing this, I am informed that the outcome of a certain test A was favorable for a certain male, then I can predict with certainty that the corresponding female will pass her test successfully. And I obtain this certainty without disturbing this female, since she is far away from the place where I have obtained my information. Hence, this is a case in which the definition of Einstein, Podolsky, and Rosen applies. I can assert that before undergoing any test, the female has a well-determined aptitude, either positive or negative (lack of aptitude) to pass the test. I may say that this aptitude is an element of reality. I can also assert that this aptitude is not the same for all the females in the sample, since the outcomes of the test taken by the males are different from one another. Finally, I can also assert that a female has the aptitude in question immediately before the test is applied to "her" male. To confirm this, it suffices, once again, to note the fact that at the time in question, the female is far away from the place where her male takes the test. As a consequence, if all the *couples* in the ensemble are—before any test—represented by one and the same wave function (this is not possible for living beings, but it is, in some cases, for pairs of particles), then I must grant that in some cases, at least, it so happens that all the couples (or "pairs") described by one and the same wave function do not have the same elements of reality. In other words, I must grant that the description of physical reality supplied by the wave function is an *incomplete* description.

In the opinion of Einstein, Podolsky and Rosen, an argument like this[5] proved the physical existence of supplementary parameters (called "hidden") not described by the wave function. And because of their existence, various difficulties (we remember Einstein's questions about the star and the fly) that are encountered in the attempts to obtain a realist interpretation of the usual quantum theory are removed at the same time in a fairly obvious way.

7.3 The Experimental Verdict

At the present time—that is, taking the most recent achievements of physics into account—what can be said about the validity of the Einstein–Podolsky–Rosen argument? Even if it is surprising, the answer is quite definite and unambiguous; the argument simply does not apply, and this is due to the fact that one of its premises is false. The premise in question is—in the example used above—implicit in the phrase "without disturbing the female, since she is far away from the place where I have obtained my information" and also in the argument "at the time in question, the female is far away," which is used a few lines later. Such a use of the word "since" is legitimate only if some principle of locality is assumed true, according to which an operation carried out at some time at a given location cannot disturb the state of a system lying, at that same time, at some other distant location. Einstein himself, after he had pondered the criticism Bohr had formulated concerning his argument, found it necessary to make this assumption explicit (although such a principle was, in his opinion, self-evident). If, in the example used above, the female is, at some given time, suitably far away from the event "the test on the male", then, Einstein asserted, "the real factual situation of system II [here, the female] is independent of what is done with system I [here the male]."[6] Again, it is only if such a principle is correct that Einstein's argument is conclusive. But this principle, which has been called the "principle of separability" is, as we know, highly questionable. Its outward self-evidence is deceptive. As shown in Chapter 4, recent experiments now make it difficult to regard this assumption to be credible. In fact, it is the opposite hypothesis, namely nonseparability, which is very much favored by the experiments in question.

To summarize, Einstein failed in his attempt to interpret quantum theory in a way that would have been compatible with the realistic point

---

[5] In fact their argument is similar, but not identical, to the one given here.

[6] *A. Einstein, Philosopher, Scientist,* edited by P. A. Schillpp, Library of Living Philosophers, Evanston, IL., 1969.

of view or, otherwise stated, with the strong objectivity requirement. And the reason for his failure is clear. Quite naturally, he introduced into his problem a principle of finite velocity of travel of any physical influence, that is, a principle that was in his opinion, a straightforward generalization of the analogous principle concerning signals, which he discovered. In other words, he combined strong objectivity with locality. Thanks largely—it must be said—to the research his questioning called forth (and whose results he could not know, of course!), we now know that this very generalization is in fact incorrect, and that, to the extent that the notion of an independent reality has a meaning, such a reality must be nonlocal (or, nonseparable, according to our definition).

But such a failure certainly does not imply that the upholders of realism must lay down their arms in resignation. Indeed, it gives no evidence whatsoever against the hypothesis of a nonlocal reality (or, otherwise stated, a nonseparable one). Besides, it does not at all diminish the strength of the general arguments stated at the beginning of this chapter and directed against the view that the philosophy of experience should be accepted; for the arguments in question constitute objections against any philosophy based on the ideas of pure operationalism.[7]

---

[7] In this connection, the following points should be made. To be sure, the philosophy of experience is at the present time not just a convenient reference for *physicists* looking for suitable arguments to clear up (or at any rate to discard) some of the acute difficulties they have to deal with! Under the names of "analytical philosophy" or "Anglo-Saxon philosophy," variants of the philosophy in question are also developed independent of physics, by philosophers who devote their research to it. These investigations are of considerable interest. Their inner dynamics, however, incline them to conceptions some of whose features the modern physicist must regard with quite definite reservations (somewhat as in the opposite case of scientism). In particular, this holds true with regard to a certain type of *pluralism* which, all things considered, arises as a distinctive feature of the conception in question. This, for example, is quite clear with respect to one of the definitions of the concept of "things" that is most favored by many philosophers. "Things"—they like to say—" are nothing but those sequences of sensory data that obey physical laws." For example, this would mean that a table is but a set of different—simultaneous or successive—perceptions that can be experienced and that are found to satisfy definite regularities. Even setting aside the primacy of the observer's consciousness that such a definition seems to imply—and which should at least deserve a discussion—it is impossible not to observe that according to the definition in question, any physical object is in fact a huge *multiplicity*, namely that of all its aspects. It is also impossible not to observe that the simpler the object, the greater and more complex the multiplicity must be; for in order to conceive of all possible "aspects" of an electron, it is necessary to maintain the notion of an infinite number of measuring instruments, all of them made up—in particular—of electrons. Such an uncontrolled proliferation of basic elements of the theory must leave physicists unsatisfied since, in contrast, they have always strived, and quite successfully for a long time, to discover beneath the complexity of appearances a deep simplicity in the underlying reality. I am grateful to A. Shimony for drawing my attention to the relevance of these objections.

CHAPTER 8

Other Approaches: Elements of a Skepticism

As we have seen, neither realism as conceived by Einstein, nor its antithesis, the philosophy of experience, is ultimately satisfactory. On examination, it turns out that neither one can fit the constraints that arise from the facts and those entailed by our legitimate demands for explanations beyond mere descriptions. But—some will stress—these are not the only possible points of view. Even if many existing pseudo-doctrines (which merely throw dust in the eyes) are discarded at the outset (as quite obviously they should be), science still presumably suggests, and philosophy definitely propounds, a variety of other approaches. Among all these, could we not at least find one that would simultaneously take into account all the constraints mentioned previously? Could it not even be the case that there exists precisely one of them which any impartial mind would consider correct?

Clearly, it would be preposterous to think that a negative answer to such a question can be justified in any strict way. Our present purpose is considerably less ambitious. It is merely to point out some reasons for skepticism in this respect. More precisely, it is to make clear why, at present, the essential core of knowledge—which in addition to science, may or may not include one or another of the better known philosophies—apparently fails to constitute a consistent scheme on which we can rely in order to reach simple solutions to the problems studied in this book.

Our first point, which will be taken as self-evident, is that if the concept of Being (also called "independent reality" or "intrinsic reality" here) is considered meaningful, then it is to the knowledge of Being and to nothing else that the development of any knowledge worthy of being called fundamental should be directed. A preliminary question of the utmost importance is then, "Does the concept of Being make sense?"

Unfortunately, this is an extremely tricky question. It has, as everyone knows, fostered philosophical controversies for more than two thousand years. The positivists, for example and, more particularly, the operationalists tend to answer negatively on the grounds that an operational definition of Being is obviously quite impossible. Yet the operationalists could be attacked on this point. Indeed, it could be claimed that *they too* refer—at least implicitly—to the notion of Being, but that to them, man is simply the ultimate Being. In this respect, they perhaps differ less than they think from a philosopher such as Martin Heidegger, since the "dasein" of the latter seems to refer ultimately to the concept of mankind. Strictly speaking, even the solipsist does not really discard the notion of Being. *He* is what is: *he* is Being.

It is easy to see where I am heading. I assert that even those philosophers who thought they could discard or surpass the notion of Being did not in fact succeed in doing so. I claim that, in effect, all they achieved was to bestow upon Being one quality and deny that it has another quality. Is this not the case, for example, with regard to both Heraclitus and Nietzsche? While it is true that, as the former said, "I never bathe twice in the same river," does this imply that hydrodynamics does not exist (or that it varies)? Obviously not. With regard to the latter of these two thinkers, to be sure he was right in emphasizing the importance Heraclitus attributes to the notion of Becoming. When Nietzsche stresses that in the endless changes of the world, Heraclitus merely perceived the plays of Zeus, he seems to magnify Becoming and Play at the expense of Being. But is it not remarkable that, for such a purpose, he could not avoid introducing Zeus into the debate? Is it not true, then, that the very necessity of constructing a meaningful sentence forced him to consider an entity that, in essence, is nothing else but Being? And does not this author finally thereby prove the exact opposite of what he meant to demonstrate? Is it not Zeus, the Supreme Being, who is in fact given preeminence in this talk? To be sure, such hasty remarks may not replace a serious philosophical discussion and may even less serve as a conclusion to it. On the other hand, they suffice for our present purpose, which is simply to explain why, in spite of many objections, the notion of Being, that is, of reality viewed as independent of man, should be considered meaningful. But at the same time, since such a meaning cannot be given an operational definition, the possibility that it should remain somewhat mysterious can obviously not be ruled out. In other words, it is wise merely to introduce the *notion* of Being and to keep an entirely open mind with regard to the question of its possible *attributes*. For, in fact, it is *a priori* conceivable that these attributes are faithfully represented by some of our mental images [Democritian atomism (reality is a set of tiny bodies); Platonism (reality is a set of essences, some of which at least are familiar to us)]. But it is equally conceivable that this is not at all the case and that, on the contrary, the notions suitable for describing these attributes have to be more or less painfully constructed.

Clearly, when we thus strive to keep an open mind about the problem, we must consider several quite different views. However, to avoid long digressions, let us confine ourselves to a few brief remarks bearing on just two examples of such views. The first pertains to the use of dialectics. This example is highly representative of the methods by means of which philosophy tried to penetrate to the core of Being by avoiding the categorization of it in preconceived mental schemes.

The basic idea that is usually put forward for justifying the use of dialectics is that of the existence of contradictions within things. In short, this thesis—mainly developed during the nineteenth century—is that, in a way, order and harmony are mere appearances (belonging to the realm of phenomena, i.e., mainly constituted by projections of our own minds) and that, on the other hand, intrinsic reality—Being—is governed by contradictions.

Here it is unnecessary to sum up the more or less obvious causes of the past and present sociological impact of this thesis. But it seems appropriate to clarify the probable reasons why it was embraced by so many different people and why it even became, for a while, the cornerstone of the world view of so many intellectual and literary sets. In fact these motivations become clear as soon as reference is made to the historical development of the thesis in question. Indeed, to Hegel, Being is of a spiritual (or mental) nature. And, on the other hand, it is rather clear that the primitive human mind is governed by contradictions (which, incidentally, may be of great emotional value as exemplified in the art of tragedy). Now it is quite natural that within such a spiritualistic view of the world, basic reality—or Being—should somehow be identified with the primitive human mind, and the existence of contradictions within things follows! It seems that the initial intuition of other thinkers, such as Nietzsche, who made the thesis fashionable, was of a very similar nature.

But the conclusion of a proof holds true only if the premises are true. So we should try to assess the value of this starting point. Is it true that basic reality is in some way identifiable with primitive human life or primitive human consciousness? In support of such an idea, Nietzsche quoted Schopenhauer, which was indeed quite appropriate. To be sure, whoever embraces the world view so clearly expressed by the title (*The World as Representation and Will*) of the famous book by this author must assume that the idea in question reflects a profound truth. But, unquestionably, a difficulty arises when it is observed that the thinkers who were most effective in popularizing the general idea under discussion (namely that of the existence of contradiction within things) were the very same ones who most vehemently dismissed the "mentalist" views of Schopenhauer. In fact, it is very difficult to understand to what consistent argument these thinkers could refer in order to justify, in their own eyes, their choice of embracing such a thesis. In all truth, the hypothesis that they simply borrowed it unaltered from their elders, without seriously trying to analyze its foundation, cannot be entirely disregarded.

It is not absurd to consider that the insertion of that very same thesis into the set of dogmas and taboos of the Western postwar intelligentsia is at least partly due to a similar phenomenon. The idea is emotionally quite attractive. It is rich in conceivable "practical" applications of many kinds and can be given some sort of rational justification on the basis of idealism, as we have pointed out. And such a justification was in fact sponsored by famous authors of the past, all of whom more or less accepted the premises of idealism. For some among us who refuse idealism, the temptation may be quite great to keep in mind only two facts—the first that the thesis discussed here is attractive, and the second that it *did* receive *some* intellectual vindication from authors who were considered difficult and deep—and to simply forget the premises on which the vindication in question was based!

Of course, as soon as the inconsistency of such an attitude is discovered, it becomes impossible to continue to uphold it. However, one could still try to discard any reference to idealism and to justify the thesis in question by means of arguments of a more modern appearance. Indeed, in the literature, many texts can be found that describe the internal contradictions of a certain social system and that—by a sweeping generalization—pass on to the idea that contradiction (or *negation,* as it is sometimes called) must also exist deep within the fundamental laws of the universe. Obviously, however, the argument—if it is one!—is of the kind examined above and is open to the same criticism. Finally, when inspired by Hegel, the argument often takes a more abstract form. Being, it is then argued, is also Non-Being, for otherwise it would be static. And this contradiction is resolved by passing to the synthesis, that is, to Becoming. To try to keep in touch with actual facts, most of the authors of such developments find it necessary, at this stage, to give some examples. They then choose systems in nonstationary states, most often living systems. All living beings must die, that is, return to Non-Being. But the decay of the seed is the Becoming of the plant, etc. In other words, these authors incite their readers (unintentionally we hope!) to confuse two notions: one is that of the *changes* undergone by a nonstationary system (changes that, as we all know, also occur according to classical physics, that is, in a domain which is certainly free of internal logical contradictions), and the other is that of genuine *logical contradictions,* of the type "*A* is *A*, but *A* is also non-*A*." In most cases the examples chosen have an appreciable emotional impact (birth, death, germination, etc.) which makes the "proof" more convincing.

It is fair to stress that even at the time they were most popular, such intellectual accommodations could hardly lure the members of the scientific community. In general, the latter rapidly understood that whenever they tried to disentangle some sound thesis out of all these faulty examples, whenever they tried to leave aside the clumsiness of illustration to discover the author's idea, this very idea always seemed to lack consistency. Hence, most of the scientists who, in spite of this, remained faithful to conceptions more or less derived from Hegelian dialectics choose a kind of middle road. When assailed by some opponent, these scientists ultimately grant that contradictions do not take place within things and insist only that they exist in our present methods of describing them. This is admittedly indisputable—models are always imperfect—but it sheds no light whatsoever on the problem of Being. Hence, a similarity finally exists between the scientists who subscribe to dialectical materialism and the positivist scientists, a similarity that is parallel to the one existing between Hegelian dialectics and positivism. To an unprejudiced mind, it becomes quite clear that the former of these two systems either does not deal with Being or can be consistent (as we have seen) only from the point of view of idealism. Similarly, the second one centers everything on observation, that is, ultimately, again on the human mind. But the scientists who are at the same time upholders of dialectical materialism do not accept such foundations, and in general neither do those who make use of positivism. Thus it happens that, in general, both groups prefer the persistence of some haziness within their basic conceptions to the disadvantage they would find in making the latter completely explicit.

Husserl's thinking, which found so many supporters among philosophers, never generated much interest within the scientific world. Apart from this, remarks somewhat similar to the preceding ones could be made with regard to his ideas. For example, Husserl—and who would not agree with him?—stresses the irreplaceable flavor of experience. Hence, it is in the things as they are perceived, in the immediately given, in the unanalyzed phenomena that he wants us to see ultimate reality. Since—his followers say—you yourself admit having great difficulty in introducing your independent reality, why not eliminate it completely? It is only by considering the apple tree as immediately given—there, in the orchard— by refraining from all the intellectual hair-splitting commonly indulged in by scientists, that you will finally succeed in capturing all of the subtle complexities of Being.

To the extent that they incite us to turn to poetry (and hence to close the most ponderous of philosophical treatises, and first of all, of course, those of Husserl himself!), such precepts undeniably have something positive in them. But, insofar as they constitute criticisms of the basic nature of rational scientific research, I think they are founded on the refusal to acknowledge two facts. One is the ability of modern physics to account in a neat and detailed way for our experience and to do this precisely *without* making any use of the concept of an independent reality, by means of a *nonontological* mathematics which, according to the already quoted phrase of Heisenberg, seeks to describe our relationships with Nature rather than Nature-in-itself. The mere existence of such an ability undermines, I think, to some extent, the basis of the criticisms that are directed toward science by some of the more or less orthodox followers of Husserl. The other fact that his followers fail to acknowledge is that simple differential equations may well have highly complex solutions and that transformation groups, whose structure can be concisely expressed, may well have extremely intricate representations. Such a fact implies that such compact formulae as the equations of Maxwell or Schrödinger can quite well underlie a dazzling variety—an almost infinite diversity—of phenomena. To he who knows this, Husserl's proposal of reduction to unanalyzed experience looks slightly naive, just as a physicist would appear slightly naive if he claimed that dropping the equations of Maxwell and of

Schrödinger would make the phenomena more easily understandable with regard to the qualitative differences between them. In short, even those among us who agree to follow or to interpret Husserl by means of some mental operation of "de-realization" of objects are in no way bound to give up the use of the concept of quantity, as this philosopher and his followers would prefer. In fact, the opposite is true, for this would barely constitute a loss. What additional insight are we supposed to gain from it? But, on the other hand, if we do *not* give up the use of quantity, then it seems that Husserl's philosophy thus modified bears a strong resemblance (although it is less definite) to the "philosophy of experience," whose advantages (but also the difficulties) have already been discussed.

Again, here it would be pointless to scrutinize in detail the attempts at a better understanding of Being made by general philosophy. These brief observations suffice, I think, for motivating an attitude admittedly of interest and curiosity but also of partial discontent with regard to them. We must therefore continue our quest and investigate other modes of approach. Here, of course, I have essentially in mind those that are peculiar to scientists.

This is really another universe. In contrast to philosophers, the men of the Renaissance who originated modern science were interested in partial specific notions and in small things. The spirit of the time, the then prevalent taste for earthly things, incited them to delve into particular problems. They were amazed to observe that in some cases such problems could *really* be solved, and that their solutions, based on experiment aided by thought, were marvelously conclusive. Since that time, the scientist, that Danubian peasant, has entertained a mistrust towards all individuals who do not cultivate some well-circumscribed little field, the mistrust, so to speak, of the scientific ant toward the philosophical cricket.

But the times of "fragmentary" knowledge, even if we still live in them psychologically, essentially ended long ago. Indeed, it was quickly found that the scientific solutions of the particular problems linked together, so to speak, in such a way that they provided stable solutions to problems of a more general nature. Without having sought this at all, scientists found themselves able to provide new plausible successful answers to difficult questions which their philosopher forerunners had bitterly quarreled over without ever being able to make any substantial advances. Today we understand the motion of the planets. We know how stars are born and die. We have vastly generalized a power that dazzled Victor Hugo: that of predicting the returns of comets. We know the "great secrets" of matter. For half a century we have been able—thanks to the advent of quantum mechanics—to calculate with remarkable accuracy the stability of atoms and molecules and the radiation they emit. We can predict in advance, quite precisely, what will happen to an ensemble of these entities under given circumstances; and our calculations to this effect are verified by experimental observation every day and everywhere. And we have found the "philosopher's stone," since we know how to induce transmutations of elements.

Indeed, the structure of the nucleus is now well known. Here it may be permissible to recall in a few words—in view of the discussion which follows—that they are composed of nucleons (protons and neutrons) and of fields called "mesic" that in a way play the role of glue and keep the whole structure stable. Since World War II, the knowledge of these fields has greatly increased, as has, more generally, that of the constituents of the atomic nucleus. This extension of nuclear physics is called "elementary particle physics." One of its most recent discoveries is that the nucleons themselves are compounds. Nowadays they are described in turn as systems of particles, called quarks, held together by fields called gluon fields. Such a description is essentially theoretical (nobody has ever isolated a quark, and it may well be that in contrast to the nucleus, nucleons are really not partitionable). Far from being arbitrary, however, this description is based on the converging results of many precise experiments for which at the present time formal (i.e., mathematical) theory has not been able to offer a synthesis other than the one described here.

Of course, on the level of the theory of knowledge, the remarkable thing is precisely that such a mathematical synthesis is possible and proves to be unambiguous. But here it is necessary to be careful. This great success—for it certainly is one!—is something whose real significance we must yet understand. Does it mean that by studying the most recent theories about elementary particles (quarks, gauge fields, gluons, etc.) we can obtain the most fundamental statements that science can make about reality? *A priori* the answer seems quite evidently to be "yes." Yet it is not. It is through the study of the general principles of quantum theory, and not through currently developing theories of elementary particles, that the deepest problems concerning intrinsic reality are best approached.

Such an assertion may appear strange and must thus be justified. For this, several points should be remembered. The first is, as already noted above, that the descriptions of particles which contemporary physics provides are essentially theoretical. Even when they use images (like that of a nucleon "composed of quarks," for example), it should be kept in mind that what gives them their value, and one could even say their substance, is not the spatial picture they suggest (this is always somewhat deceiving), but the mathematics that underlies these descriptions; or, more exactly, it is the theory of mathematical physics which they merely translate. This expression—namely "mathematical physics"—denotes not only a collection of mathematical entities—functions, functionals, operators, etc.—but also, and above all, a set of rules establishing a correspondence between these entities and the observed physical world.

The second point is the following. Admittedly, current mathematical physical theory of elementary particles brings into play a certain collection of mathematical entities—the S-matrix, renormalized Lagrangian field, etc., whose enumeration would be boring and unnecessarily technical—that are rather specific to it. Indeed they are tools largely fashioned for the specific purpose. However, the very general rules establishing the correspondence between these entities and the physical world, the general rules, in other words, that place the mathematical formalism in correspondence with the experiment, are merely borrowed from atomic theory; they are nothing other than the fundamental principles of quantum theory which our fathers possessed. In spite of all their efforts, the theorists of today have, in this respect, not been able to discover anything better.

The third point, perhaps the most essential one, is that to the realist, the interpretation of these fundamental principles is very far from obvious, as we have seen. Hence, finally, the realist thinker who tries to understand physical reality by means of modern physics should soon observe that for his purpose it does not matter very much whether he thinks in terms of a particle whose existence has been known for a long time, such as the electron, or in terms of one of the most recently discovered or imagined particles, such as the quark. In any case, his reflection should automatically return him to the most decisive problems, which are not to know into what kinds of families the particles should be gathered or other questions of this type, but rather what is the significance of the language we are using here; what meaning can we legitimately give to the translation of the formalism into experimental data and of the experimental data into formalism; in short, what can we assert with regard to the general rules that govern these correspondences? This means that, in fact, he should study the fundamental principles of quantum theory. This justifies my assertion. If he does not, then he is in danger of interpreting the descriptions of matter provided by elementary particle physics in terms of the naive Democritian atomism, which admittedly is, as a first approximation, quite an acceptable model for the physicst, but which nevertheless constitutes a fallacy for any thought concerned with Being (as Chapter 6 has shown, I hope).

Such a remark is serious and disconcerting. It renders the huge body of facts and data constituted by elementary particle physics almost useless for the kind of investigation considered here (namely the search for an adequate approach to the description of independent reality, or Being). More precisely, it implies that the only piece of information provided by particle physics and which is useful for such a purpose, is just the one noted above, according to which even at the subnuclear level the basic principles of quantum theory continue to apply. To be sure, that one piece of information is of fundamental importance. All by itself it is sufficient to vindicate the huge collective undertaking that has been going on for thirty five years in the field of particle physics. But once I have duly noted this one basic fact, I cannot hope to obtain any better knowledge of independent reality by making essential use of all the physical and mathematical details I know concerning particle theory. With regard to this purpose, these details thus become, if not useless, at least secondary.

Could I then at least state with certainty that "all is geometry"? More generally, could I embrace Einstein's view of the world, described in Chapter 2 under the name (admittedly ambiguous, but I have explained its meaning) Pythagorism? The question is a delicate one, since by definition any sort of Pythagorism aims at being an ontology: it strives to describe "what is." If I interpret the question as, "Can quantum theory, together with all the other parts of present elementary particle theory, be considered as constituting elements of an ontology?" (in the same way as general relativity was given by its discoverers the status of an element of ontology)—then the answer is "no." This is so because the basic principles of quantum theory—on which, again, all present-day theoretico-experimental developments are grounded—can in no way (at least in their present stage) be interpreted to be elements of a description of "what is." As recalled in Chapter 3, they can only be viewed as a description of that which is definite and unambiguous in the observational predictions we can make. Here, also, the question under study could conceivably admit a positive answer only in connection with some future theory based on principles that would differ from those of the present-day theory and that would permit a realistic interpretation of the fundamental elements of quantum theory. But the search for such new principles meets with considerable ambiguities. Up until now, these difficulties have practically discouraged an international community of physicists which, on the whole, is very much under the influence of the positivist philosophy and which therefore questions—moreover!—the very idea that such a search might be warranted.

I believe that the foregoing developments prove the statement made at the beginning of this chapter. From any point of view, the bulk of present-day human knowledge does not constitute a completely consistent whole, and none of its parts is sufficient for opening to us a royal road towards a knowledge of the essential: of what *is*.

CHAPTER 9

Veiled Reality

In their beds at night, children ask for details about a fairy tale. How big was the pumpkin? What color were Puss-in-Boots' boots? In the same way, our reason questions our positive understanding. Now then, all this physics! Does it really disclose nothing but rules and recipes?

Admittedly, precise details are not lacking! They could fill hundreds of books. The real difficulties—slurred over, it must be said, by learned books as well as by popular ones—begin when we consider the problem of making a selection. They begin when we try to put aside all that is merely a description of models and see whether anything remains. This is all the more so because, in this field, the search for thoroughness may paradoxically appear to some to be somewhat simplistic. Indulging in the search entails laying oneself open to the criticism of those—physicists or philosophers—who set up as a principle that "of course, in the final analysis, everything is a model," and who will insist that what is subtle and beautiful is to establish a hierarchy of models ranging from grand general theories like quantum theory, which apparently covers all exact empirical sciences, to the multitude of particular little models, with very limited value, like that of the celestial sphere or the ecliptic, or those which abound in particle theory.

The concept of a model will be further studied below, but since it is a concept familiar to most, at least in its outline, it is legitimate to refer to it here.

To view scientific research as a hierarchy—or as an aggregate—of models is, to be sure, a healthy and fruitful attitude of mind for a scientist. Nay, for him who takes part in the development of science, this may even be the most appropriate conception he may have of his professional activities. One could even go so far as to concede that in some way such an attitude of mind is essential to the thinking of any even slightly educated person! Thus, for example, according to the classical principles of general relativity—whose consequences have been so well verified—the Newtonian gravitational force, strictly speaking, does not exist. It is nothing but a guise, reflecting, for our senses, the reality which is the curvature of the universe (as opposed to other forces, which seem to defy a geometrical interpretation). Gravitational force can therefore be taken into account only as an element of a model. But whenever matters having to do with daily life or with down-to-earth engineering are considered nobody would even dream of denying the intrinsic reality of gravity; and descriptions of machines or of works of art would be completely incomprehensible if we had to give up that model and could speak only in terms of the curvature of space. Moreover, rigor would be gained only if that notion of space curvature were not at risk of being itself abased to the rank of a mere element of a model, especially if the latter were meant to give only positivistic recipes. And this would be precisely the case if the views of the upholders of a quantization (still to be achieved!) of general relativity were confirmed.

It must be acknowledged that, with regard to scientific knowledge, a reasonable attitude consists not of demanding the almost impossible, but rather in being satisfied with overlapping, or hierarchical, models based on realistic images. Under this condition, science can supply infinitely precise information about the universe, its birth, its evolution, its composition, the galaxies, stars, macroscopic bodies in general, life, atoms, particles, etc. Hence, if—knowing general relativity and sharing the opinion that it should be quantized—I am *nevertheless* prepared to hold that the pencil which just fell from my hand responds to a *genuine* attractive force due to the earth, then I can reasonably believe—through a similar slippery move—that (in a sense I find sufficient) all the above-mentioned information is also true. Thousands of books, popular and purely scientific, are then at my disposal to inform me on the details.

9.1 Beyond the Customhouse

Again the attitude described above is unquestionably the "reasonable" one. However, it is *not* the one that will be considered here. For who does not see—having studied the content of the preceding chapters—that, after all, it leaves a void of comprehension that, properly speaking, is unacceptable? Who does not see that the questions such an attitude leaves unanswered are precisely the essential ones: those that are not "vanities"? Thus, I must try to venture beyond the border marked out by Heisenberg, for example,[1] and must attempt to interrogate physics on the question of knowing which descriptions of "nature in itself" remain admissible. Certainly the difficulties encountered by Einstein show that this attempt is daring. Nonetheless, it should be made. How could I ever form for myself a trustworthy idea of this vast world if I constantly refrain from venturing beyond the safe borders of my own country?

---

[1] Cf. page 23.

At the beginning of such an attempt, it is necessary to have a broad overall view of current physics. Among the experts concerned, it is generally admitted that the physics in question is basically a theory of quantum fields. In fact, those objects which appear to be particles are interpreted by the theory as manifestations of such "quantum fields." An electron in a certain state of motion is thus nothing more than the manifestation of a particular "excitation" relative to the universal "electronic field," and so on. (The creation and annihilation of particles are thus reduced by the theory to simple modifications of the state with respect to universal fields.)

But quantum fields are not beings. In this, they differ from the classical fields, which could always be interpreted as such. Their status is nearer to that of observable physical quantities. To the extent that such a gross image can be tolerated, they resemble less the Eiffel Tower than the height, or the size, or the shape of the Eiffel Tower. Or even, if a somewhat more refined and learned comparison is desired, they resemble less an electron of elementary quantum mechanics than they resemble the observable properties "position" or "velocity" of an electron (hence, the formalism of the theory associates them with mathematical entities, called "operators," of the same kind as those entities associated with the observable properties, such as position or momentum, of the particles in elementary quantum mechanics; but this comment is addressed exclusively to the reader whose college encounters with quantum mechanics are still fairly recent).

To common sense, the preceding statements may come as a surprise at first. All knowable entities are thus mere properties, but properties of what? By its very definition, a property is an attribute of an entity, even if this entity is rather hidden. This is the obvious truth which, for example, Einstein and, even more clearly, some of his successors, like Wheeler, seem to have seized upon when, the former in constructing general relativity and the latter in refining it, expressed (after Descartes!) the idea that "all is geometry." Pushed to its limit, within this conception particles are admittedly given the status of mere properties, as in quantum mechanics. But they are properties of something. This something is nothing other than space or space–time, which, being locally structured (variable curvature), have indeed enough "flexibility" to possess infinitely many "properties" or particular local configurations. In this sense, even pushed to the extreme, classical general relativity remains faithful to the postulate of physical realism.

But, however, after a great deal of research, scientists today are almost unanimously convinced that the following statement is true: *classical* general relativity cannot constitute the ultimate foundation of physics. The world of elementary particles has proven to be too rich and too subtle to fit such a mould. Quantum field theory is essential. The question formulated above is therefore essential as well: Fields are properties of what?

Quantum field theory opens up the possibility of an answer to this question. In fact it introduces mathematical entities[2] analogous to the wave functions of elementary quantum mechanics, and which, like these functions, play the role of describing the state of an underlying reality. The particular value of some given field at a given point, or, again, the number (positive or zero) of particles of a given type finding themselves in some state of motion, are quantities which therefore appear in the theory as simple properties of this underlying reality, which I will from now on call "the reality," for short.

Therefore, it appears that, in quantum field theory, reality lies at a deeper level than could be imagined by common sense or even by elementary quantum mechanics. A particle is not in itself "a reality"; it is simply a more or less transient property of reality, a level of excitation (to speak as physicists do) not, properly speaking, of a field (my language has necessarily been somewhat schematic), but of reality, excited in a fashion corresponding to the field in question. Apart from this, the fundamental mode of description of quantum field theory is in no way qualitatively different from that of elementary quantum mechanics. On the one hand, the two theories are founded on the same general mathematical formalism and, on the other hand, the purpose of both is the study of observable properties of an underlying reality, which in the first case is simply more general and more "remote" than in the second. But an assertion that has already been stated in previous chapters finds its justification here: The fundamental principles of quantum theory are the real clues to the descriptions of the reality provided by contemporary physics. Now—once again!—these principles, as has been amply emphasized above, forbid us in general to speak of properties of reality as if reality *possessed* them. Whence the practical success of the positivistic interpretation! Whence, on the contrary, the failure of all tentative interpretations founded on physical realism! Unavoidably—as I could well expect!—I again meet the fundamental problem so often encountered in these pages and so highly specific to quantum theory: How can strong objectivity be restored? How can we attain a conception of the notion of an independent reality (which, on the other hand, it is conceptually impossible to do without)? In comparison to elementary quantum mechanics—which conserved the idea that, lacking properties, a particle could at least have an *existence* of its own— what quantum field theory (and, therefore, all of contemporary physics) achieves is a mere postponement of the point of application of the

---

[2] These are called "state vectors." Note that the notion of state vector in quantum field theory, here and in the following paragraph, refers to an elaborate and delicate—even very subtle, if one may say so—aspect of theoretical physics; an aspect which at first sight it would seem best to disregard entirely. Such a simplification does not hinder—perhaps even aids, on the contrary!—the understanding of the general lines of reasoning on the present subject, those which the study of the simpler notion of a "wave function" already reveal (pp. 86–92 below).

fundamental problem. It has not modified it. Hence, in order to study the
possible solutions to the latter—all of them hazardous, as we have said—it
is legitimate to place the grand but difficult vision of quantum field theory
in parentheses, and we are permitted to *imagine* that particles are themselves basic realities. To be sure, proceeding this way requires that we
momentarily suspend taking the phenomena of annihilation or creation of
particles into account in any elegant way; but it may be a good idea to
divide the problems in order to better visualize them. The following considerations are not dependent on this procedure; but the procedure does
make representation easier. It entails returning to elementary quantum
mechanics, so that I shall henceforth be allowed to make use of the
quantum-mechanical notion (which was introduced above) of the "wave
function," instead of the corresponding notions—more subtle but equivalent for the present purpose—of quantum field theory.

The outstanding role of the wave function (the "orbital," in the language of contemporary chemistry) is well known. Therefore, if we seek a
realistic interpretation of fundamental physics, the first idea that comes to
mind is obviously to consider the wave function—or its analogue in quantum field theory—as *being* reality. Of course, this implies that an exact
knowledge of this wave function constitutes in itself a complete knowledge of the corresponding reality. But, at the time of an observation or
measurement, this wave function will generally change (or "collapse")
abruptly. One apprehends that there is a grave difficulty here. Some
physicists have solved it by refusing to consider (in a basic sense) anything but the wave function of the whole world, including the observer and
his "consciousness." The difficulty encountered here is that, at least in
some cases, it follows from the mathematical structure of the theory that
the observer must necessarily find himself split between different macroscopic states. In extreme cases, he must be alive and dead at the same
time! Should we say that in such cases the whole universe has split into
two "branches," one in which the observer is alive and another in which
he is dead? Some physicists have gone so far as to assume this.[3] In
support of their thesis, they have shown that if this were the case, another
consequence of the mathematical structure of the theory is that we could
not perceive the split. This is analogous to the fact that we cannot "feel"
the earth move, a consequence of the principles of mechanics. This remark ruins the simplistic objection which "common sense" could have
made against Copernicus in his time.

To be sure, the above idea is startling! Perhaps even more startling is
the fact that, as soon as I agree not to laugh at it, I have difficulty finding a
simple and obvious argument to show that it is false! However, it seems
that even its upholders have difficulties in specifying the precise nature of

---

[3] Cf, for example, *The Many Worlds Interpretation of Quantum Mechanics,* edited by B.
de Witt and N. Graham, Princeton Series in Physics, Princeton University Press, Princeton,
NJ, 1973.

the phenomena of duplication (or multiplication) of the branches of the universe and in accounting for the apparently quite strict correlation of these phenomena with measurements. Do universes devoid of conscious beings multiply, and if so, according to what rules? The supporters of the theory have so far been unable to answer questions of this kind in a completely unambiguous way. Besides, I am, right now, a conscious living being, and it therefore seems that the branch of the universe in which I am alive distinguishes itself, at least in this respect, from those in which I am dead. But this distinction is not specified by the wave function of the universe. Additional parameters are therefore necessary for a complete specification of reality. Consequently, this theory seems to be a special case of the theories with supplementary parameters, on which we shall say more below (and the question of knowing whether or not this theory conforms to the principles of physical realism must be reduced to the question of knowing whether the latter do).

A different theory[4] consists of taking seriously the abrupt changes of the wave function that must take place together with the measurement processes in any theory that does not incorporate the observer's consciousness within the wave function of the system. Such a theory is avowedly dualistic; according to this, there exist two kinds of realities, one described completely by the wave function and the other composed of the consciousness of the observers. Matter and mind. From a view of the world which, by its revolutionary character, startled even the nonconformists among us, we thus pass on to a conception which, on the contrary, surprises us with its apparent traditionalism; and this, strangely enough, on the basis of the same science and by only a "small" change in interpretation, a change, moreover, which is practically devoid of verifiable consequences. The "technical" possibility of a modification which is at the same time so momentous and so simple is disconcerting at first. It does, however, show quite vividly the purely subjective and "epidermic" character of such labels as "new" and "obsolete," with which we are often content to judge the essence of ideas. Contrary to the Copenhagen interpretation, the one we have just described has the advantage of being explicitly realistic. It therefore deserves an examination of its qualities and defects, even if only a brief one.

In view of such an undertaking, it is simplest at the outset to return to Einstein's position, discussed in Chapter 7. Concerning the thesis, also underlying the interpretation presently under consideration, that the wave function provides a complete description of the matter constituting physical objects, Einstein, it will be recalled, formulated this objection: if such a thesis were true, then the center of gravity of a macroscopic body could not continue to occupy a well-defined position, and not even a quasidefinite one. Pondering this remark, we might first wonder whether

---

[4] Cf., for example, E. P. Wigner, *Symmetries and Reflections*, University of Indiana Press, Bloomington, IN, 1967.

the interpretation under study does not suffer from the same defect as that for which idealistic philosophies are blamed with good reasons, the defect that rests on the impossibility of accounting for any permanence in the localization or the properties of objects that are perceived solely in an intermittent manner. Hume says, I leave a room where a fire is burning in the fireplace. I reenter moments later and ascertain anew the existence of a fire in the fireplace. Is not the simplest explanation to assume that, even without a direct perception on my part, the fire continued to exist in my absence? In the same way, I observe the existence of a macroscopic object in a certain place and at rest. Then I leave it by itself. Necessarily, according to the theory, its wave function changes and spreads out. If such a function were to constitute a complete description of the object, the probability of not finding the object at its initial place would be appreciable. But, systematically, I find it there every time I return. Is not the simplest explanation again to assume, like Einstein, that, independent of the wave function, the center of gravity of the object has always had a well-defined position?

Formulated in this way, the objection could be discarded by simple "technical" arguments. As with any measurement, the first position measurement is necessarily imperfect. And even if the corresponding uncertainty is very small, the ensuing spreading of the wave function of the center of gravity of a macroscopic body proves to be extremely slow. An appreciable variation requires a duration to be reckoned in astronomical units.[5] The relative stability of intermittent perceptions thus receives an explanation which seems satisfying enough. The realist who wishes to adopt this interpretation may nevertheless remain worried by Einstein's objection applied to the very first measurement. For the reasons given in Chapter 7, it seems rather unlikely that before this measurement the wave functions of all the centers of gravity had quasilocal supports. Did the first measurement of Jupiter thus fix Jupiter's position? Here it seems that the requirements of realism cannot be satisfied with simple human consciousnesses, and that a Demiurge is necessary; an observing Demiurge whose very perception of the stars fixes them in their courses!

With regard to Einstein's second objection (see Chapter 7), it leads to a nonseparability which today it is no longer possible to regard as not real. In the interpretation under study, nonseparability follows from the fact that the wave function is nonlocal and therefore a measurement performed at one location influences instantaneously, and sometimes quite appreciably, what occurs at other locations arbitrarily far away. In other words, the observing consciousness is thereby endowed with strange powers of bridging distances. In this regard, however, a warning is quite necessary. As we have seen in Chapter 4, nonseparability never allows

---

[5] Except, perhaps, for objects having a velocity so poorly defined that the objection does not apply.

instantaneous transmission of signals or decisions over distances. We must not rely on it for an elementary explanation of parapsychological phenomena. Moreover, in this interpretation, it is not so much consciousness which is nonlocal as the wave function, that is to say, the *physical part* of total reality.

The interpretation whose outlines have just been described is a realistic interpretation. But it does not satisfy the postulate of physical realism, for the consciousness it brings into play is not described by physics. Whether or not it must be believed is a question everyone will answer according to his own taste, having taken note of two things. First, the interpretation is flexible, for the domain of consciousness can be extended either "upwards" (the Demiurge already described) or "downwards" ("so all is sensitive," as Pythagoras allegedly stated). Second, this interpretation is not the only one possible.

A final acceptable realistic interpretation can be found in the concept that introduces "hidden" or "supplementary" variables.[6] This theory consists of assuming that the wave function is not the entire reality but only one of its aspects. The state of any physical object is then characterized not only by a wave function, but also by other parameters or variables. These have often been called "hidden variables," since the measurement of the most usual physical quantities, such as the binding energy of an atom, cannot reveal their value in any sense in which such information could be useful. This, at any rate, was the first and simplest idea physicists formed concerning these variables. For example, as we have seen, it was the conception held by Einstein (at least at a certain time in his life).

As we have also seen (Chapter 4), through the fable of the twin brothers, the discovery of nonseparability has shown that this simple concept is false. Any hidden-variable interpretation in which, under any circumstances, the results of future measurements that we intend to perform on a localized object depend *only* on the state of this object and on that of the instrument used (regardless of the nature of the object) is an erroneous interpretation. In fact, applied to certain pairs of particles, it necessarily implies (whatever the details of the theory) the Bell inequalities which, as we have seen, are violated by experience.

Hence, the only hidden-variable interpretation that is still acceptable is a nonlocal interpretation. In such an interpretation, as in a local hidden-variable theory, the results of future measurements performed on a localized object depend not only on the wave function of the object, but also on supplementary parameters. What is new is that these parameters are not all exclusively attached to the object in question. They include quantities attached to other objects, which may have interacted in the past

---

[6] Compare, for example, L. de Broglie, *J. Phys.* **5** (1927), 225; D. Bohm, *Phys. Rev.* **85** (1952), 166.

with the object considered but which may now be far away. In other words, in certain cases, the behavior of the now-distant objects influences the behavior of the object under study, and does so immediately.

The interpretation we have just outlined also satisfies the postulate of realism. Is this a "physical realism"? A positive answer could be given only if one and only one of the interpretations surveyed above were supported by a theory that would itself be unique and sufficiently anchored in the rest of theoretical physics in order to impose itself convincingly. But this is by no means the case. In fact, interpretations of this nature are interesting only because their existence proves the possibility of non-paradoxical solutions to the problem of realism. On the other hand, it is impossible to cast them in a concrete form except by means of ingenious models, none of which are convincing.

The restriction we have just stated is essential. However, it does not deprive all of these models of interest. For example, the model of Louis de Broglie and David Bohm (to which we have already alluded above) remains quite interesting. In fact this model succeeds in accurately reproducing the verifiable predictions of quantum theory without having to introduce an essential distinction—an apparent "dualism" of essences—between physical objects on the one hand and instruments or observers on the other. This feature distinguishes it not only from a few other hidden-variables models (such as the model of a "branching universe" discussed above) but also, it seems, from all other interpretations of quantum theory. For this reason it is interesting to summarize its most essential aspects in a qualitative way.

In this model, the particles are definitely real. They are pointlike and each one occupies, at any time, a well-defined position (and has a definite velocity). The supplementary variables are these positions. In addition to the forces of the usual theory, other unusual forces act on the particles. These can be calculated with the help of the wave function and a general formula, and they have the following effects. If, at an initial time, a batch of particles is statistically distributed according to the probability distribution provided by the wave function evaluated at this time, the batch remains, at any time, statistically distributed according to the probability distribution provided by the wave function evaluated at this new time. Thanks to this property, the observable predictions of quantum theory are correctly reproduced by the model. It is important to note that in this model, on the one hand, the wave function is a real entity which plays the role of a system of fields of forces and, on the other hand, the supplementary variables which are just as real play a dual role. In one role, they specify the localization of the particles, and during a measurement it is they that an observer definitely "sees" directly (for this reason, some have suggested that they should not be called "hidden"). In the other role, because of nonseparability, those attached to an object are capable of immediately influencing not only the supplementary variables (positions) of nearby objects, but even those of objects lying arbitrarily far away.

Compared to the other realistic models described above, which all required that the concept of consciousness, or perhaps even that of a Demiurge, be taken into consideration, this one appears to be very "mechanistic" (since it seems to reduce reality to a great system of particles and forces). It even gives the illusion of "multitudinism" (see Chapter 6). Is its existence a valid argument in favor of a vision of the universe that would be not only realistic but even mechanistic, and indeed multitudinistic? It is *not,* for the following reasons. In the first place, and this must be stressed, this is merely a model. In the eyes of a theorist of quantum field theory, its description of reality by means of a fixed number of particles is naive. Such a theorist must question that the true supplementary variables, if they exist, have the ontological status of positions of particles. And if they do not, many mechanistic aspects of the model disappear. As to its multitudinistic aspects, they are only superficial, due in part to the picture we have just denounced as too simplistic, and also to the fact that within such a frame we have a natural tendency to forget nonseparability, or at least to minimize it. In fact, whenever two objects have interacted, the hidden variables of the one could influence the behavior of the other whether they are close or distant. And the simplest manner, the one least dependent on the model, to express this fact is again, without doubt, to say (as suggested even in the usual theory by the nonlocality of the wave function of a pair) that after their interaction, the two objects actually constitute only one object, even if they appear to be distant. We are thus led back to a type of consideration which emphasizes the notion of globality (by the argument that in the long run all objects interact) and which leads us to believe that space is definitely nothing but a mode of our sensibility.

Finally, this model leaves unanalyzed the following question: through what process are the supplementary variables directly connected with perception and determine it causally while, at the same time—still according to the model—these variables are completely dependent on fields of forces, classical and quantum, which they in turn do not influence at all? In Young's double-slit experiment (compare page 18) modified by placing particle counters before the two slits, *both* counters are under the influence of comparable quantum fields associated with the particle passing through the device. The quantum fields associated with the particles which compose these two counters, themselves undergo comparable evolutions (which are inseparably connected). Yet, since the particle passes through one slit only, we as observers will discern only one counter being triggered. To say that only one is "really" triggered would mean that we arbitrarily bestow on the supplementary variables an "ontological status" which in a mysterious way would be superior to that of the fields, whereas their complete dependence on the latter would suggest the opposite. Ultimately, only the explicit introduction of a postulate according to which "we perceive supplementary variables and not fields" would allow us to justify such a difference in status. But the notion of consciousness, which in this model we thought we had expelled through the front door, thus enters again, not at all timidly, through the back door! It could certainly be warded off once more by modifications of the model. But the modified models are rather arbitrary and tend to lead to predictions that differ from those of usual quantum mechanics, with respect to some phenomena. But, up until now, these new predictions have not been confirmed experimentally.[7]

9.2 Veiled Reality

In view of so much diversity and so much uncertainty, several attitudes are conceivable.

The first one could be called "the attitude of Wittgenstein." This philosopher's saying is well known: "Whereof we cannot speak, thereof we must keep silent!" The obvious wisdom of this aphorism won the consensus of almost all physicists of our time. Acknowledging the general inaptness of man—and of themselves in particular—to assert anything certain about reality, they satisfied themselves with a mere description of measurement results. In other words, they were content to merely be able to state mathematical abstract rules aimed at correctly predicting the results of observation. The theoretical physics they constructed along these lines is powerful and general, but its expression—even if it brings into play words which allude to a realistic imagery—must always be translated into the language of preparations of states and of measurements of observable quantities in order to be understood correctly.

Plausible as it is, Wittgenstein's statement—or, more precisely, the radical positivism which generalizes it—is, however, less unobjectionable than one would think. On a practical level, positivism favors the advancement of science, but merely horizontally. If an idea is truly new, one has in general only a very faint insight into the means through which it could be verified by experiment. Based on positivistic arguments, the criticism of the theory of atoms by Berthelot in the course of the nineteenth century is a celebrated example (there are others) of the practical dangers of positivism. On the theoretical level, we now know that in physics operationalistic methodology was fruitful only in proportion to the accepted extensions of its principles. Taken in its absolute purity, the famous principle of verifiability has, in effect, progressively been recognized as almost completely unproductive even by philosophers who ini-

---

[7] This mainly concerns the models of Wiener and Siegel and Bohm and Bub and the experiments of Papaliolios. See, for example, F. J. Belinfante, *A Survey of Hidden Variables Theories*, Pergamon, Oxford, 1973, where more complete references are given.

tially viewed it as some kind of panacea. Finally—but this judgement is to some extent a subjective one—radical positivism, while it makes answers to practical questions possible, discards, in principle, all the questions that could rightly be regarded as essential, by simply asserting that they are meaningless. Even worse, Wittgenstein's statement subtly suggests another one, one that is quite definitely mischievous, namely: "What we cannot describe does not exist." It is not certain that no positivist and no disciple of Wittgenstein ever succumbed to the temptation of passing from the first statement to the second.

The second attitude is that of pure and simple rejection. Science is identified with a collection of recipes of purely practical interest and, in order to learn about being, the instruction is to turn towards other sources and completely discard all the information provided by science. Criticism of that attitude has already been outlined in the preceding chapter. It can be summarized as follows: it does not seem certain that the other sources have ever been able to provide any sure knowledge; it is quite clear, on the other hand, that they misled several reputable thinkers into rather gross uncritical mythologies. Undoubtedly, this is due to the fact that, except in the domain of daily action, the human mind often makes great errors. And it is also connected with the fact that for persons unfamiliar with the exact sciences, it is somewhat difficult to become conscious of that frailty of human reason (a defect that, to be sure, is not irrevocable but which is, however, a very serious one).

Finally, there is a third attitude that could be adopted. It essentially consists of aiming at an impartial conception. Realizing that empirical-deductive certitude is impossible in this domain, those who choose such an attitude search for some reasonable equilibrium. In other words, they return—for lack of something better!—to the old beautiful concept of *reason* as this concept was understood during the seventeenth century; that is, to a reason that does not really "prove," in the modern sense of the word, but whose scope is greater than that of modern reasoning. They look for the "reasonable choice."

To guide such a research, a sound principle is to renounce precision and details. The situation being what it is, the choice of a very precise view of the world would be completely arbitrary. It is preferable to inquire whether in spite of their differences—and even their oppositions—the realistic concepts described above have anything in common.

To obtain a first answer to this question, it is sufficient to remember the nature of the descriptions of the world that, *a priori*, could legitimately be hoped to emerge from physics. In deciding to build up this science, man could reasonably think that it would provide him with a representation of all phenomena, in both the short and the long range, and that it would do so with the help of a system of concepts that, at the same time, would be operationally defined (or serve to connect operationally defined concepts) *and* would be capable of being understood consistently as corresponding to elements of independent reality. He could also hope that this representation would be unique. In short, he could expect to witness the gradual development of a description of independent reality that would conform to the postulate of physical realism as stated in Chapter 6, a postulate which implies, as we know, that independent reality must be describable without ambiguity with the help of physics.

The falseness of such a hope (if false it is) can certainly not be proven, since we cannot know the physics of the future. However, it is important to recognize that the present development of this science gives strong indications that this hope is illusory. The fundamental concepts that are operationally defined by contemporary theoretical physics cannot in general be considered, in a strictly consistent way, to correspond to elements of independent reality. Those introduced by the models we have considered, out of a concern for "realism," have not been defined operationally. Nor do they unambiguously constitute definable links between operationally defined concepts, since there seems to exist *several* such inequivalent models among which it is impossible to choose on the basis of purely rational criteria.

However, a common element in all three of these models is thereby revealed. It is that, partly because of intrinsic deficiencies and partly because of the existence of the other two, none of these three models can be said to satisfy the principle of physical realism. If I want to retain my realistic requirements, I am thereby compelled to embrace a nonphysical realism, which might also be called a *theory of veiled reality*. This choice still remains quite open, yet it is significant. I understand nonphysical realism or the theory of veiled reality to mean any realism that does not satisfy the hope described in detail above and which the postulate of physical realism summarizes.

Since it is necessary to make a choice, I think I am reducing the arbitrariness of my choice to a minimum, by making the choice of the theory of veiled reality and by inscribing into it the vision of the world that I am seeking.

Having made the reasonable choice of nonphysical realism, can I now construct an ontology according to my whims? If I am a scientist, certainly not. To be sure, I am not guided along a strict course. There remain several possibilities. But all my knowledge is not suddenly rendered useless, for it continues to allow me to dismiss some ideas by making them indefensible. Thus—to continue an application of the preceding method—it seems convenient to introduce a distinction between "near realism" and "far realism." Let me define "near realism" to be any vision of the world in which all the elements of reality are supposedly adequately described by notions which to us seem near and familiar. Let me define "far realism" to be any conception not satisfying this condition.

The view of the world of the man-in-the-street is that of near realism. The same holds for Democritus (what is easier to grasp than a "little body"?) and of most molecular biologists if they are judged from their writings. This also holds for the vision of the world of the majority of the archaic religions. And even, it might be said, for that of Plato whose "essences" coincided in general—as has already been noted—with the most familiar concepts. On the other hand, the visions of the world of Buddha, of the Tao, of the gnostics, and of general realitivity are some examples (more or less) of far realism.

Having introduced such a distinction, we have quite obviously rendered near realism very unlikely by our knowledge of present-day physics. Just to consider the realistic models, all those described above bring into play, in an essential way, the concept of the wave function, the idea of non-separability, etc., in short, notions that do *not* naturally emerge from our infantile or ancestral experience and that—on a first view—do not even seem related to it. Hence, again, it is not very risky to choose far realism rather than near realism.

As an aside, let us say that discarding near realism is certainly not surprising nor hardly original. Nevertheless, it is worthwhile to ponder this step for a moment, for the fact that it seems rather seriously motivated is of more than academic interest. In fact, it could even be of some "practical" use. Indeed, although it is true that a certain amount of culture spreads—thanks to secondary education, to mass media, etc.—it can easily be observed that such a culture is superficial. As a consequence, it fails to compensate the positive character it bestows—quite rightfully by the way!—to the process of challenging every accepted view by a parallel requirement for *rigor*. In other words, although it favors the public dissemination of brillant new ideas, it also favors all sorts of superficial intellectual fashions and even very gross superstitions. For a long time— and even up to the present day—the very existence of science was in part a counterbalance to this effect. Though quite ignorant of all the details of research, the general public nevertheless kept in the back of its mind the idea that, working quite apart from the above-described futility, teams of scientists were setting into play precise and difficult methods in order to develop not only the technical power of man—his knowledge of the good recipes—but also his knowledge of the world as it really is, discarding all superstitions. If the rumor were now to spread that, according to the opinions of those very scientists, science ultimately misses reality or should not bother with it, then, undoubtedly, the portion of truth that such an assertion contains would at once be simplified and distorted by thousands of commentators little used to restraint and nuances and very happy, perhaps, to be able to thereby justify some superstition or some momentary fashion. In order to thwart the song of these sirens, one must remember that, with regard to the question of reality, science indeed is not mute, since it excludes near realism, as noted above. In view of the fact that all superstitions, all the magic of all times (including ours), are—by definition, it could be said—theses of near realism, a reminder of the very simple circumstance just mentioned should suffice to refute them.

The exclusion of near realism and that of physical realism obviously leaves open innumerable possibilities, and henceforth the choice is uncertain. For example, should a dualistic vision of the world or a monistic one be adopted? Physics alone is not sufficient to enlighten us with regard to this question. Indeed, of the three great realistic conceptions (or models) described above, two are openly dualistic, whereas the third move closely approaches the ideal of monistic thinking, at least because of the fact that the concept of consciousness is not required for founding its *bases*. On the other hand, our direct perception of the supplementary variables remains unanalyzed in this model, as we have seen. But, more generally, and quite independent of any physical knowledge, it is quite clear that consciousness exists. It also seems clear that it cannot be reduced to the notions physics makes use of as a technique since, to take a well-known example, it is impossible for me to make a person insensible to pain understand—whether by means of an experiment or by means of a theoretical demonstration—what I really mean by the word "pain." But certainly this does not imply that the sensation or the feeling of being conscious of something is not associated with some mechanisms in the brain. Indeed, it definitely is. In the old multitudinistic view of the world, founded on Democritus' atomism, by assumption, the particles of the brain constitute true reality, and, because of this, the idea that consciousness—in spite of its irreducibility to usual physical notions—is nothing but an emanation of these particles was a natural idea to uphold. In a vision of the world that partakes of far realism, the situation is very different. In this view, it becomes increasingly clear that reality escapes all easy descriptions and even those of physics. Although, to be sure, in such a view consciousness is still nothing but a *property* of that reality, exactly the same holds for the particles of the brain. And if it remains clear that there is between these two types of properties a *phenomenological* hierarchy, it is much less clear that it should remain necessary to conceive of a corresponding *ontological* hierarchy, or, in other words, of a relative primacy. Such a necessity looks even more questionable when it is observed that in the more monistic models described above, space appears to be less a feature of (intrinsic) reality than a mode of our sensibility; for such a circumstance weakens the strength of the arguments in favor of the ontological hierarchy that are founded on the fact that consciousnesses exist only in very small regions of space.

For these reasons it seems that we would narrow our vision of the world extremely arbitrarily if we continued to claim that consciousnesses are but emanations of particles or fields. Less restrictive and, hence, more attractive is the view that places all of these notions on more or less equal footing.

We could attempt to go even further. Apparently, a major lesson of fundamental contemporary physics is again that the spatial separation of the objects is in part a mode of our sensibility. It is thus quite legitimate to perceive in the whole set of consciousnesses, on the one hand, and in the whole set of objects, on the other hand, two complementary aspects of independent reality. This means that neither one of them exists in itself, but that each one comes into existence through the other, somewhat in the same way in which the images of two mirrors facing one another give rise to one another. Atoms contribute to the creation of our eyes, but also our eyes contribute to the creation of atoms; that is, they allow the particles to emerge from the *potential* into the *actual*. Our existence contributes to causing particles to emerge from a reality, which is an indivisible whole, into a (phenomenal) reality extended in space–time.

Thus, different views remain possible. But in spite of their diversity—which cannot be denied!—a thesis can be upheld which, to be sure, is somewhat schematic, but which seems to more or less fit them all. Such a "greatest common denominator" is the notion that independent reality—or "intrinsic" or "strong" reality—is situated beyond the frames of space and time and cannot be described by our current concepts. Again, in this view, empirical reality, that of particles and fields, is, like consciousness, merely a reflection of independent reality. And these two reflections are complementary in the sense specified above. One could say that both are realities, but merely "weak" realities, not totally describable in terms of strong objectivity.

A thesis like this reconciles our need for a true explanation of the regularities of phenomena (the point on which radical positivism is faulty, since it settles on a mere statement of these regularities) with our scientific knowledge. The difficulty is to make this thesis expressive and evocative. For this purpose, establishing a link with some philosophical or cultural tradition is necessary. That of the realists of the seventeenth century is apparently the most appropriate. The philosopher M. Merleau-Ponty distinguished between *great* and *small* rationalisms; small rationalism is that of nineteenth century science; great rationalism is that of seventeenth century philosophy. Both open ontological perspectives so that it is permissible to adopt this language and call the corresponding realisms *great* and *small*. We will then denote "small realism" to be near realism and physical realism, both refuted above. There remains "great realism," which was the basis of the thought of thinkers such as Descartes, Malebranche, and Spinoza. But, of course, concerning such a subject, only some very brief suggestions can be ventured here.

First, a word of caution must be expressed. An unconditional return to the ideas of the thinkers of the seventeenth century is certainly out of the question. In fact, since that time, not only science, but epistemology, too, has undergone such considerable advances that—whether it is deplored or not!—most of the statements of these philosophers must be regarded as null and void. To give just one example, it has already been noted that in the domain of the philosophy of mathematics, these thinkers appear to us today to have been victims of somewhat naive illusions. On the other hand, their use of reason, conceived by them as reconciling restraint and extension—a reason surpassing simple understanding and syllogistic narrow-mindedness—permitted them to give life to their great intuitions about Being. And it lead them—sometimes in spite of themselves—to associate these with the reality of desire. For any vision of the world, such an aura is necessary and, as we see, studying these intuitions may be useful for capturing it.

Within such a program the question of which thinker to choose for inspiration is not of crucial importance. However, it seems that the general aspects of Spinoza's view of the world is the least remote from the general thesis described here. Some of Spinoza's conclusions are very different from ours, since he rejected experience, considered sensory data to be extremely deceiving, and maintained that reality is completely and unambiguously intelligible. Moreover, the pseudomathematical camouflage of his *Ethics* makes us quite uncomfortable today because of its apparently intentional illusion of rigor. But within the perspective chosen here, such differences are inconsequential. What is really important is the parallelism—imperfect but quite definite, nevertheless—between the conception, introduced above, of a "far" reality and the substance of Spinoza's ideas.

Certainly the parallelism is quite imperfect. In Spinoza's view, the two "attributes" of Substance, namely thought and extension, separately exist, both having a kind of intrinsic existence of their own. In this regard, Spinoza's idea partly foreshadows that of Einstein. It is realistic with regard to the existence of space–time. But the facts that may be grouped under the heading "nonseparability" seem to me to impose, with regard to this point, a revision of their common doctrine. This is why the thesis described above considers thought and extension to be nonexistent in themselves but mutually generating within Being (or Substance). However, once such a difference has been duly noted, the important elements of similarity are no less evident. Spinoza's Substance is what exists in itself. In other words, it is that which is neither a quality of something nor a phantasm of anyone. In modern physics, this Substance of Spinoza could be neither an assembly of particles nor an ensemble of observables. But it undoubtedly resembles the universal reality mentioned above and to which some symbols of quantum field theory could not improperly be considered to refer (I am thinking, for example, of the symbol $| \ 0 \ \rangle$, the vector describing the "void" for a theoretician, this void which, as specialists know, is full of things all situated midway between the virtual and the actual).

In this respect, a remark should be made with regard to the inadequacy—in modern physics—of the concepts derived from our experience (or from our action) for the description of anything that could be thought of as being independent reality. The remark is that such an inadequacy is also a distinctive trait of, for example, Spinoza's idea, for, in the latter, Substance is infinite, whereas in our experiences we deal exclusively with the finite. Sometimes Spinoza gives Substance (intrinsic reality) the name *Natura naturans*. That name opposes the expression *Natura naturata* which, in our present language, means the phenomena, in short. Such a contrast quite clearly expresses the difference that must in fact be established, as we have seen at length above, between the intrinsic reality, or Being, and the empirical reality that we describe by means of our usual concepts and in which we project so much of our own selves. Here we thus observe that Spinoza's language (and as much could be said of that of other philosophers of his time as well) is better adapted to the truth than the language of modern authors, in which the use of the single word *nature* blurs that distinction (the same objection could be made to the use of the word *matter,* which often serves to designate without distinction either Being in its totality or some of its parts (or, again, the empirical reality of phenomena).

More remarkable still is, without doubt, Spinoza's use of the word *God* as a synonym for the word Substance. To be sure, the use of that word, if it were carried over here, would meet with an objection similar to that which was formulated concerning the use of the words "nature" and "matter"; it could easily lead to an erroneous attribution to "independent reality" of qualities that could only be elements of "empirical models," qualities such as will, omnipotence, and so on, all of which, when attributed to Being itself, always bring about insoluble problems. But, in other respects on the same point, Spinoza should be credited with a certain wisdom worthy of imitation. Attributing the name "God" to independent reality strongly marks the difference between that reality and the purely phenomenal reality, and this is quite in agreement, as we saw, with the teaching of contemporary physics. Such a denomination also has the advantage of leaving open the possibilities of some attributions. Again, to be sure, these (such as divine love) can only be interpreted to be elements of a model. But it is permissible to be somewhat pragmatic here, in the original sense of William James. To the extent to which such a model is fruitful (that is to say, according to James, to the extent to which it contributes to the welfare of men, both with regard to emotional life and a certain feeling of security in knowledge), we may perhaps conjecture that the model is significant. A great advantage of physical models is, as all physicists know, that as long as we remain conscious of dealing with a model (and not with an alleged description of the reality itself), we need not worry about the possible contradictions that would unavoidably follow from the extrapolation of the model to phenomena different from those for which the model was intended. It is not absurd to extend this notion and its advantages to metaphysics, and, thus, to speak of divine love in spite of earthquakes and their effects. He who reflects on this will perhaps discern here a starting point for a new theodicy. Could it compete with that of Leibniz? Yes, at least in that it would probably be better adapted to the mentality of our times.

In spite of its dangers, Spinoza's use of the word God to denote Being has another advantage which should at least be mentioned. In view of the immemorial traditions of almost all civilizations (with the possible exception of the Chinese), the use of that name is the most direct procedure for comprehensibly expressing the idea that Being is not blind mechanics; or at least it leaves room for the hypothesis that it is not. Admittedly, as soon as we introduce a spiritual element into our assertions about Being, we run a risk which in a way is symmetrical to the one we come across when we base such assertions exclusively on the notions of particles or fields: that of attributing incorrectly to Being properties or "qualities" which (as the analysis of the principles of quantum theory has shown with regard to the properties of a "physical" type) can merely be referred to our experience. The danger of mixing up models and reality or, in other words, of aiming at a description of Being in terms of near realism is then great. The failure of physics to achieve such a description lends little plausibility to any attempt in this direction. In our ways of thinking we are, however, conditioned in such a manner that it is almost as misleading not to introduce spiritual notions into our assertions about Being as it is to introduce them, for if they are not introduced, our consciousness—which hardly tolerates the absence of images—spontaneously fills the void thus created. And it fills it either with the image of a *mechanism* or (if it is wise and therefore cautious) at least with a more or less conscious reference to the postulate of physical realism, implicitly considered to be necessary. But even in this case—that in which our consciousness believes it is cautious—it is still, in reality, very adventurous since—we must always return to this!—the postulate in question is highly objectionable due the fact that today physical realism can no longer be considered a workable basis for physical theory. Apart from human experience, we know nothing with certainty. In view of this, should we hastily jump to spiritualism? Definitely not, since, as Aristotle noted, that which is first in knowledge need not be first with regard to Being. But at least we must guard against jumping—even more arbitrarily!—to the opposite conclusion. In this respect, the use of the word God as a name for reality has the advantage that it leaves some outlets open, though again some mistrust is appropriate with regard to all the models of the divine which were abusively considered absolute.

Finally, a last argument in favor of using the word God for intrinsic reality is as follows. Every kind of understanding need not necessarily be intellectual. Our intelligence is not transcendent. It has been formed by evolution in the same way as our muscles or our skeleton and in the same way as some of our elementary concepts, that is to say, some of our old terms. Moreover, it is not absurd to believe that we may have developed other forms of comprehension as well. But then, whether intellectual or not, any form of understanding should be inextricably linked with *the old terms* expressing it (as Bohr's analysis of quantum theory has explicitly shown with regard to our intellectual understanding of "matter"). Hence, if there exists a nonintellectual understanding, it too is presumably linked to the *old terms*. And, in particular—to some degree at least—with this old word, "God", slowly coined over hundreds thousands of years from the infancy of the human species (a fact the anthropologist Leakey has especially stressed).

But, of course, it is also quite permissible *not* to like that word. In support of such reticence, the history of Western and Islamic civilization—to mention just these—indeed provides a great number of powerful arguments. Here we should recall Blaise Pascal's Golden Rule: "I never dispute about a name as long as I have not been told what meaning it has been given." Here the corresponding meaning has been specified as well as possible in the preceding pages. "God" means Being, and above all the unity of Being common to the indications of physics and to the most essential of Spinoza's intuitions.

Again, it turns out that this old philosopher may be helpful to the modern searcher. Having arrived at the essential notion of the unity of "eternal" Being (eternal here means beyond time), such a searcher could indeed have reached the disturbing impression that he had come to nothing but a dry and abstract view or, in other words, to a concept which is purely theoretical and somewhat too general to enlighten the existence of anyone. But, when reading Spinoza (or other realists of his century), it appears that such a feeling of discouragement is not motivated at all, except perhaps by the fallacious activist criteria that the imperatives of the scientific-industrial revolution and the cult of subjectivity have imposed upon contemporary mentality. In fact, under the apparent impassibility of an attitude like Spinoza's, good analysts have for a long time known of the flow of an intense impetus of an emotional kind. The existence and nature of this impetus can easily be understood. Although it is true that—as noted above—any conception of "love felt" *by* the eternal Being *for* mankind can be understood, in a philosophy such as that of Spinoza, only as an element of a fruitful model, nevertheless, the reverence and love human beings legitimately feel, and *must* feel, for the eternal Being *are* quasinecessary requisites in such a philosophy. It is rather charming but no less suggestive that in one of the first works of the philosopher of Amsterdam, the *Short Treatise* (first dialogue), it is the allegorical character *Love* who, in search of an object able to give him complete contentment, asks *Reason* and *Understanding* to let him know such an object. And it is even more suggestive that the result of the dialogue is the statement that finally, to *Love*, the *Unity of the Being* appears to be the only certain guarantee that his satisfaction is not illusory.[8] Here Spinoza allows us to catch a glimpse that might help us connect his views—and the ones presented here, too—to those that under different guises and through enigmatic images constitute the main intuition of all cultures and of all times.

9.3 Empirical Reality

The foregoing paragraph contains what I consider to be essential. It describes the central point from which I think the more detailed views

---

[8] V. Delbos, *le Spinozisme*, Vrin, Paris, 1968.

which can be formed on such and such particular problems can be seen in the proper perspective. But I will not claim that these other views are unimportant. Quite the contrary, the "far" and almost unknowable nature of Being amply justifies, it seems to me, the interest we take in this intermediate realm. Does not this realm, empirical reality, contain practically all we can apprehend—even entities which in our eyes are as fundamental as space–time, the universe and its history, the irreversibility of time, life?

A great question that has been continually asked for more than a century with regard to such apparently fundamental realities is whether their study belongs in the realm of philosophy or that of science. Hegel, Husserl, Bergson, Sartre: there is no end to the number of philosophers who believed that this kind of investigation belongs more or less exclusively to their domain. Their basic argument is well founded. Above we have underlined at length the eminently positivistic nature of the foundations of contemporary physics (which is itself an anchoring point for other empirical sciences). However, this argument misses its mark to the extent that—with regard to empirical reality—*any* kind of knowledge—indeed!—is but a "recipe." Because of the universality of science, all the phenomena constituting empirical reality fall without exception under this universal law. The philosopher who rejects science because of its positivistic aspect must then, for self-consistency, not only confine himself to pure metaphysics, but also restrain himself from ever founding his intuitions in this domain on any phenomenon belonging to his experience.

Phenomena—as we have just stressed—are all within the realm of science. Is life an exception? Some philosophers have maintained this, among them even some who, like Bergson, never embraced an attitude of systematic refusal toward science, as many of their colleagues did. Bergson based his conception primarily on the undeniable fact that life is inseparable from duration, or, in other words, from irreversible time. But, he claims, physical time is nothing but reversible time, or, in other words, space. Hence, that which is properly *temporal* in time, the flow of duration, escapes physical time. Moreover, this philosopher notes that human intelligence—and, in particular, scientific intelligence—is above all a knowledge of solids: this is a result of the evolution of our species, whose struggle for life was specifically based on armaments and on tools made of solids, in contrast to the animals. Consequently, science moves with ease only in domains in which the mental operation consisting of splitting reality into little separated objects is a fruitful undertaking. It is thus incapable of capturing life, to the extent that the essential thing in the latter is the fluid, the continuous, the moving.

In some respects, the analyses of Bergson, and of other philosophers having similar views, remain up to date. In fact, they express ideas which are intuitive and quite widespread in an implicit way. Most ecologists are latent Bergsonians. With regard to ideas, it must however be stated that, although partly justified at the time at which they were stated, Bergson's doubts concerning the capacity of science to undestand life are much less well grounded today. This is so, in part, because physics has now better assimilated the essence—and the specific features which are irreducible to elementary kinetmatics—of irreversible phenomena, and so on, and because it is, for that reason, able to quantitatively predict, under specified conditions, the evolution of spatially homogeneous substances toward the nonhomogeneous, or, in other words, the emergence of order out of fluctuations. The emerging structures, which have been called dissipative structures, can develop to ever greater complexity and they can endure only because of continuous exchanges with the environment. It seems legitimate to recognize in them at least *some* of the traits of life; others (those studied mainly by molecular biology) can more or less be identified with highly complex processes belonging to the realm of the mechanics of solids.

Thus, finally, it seems to me that what has been called the "intermediate" realm above belongs mainly—perhaps even exclusively—to the exact sciences. This is a vast domain in which problems belonging to many conceptual levels are entangled. Some refer to applications; others are very fundamental. Even if some shifts in the relative importance attributed to them must continuously be made, it must not be feared that, in the near future, researchers in the field of pure science will lack legitimate motivations. And it would be a misunderstanding if the preference given above to nonphysical realism over physical realism were understood to entail denying the interest of positive scientific research as far as pure knowledge is concerned.[9]

---

[9] Concerning this choice, we need to answer some technical objections that the notion of "veiled reality" or "nonphysical realism" could easily give rise to in the minds of some epistemologists. It is in fact quite certain that according to most of the qualified representatives of contemporary Anglo-Saxon philosophy—which at present appears to extend whatever has endured from the positivistic message—such a notion must *a priori* give rise to serious reservations. With the help of valid arguments, does not this philosophy condemn metaphysical realism? And is it not true that metaphysical realism is very close to the nonphysical realism introduced here?

With regard to this subject, this book is not the proper place to enter into very specialized developments, no more, indeed, than with regard to particle physics. Let me merely observe that such reservations are mainly based on an ambiguity of the expression "metaphysical realism." *A priori* this expression *could* indeed be used to denote a conception of reality that would be very close to the conception of "veiled reality." That is to say, it *could* be used to denote a conception in which the notion of an independent reality is considered to be "far" and even as almost unknowable. (In fact, although the postulate of the existence of that reality is useful to account for the existence of the regularities of phenomena, that postulate does not allow us to infer anything certain about what the study of the latter could teach us about the reality in question.) But this is not the meaning Anglo-Saxon philosophy attributes to the expression "metaphysical realism" when it aims at refuting the conception denoted by these words. On the contrary, it understands it to denote a theory in which man supposedly possesses, or may acquire, an unquestionable detailed knowledge of a reality supposedly fully independent of him. It is true that such a conception is, at any rate, subject to strong criticism. Thus, for example, one could develop arguments aimed at showing the impossibility of a proof that a particular description of a particular element of reality is more exact than another. Attempts at generalizing a famous theorem of mathematical logic—due to Gödel—have sometimes been proposed for this purpose. These attempts easily lead one to infer that the definition of truth as an "adequation of intellect to things" cannot be upheld. But, dealing with partial and specified truths, such a conclusion, far from refuting the conception of veiled reality, is on the contrary quite in line with it. And, more generally, it appears that the "metaphysical realism" which one strives to refute in this way is of a very different kind than any theory one could try to identify with nonphysical realism as considered here.

Another objection could admittedly be formulated by these philosophers, referring now to the alleged arbitrariness that exists in postulating an independent reality that would remain, to a great extent, unknowable in any sure way. Contrary to the preceding one, this objection cannot be refuted by any analysis. What is called "arbitrary" and what is not seems to depend, to an appreciable extent, on individual dispositions. Those persons who believe that only questions beginning with the word "how" are significant and who consider meaningless all those that begin with "why" have good reasons, from their point of view, to take this objection seriously. Those who ask why there are regularities in the phenomena perceived by our subjective consciousnesses (and who regard *this* question as meaningful despite the fact that it begins with "why") require a concept of an independent reality. Since physics practically forbids them—as we have seen—to consider such a reality to be a "near" reality, and even to be one that would be "describable by physics," is it not true that a realism that is "far" and "nonphysical," far from being "arbitrary," is for these persons the only possible solution?

CHAPTER 10

Myths and Models

Thales believed that "everything is made of water." At the dawn of mathematical physics, Descartes thought he would be able to produce (all on his own) an exact picture of *reality as it is*. At the start of an unprejudiced questioning about the world, a fresh mind, aiming at lucidity, imagines quite naturally that it is possible to *say what is*. It does not pause to ponder that in order to "say" something, words are needed, which, in turn, express concepts, and that our concepts—reflecting as they do the conditions under which *action* was possible, either for the children we were or for our prehuman ancestors—are not necessarily adapted to the description of a reality considered, by assumption, to be independent of man.

But it is not necessary to be a philosopher or a great geometer to cherish such a delusion. In these matters it is common. Usually the delusion is only dispelled by a gradual experience (founded on science, on philosophy, or, to some extent, on mysticism) of the unproductiveness of attempts aimed at raising to the absolute the concepts of our daily life. To be sure, he who has had such an experience does not necessarily renounce the attempt to know Being, but at least he weighs the hazards of this enterprise.

The renewal of generations, though, has the effect that these hazards are perceived during each epoch only by a minority and that the delusion can remain rooted. A competent architect, able to supply upon request all the most complex details of his work, can equally well, if necessary, describe the essential features of his present work in a language that is at the same time fully elementary and thoroughly exact in its statements. A sentence such as, "The house I am building will have a door and three windows" completely satisfies requirements of this kind. Why then, the general public will ask, should it be different with regard to the scientists? When necessary, can they not, like the architect, skip the technical details and provide us with an elementary but literally exact (even if simplified) description of what *is*? Quite generally, the persons who—for some reason—are believed to know a part of the universal truth are always urgently requested by the public "to describe things as they are," "not to hide the facts behind the symbols," and "to express themselves quite simply, just keeping to the essential."

The profound reason for the impossibility of satisfying such demands without cheating has already been mentioned. It is not a taste for the esoteric; it is simply the *relativity of language* that in some cases imposes symbolic models. Before trying to analyze this notion of models and its relationship to the notion of myths, it seems appropriate to again stress the urge and the generality of the demands described above and the great difficulty of not yielding to them. In fact the great religions never resisted them, often in spite of their founders' misgivings. Did not even Buddhism, notwithstanding the expressed teachings of the Master, very soon disperse in visions partaking of near realism under the unavoidable pressure of popular demand? And what about Christianity or Islam! But, in this domain, it is not for the scientist to throw the first stone. At all times, some scientists anxious to express themselves clearly to everyone, and distressed at not being able to do so, have followed the example of the theologians and reconciled themselves with the notion of presenting as literal truths some detailed interpretations that, in fact, were merely symbolic. It is true that most of them had the excuse of a conceptual doubt: "After all"—they presumably thought—"the expression 'everything happens as if' which I am omitting in order to simplify my description may perhaps in the end be unnecessary; it is conceivable that everything *does* in fact happen as I describe it." And for a long time they took care to use the simplified mode of speech only as long as such doubts remained possible.

Do scientists behave in such a responsible way even today? The question is not a fundamental one. But it is worth a digression, for its study should allow even nonscientists to obtain, with the help of such a concrete example, a better view of the unavoidable "dialectics" that both unites and separates the concepts "model" and "reality."

The facts of the problem can be analyzed as follows. Quite generally, scientists believe that science should be better known. They see in science, and with good reason, one of the fields in which intelligence exerts itself most seriously and one of those that are least vulnerable to the poisons of fashion and charlatanism. They also believe—for the same reasons and for others having to do with efficiency—that in all applicable domains, scientific research should continue. But, in order for science to become more familiar to the public, access to it must be made as easy as possible, instead of being studded with disconcerting epistomological or conceptual difficulties. Likewise, in order for scientific research—which in our day, in many areas, is quite expensive—to be allowed to continue, it must receive governmental financial support, support which, in the long run, can be maintained only with the consent of public opinion. So the latter must be, if not lured, at least humored. Again, this is conceivable only if maximal simplicity in the exposition of ideas is given high priority. In particular, it is then advisable—since no intellectual strain should be imposed on the persons whose interest is requested!—to use only concepts that are already quite familiar to the public. To avoid elitism, which in time could be destructive, both the scientists and the authors of popular works on science are forced to adopt, to some extent, the behavior of the popes who were in charge of building St. Peter's in Rome. Like them, they must "express themselves in a pictorial and very simple way." In other words, they are committed to the use of words pertaining exclusively to near realism, even in cases in which they know that if what they say is understood literally, then it is false. But how would their message be transmitted if they introduced shades of meaning and if they recorded in detail those points they can express in images only?

Thus we find several simple models implicitly presented as being faithful descriptions of independent reality, models developed and distributed among the public by all sorts of media, and with the approval of scientists. In the case of, for example, atomic or nuclear physics, films and books are produced that describe the atomic nucleus as an aggregate of little spheres, or that represent the simplest atom—the unexcited hydrogen atom—as a miniature solar system. The request for a simple language, this urgent request from the general public, has in this way been fulfilled.

Should these practices be condemned, or is it more appropriate to forgive them? In favor of forgiveness, one could advance State policy or whatever takes its place here. After all, it will be argued, in this domain it is impossible to simplify without lying a little bit, and our lies are minimal. They make it possible for the general public, which is relatively indifferent to these problems, to quickly construct an approximate idea about the nature of things, an idea which is rough but is nevertheless preferable to no idea at all. For such an idea may, after all, encourage an interest in a deeper understanding of the subject. And, moreover, that interest may foster the financing of such research, a result which surely should not be underestimated!

On the contrary, in support of condemnation, we could stress the particularly mischievous effect of even a small lie when its formulation is such as to implicitly favor, through the very words it contains, an erroneous conception of reality, a conception which reduces to near realism. This has happened once already, in the description of hell and paradise by clerics of the Middle Ages. This happens today—on a different scale—in the "planetary" description of the unexcited hydrogen atom. For indeed such a description must necessarily be based on an equilibrium which is *not* possible in that case, since it should take place between the force of attraction, which is quite real, and the centrifugal force, which in fact is nonexistent in that state! But there is here also a deeper reason for the impropriety of the description in question. If this description cannot even withstand a summary analysis, this is because—concerning a problem of quantum theory—it aims at describing its solution in terms of strong objectivity whereas the solution in question is really consistent only within the epistomological framework of weak objectivity.[1] Juggling away the

---

[1] The interpretation using hidden parameters does admittedly allow for a description of the considered physical system in terms of strong objectivity as was indicated above. But even within this framework, the planetary description is not valid, since calculation shows that the electron then remains fixed, see D. Bohm, *loc. cit.*

difference evidently entails betraying truth on an essential point. It amounts to attributing to science a message that is quite opposite to its real one.

Concerning a topic which is so general and partly deontological in nature, the few preceding remarks obviously do not exhaust the controversy. Thus the advocates of popularization by omission (by omission, I mean, of the preceding distinction) will not fail to point out that the intended goal is that of kindling public interest in science, not in philosophy, and that the "epistomological digressions" are therefore improper. There is some good sense in such a remark, and, we could even say, a sort of rationality. In fact we could go as far as to put forward the idea that, with regard to both science and religion, the illusion of near realism is a necessary illusion. In science, anyway, the firm belief of the searcher that he is dealing with things themselves, as they really are, undeniably generally constitutes a very strong incentive. For that reason, no criticism of an ethical kind is proposed here. The sole purpose of the preceding observations is to show, in concrete problems and with specific examples, that a customary opinion is false; contrary to a spontaneous intuition (that opens the way to strong but untenable claims), it has now become impossible— considering the state of our knowledge—to describe concisely and without cheating the essence of reality exclusively in terms borrowed from everyday language.

10.1 Convergences–Divergences

We must thus turn to myths or to models. This is a truth of which, at all times, lovers of ideas have had a foreboding. Hence, it would be quite absurd if we grieved about it today. Does it not simply express the fact that reality is very "deep"? And is not that, after all, a cheerful piece of news after all the platitudes that a certain "scientificity," inherited from the nineteenth century, tried to make us believe? But we should not be satisfied with a mere general idea. Are scientific models the myths of our time? Are they, on the contrary, antimyths? Clearly, as soon as I try to evade an elementary syncretism, I must ask myself this kind of question, just as I must inquire about the word "model" itself, which is used so often today and covers a vast range of ideas.

In fact the relationship between myths and models is rather subtle. There are at the same time similarities and differences.

The main similarity is, of course, that both are symbolic. It is always an error to take them literally. In this respect, the myth of Prometheus, the myth of Paradise on earth, and the planetary model of the atom are quite obviously similar. Another similarity is that, nevertheless, neither myths nor models should be considered to be arbitrary inventions. Both are viewed as symbolic descriptions of something real. A third similarity, the most essential perhaps, is that myths and models play a positive role. They have no substitutes or, in the best cases at least, no easy substitutes. In other words, it is not just as a result of a taste for complexity—for "preciosity," one might say—that the poet of old chose to express himself through myths and that the modern scientist resorts to models. In both cases the choice was (and is) motivated by the impossibility of exactly conveying a particular truth through everyday language. Moreover, such an impossibility is in both cases most often to be attributed to the same cause, that which, as we have seen, lies in the fact that everyday language presumably reflects above all the possibilities for action of the infant we were or of the men of long ago (in the second hypothesis, these possibilities must have been incorporated gradually into our genes by natural selection. But, in both cases, they can refer to hardly anything other than material objects and even, among those, macroscopic objects). Hence arises an imperious necessity to resort to this language, with its restricted and particular range, even for talking about phenomena or ideas that in fact escape this range. Consequently, the necessity of using symbols arises.

These similarities to some extent justify our favorable appraisal of the old myths. If even the most competent physicist, when describing such a trivial thing as an unexcited hydrogen atom to a public unfamiliar with mathematics, is forced to resort to a rough pictorial description, it is not surprising that, on the subject of Being itself, those individuals who in the past benefitted (or believed they benefitted) from great philosophical or religious intuitions could also only express themselves through mere images. Correlatively, by the way, it should be noted that for the same reasons any religious dogma demanding to be understood literally must be viewed with great suspicion. How could we believe that everyday language is able to express otherwise than symbolically the truth about Being itself if it is not able to express the truth about such a trivial object as an atom, except metaphorically? To be sure, such a dogma might still be defended, but only on behalf of the fruitfulness of the illusion it proposes. The latter is, in effect, comparable to the fruitful illusion of the supporters of near realism, who believe that atoms exist by themselves. It should merely be granted in this respect that such a defensive argument remains intellectually valid at least as long as the defense of the dogmas of naive scientism is considered acceptable.

Moreover, the similarities between models and myths must not conceal the differences between them. These mainly bear on intent. Schematically, it could be stated that myth aims at Being and, more precisely, that it strives to make us pass from sensory experience to a knowledge of the general relations that unite man and universal Being. If not misused (which happens all too often), a model, on the contrary, aims essentially not at Being but at experience. A good scientific model is an antimyth in the sense that it makes use of one's prejudices concerning Being to guide one toward an enlargement of personal experience, for example, by suggesting new verifiable predictions. This having been said—which is true for all the meanings of the word "model"—it must be pointed out that in the language of contemporary science, this word, which is used profusely, covers several concepts which it is useful to distinguish and whose relationships and contrasts with myths are not fully clear. Without trying to overstress this last point, we outline in the following paragraphs a classification of the different meanings of the word *model*.

A first meaning of this word is: a simplification that the mind performs on the real facts which are considered to be highly complex and hardly manageable. In technology, the "reduced model" is to some degree an example of this conception. In physics, it is, for example, a trivial statement to assert that there are no strictly isolated physical systems. Now, the human mind is unable to deal with everything at the same time. It therefore finds it necessary to bring some order into problems and, in particular, to argue as if some physical systems were completely isolated from the rest of the world in spite of the fact that, strictly speaking, they are not. We thus arrive at "simplified models" which are models of the first kind. These models lend themselves to computation and to verifiable previsions. And, in numerous cases, experiment confirms the validity of the approximation thus made; the quasi-isolated system could actually be considered to be isolated. More generally, when confronted with a highly complex problem, the physicist does not hesitate to set inessential influences equal to zero and thus to construct, starting from real facts, an idealization which conforms to them on some points and differs from them on other points which he considers less important with regard to the phenomenon he intends to study. He thus builds a model of the first type, and sometimes even a hierarchy of such models. It is quite clear that he would not arrive at any results if he did not resort to this procedure. And the success of physics is amply sufficient to justify *a posteriori* the procedure in question.

A second meaning of the word "model" originates from the time history of a theory. In ancient times, the theory according to which the sun, the stars, and the planets move, according to different laws, around the earth—which remains motionless—was, as we all know, considered to be true. The celestial sphere bearing the stars was generally viewed as a real entity, revolving within twenty-four hours about the polar axis, and the astronomers had discovered the path of the sun on this sphere. In spite of its elementary character, this theory made several computations possible. Of course, with the Copernican Revolution all these conceptions collapsed. The celestial sphere does not exist, and the path of the sun in this theory is not a reality. However, the computation procedures that were based on this image and that—with an admittedly rather poor accuracy—were valid for a variety of predictions remain valid today with the same margins of error. With regard to them, the old theory, though disqualified, remains usable. It has not fully disappeared; it has merely been abased—so to speak—to the rank of a model. This type of model—

which is here called the "second" kind—is different from the first type which is usually regarded to be a simplified but essentially correct description of the "reality of things." Here, obviously, there is no claim that the old description is "approximately exact," that the earth is "almost" motionless, that the celestial sphere and the path of the sun are "nearly" existent. Such statements would be meaningless.

As is well known today, the transition from Newtonian physics to general relativity was a conceptual revolution of a somewhat similar type. Today, physicists who believe that the conceptions of an absolute Euclidian space, of universal time, and of gravitational force are anything more than elements of a "model of the second kind" are very rare if not nonexistent. In other words, all of Newtonian physics has been abased to the rank of a mere model, one which, admittedly, may be useful for some calculations (we think here of the trajectories of artificial satellites which are computed on that basis), but which is no longer considered to be—even approximately—a description of Reality as it is.

The transition from classical mechanics to quantum mechanics represents, in some respects, a similar development. However, it is more subtle because of the epistemological transition from strong objectivity to weak objectivity that must be made in conjunction with the transition in question. (The least one can say on this subject is that quantum physics must still make use of the basic concepts of the classical model for formulating its own basic principles; as is well known, this is the way in which the Soviet physicist Landau depicted the weak objectivity of the Copenhagen analysis.) Such a transition could indeed serve to characterize what could be called the "models of the third type," of which the planetary model of the atom is by far the most remarkable. As we have seen above, with regard to this example, a model of the third type is a metaphor which aims to express in the language of strong objectivity a truth that, in reality, is consistent only within an epistemological framework based on weak objectivity. A demand for strong objectivity (and a transition to it with the help of hidden variables) would change the metaphor into a falsehood, since, as mentioned above, the electron must then be regarded as fixed. Hence, such a demand cannot be made if the model is to be valid.

In physics there are other meanings of the word "model." One of the most widely known is that of a "mathematical model." This is a recipe for calculation that may well be founded on no physical image at all and which is successful in the calculation of phenomena of a certain kind. The elaboration of such models has turned out to be essential for classifying some experimental facts and for transforming them into self-consistent systems. One of the main points of interest in such models is that they may sometimes be elevated to the status of theories. But against this the obstacles are so considerable that this goal is seldom reached. Even if "formal" ("positivist"!), the presently existing theory is in fact extremely powerful in a domain which encompasses almost all of known physics. Hence, in order to acquire the status of a true theory, a model must, in principle, *either* merge into the existing theoretical framework *or* develop to a point at which it can replace the latter. (This happened with quantum mechanics when it took the place of classical mechanics.) Or, again, it must be related to special phenomena whose description turns out to be only weakly related to the description of the rest of physics. Such cases are in fact quite rare. It should be noted that among the foregoing conditions, none is listed which demand that the model be interpreted as an intelligible description of *reality as it is*. Again, this is so because of the deeply positivistic nature of contemporary physics.

Finally, as a reminder, it should be recalled that the word "model" is also used in relation to theories that *do* claim to describe reality itself but whose validity in this respect can neither be proven nor refuted for lack of the means of verification. This is indeed the meaning attributed to the word model at several places in the preceding chapter.

In general, models are less ambitious than myths. Accordingly, they are more reliable. Hence, the idea of comparing them to beautiful primitive legends may seem naive. Does this comparison not result in ignoring the virtues of critical analysis? As it has been practiced by science over the last three centuries, this analysis represents a huge and fruitful effort, which seems to have no equivalent in all of human history. To be convinced of this, it suffices to note that during these centuries successive generations have succeeded in uniting their intellectual forces instead of allowing their members to strive each on his own, and never before had this happened in a domain in which emotion did not take the lead.

However, in spite of their greater reliability it must be acknowledged that the models still remain ambiguous in some respects, and that even the criterion of fruitfulness does not always have the power that we would be prepared at first to attribute to it. It is truly very remarkable that in the course of the development of physics, false ideas have led to strangely exact predictions. This point can even be stressed by considering cases in which such false ideas led to predictions which were quantitatively correct with surprising precision. Such was the case with the Bohr model of the hydrogen atom. With regard to the handling of human reason for the discovery of things, such circumstances must again reinforce not, of course, unfounded suspicions, but rather our caution and our demand for control. Anyway, it is appropriate here to again point out that, unlike a theory, a model, as soon as it has been acknowledged as such, is not *discredited* by some false consequence of it, but that, quite the opposite, it often remains useful in its own domain long after such an imperfection has been discovered. Correspondingly, the knowledge of this fact could again induce us to apply similar standards to some great myths which, taken literally, would have absurd implications. Contrary to the rather too abrupt judgements of some nonphysicists, such a circumstance does not suffice to demonstrate that the myth which is found wanting in such a way is without truth.

In the field of religion, it is clear that the foregoing considerations lead to a kind of syncretism. Any great religion is a carrier of myths, which aim at acquainting us with certain modes of Being and of its relationship with mankind and observation. With regard to these myths, it is—for lack of a criterion—legitimate, *a priori,* to entertain more or less indistinctly some favorable prejudice. Such an attitude should, I think, as a clear consequence of the content of the preceding chapters, be that of any lucid scientist. That is, the fact that the information science can provide about all such questions (the questions about Being and about its relationship to mankind and observation) is ultimately only a rather ambiguous one.

Unfortunately, if the scientist reaches the conclusion that, after all, he must concede this to the faithful, he cannot at all feel certain that once he has taken this step he will obtain a *satisfecit* from the latter. There are psychological difficulties here. Undoubtedly, the main one is the fact that a religious attitude of mind often leads to sharp reservations towards any kind of *symbolical* interpretation of the dogma, and that a specific faith does so even more. Admittedly, this is a serious objection. The attitude of mind of the faithful demands self-denial. And while any self-denial for the benefit of another person—or with reference to some ideology—is already quite difficult, still infinitely more exacting is self-denial with reference to some badly defined—since ineffable!—entity, of which myths alone, understood as parables, can sketch the traits. The heart of man instinctively rejects such an attitude. While it craves for the far and the ineffable, it needs—through a strange contradiction!—to feel itself infinitely close to the far and the ineffable. Such a demand may, in part, be the basis for his "infiniteness." But since this is irrational in character, it would be hopeless to try to dissipate the contradictions it implies with the help of some intellectual scheme. Still, a point to which attention should be drawn is that agreement should be reached with regard to the meaning of the words used here. While it is true that I grant the mere symbolical nature of the religious descriptions, I acknowledge *also* (and this must not be forgotten!) the ultimately purely symbolical nature of the *usual description of objects* as entities existing in a three-dimensional space where they can be considered to be approximately or rigorously separated from one another. It is permissible to proceed mentally to a "realization" of the content of one or the other of these descriptions. In other words, it is permissible to forget for a moment that they are only symbolic. As far as objects are concerned, this is an operation of the mind which—in view of its practical quasinecessity—is recommended even by the highest authorities in the field of thought. The concept of empirical reality is intended to facilitate this, and, again, numerous philosophers, among them a great number of epistemologists, have redefined the notion of *reality* in a way in which it coincides with empirical reality, and this for the very purpose of facilitating and legitimizing the operation just mentioned. Hence, it is not quite clear on what kind of well-founded intellectual requirements these very authorities can base their case when they condemn *a priori* the mental operation of "realization" of religious descriptions to which—in most religions—the attitude of faith unavoidably leads. Even though they concern highly different domains, the mental processes are in both cases centered on the same principle, since both sacrifice complete accuracy and consistency in order to approach a view that should be expressive, in the one case for the technical instinct and in the other for the love of Being (the importance and justness of which have been acknowledged above).

Certainly, the scientist here has good reason to observe that in order to be led to an admission of the validity of a statement, it is not enough to have discarded, in one way or another, the objections that could be made against it. The statement must furthermore not be arbitrary. In other words, there should be *positive* reasons for accepting that statement rather than any other one. With regard to the great religious or worldly myths, he may request these positive reasons. More definitely, since his habit is to justify statements on the basis of their power to explain phenomena, he will presumably—just like the primitive people for whom most of the myths were originally designed—be led to inquire about the explanatory power of these myths. And he will make the existence of such a power the criterion for his acceptance of them.

According to this criterion, it is quite clear that many of these myths must be rejected. That of *original sin*, for example, is presumably not the right *explanation* of the phenomena of pain and death. But such a criterion is, with regard to myths, not acceptable. In fact, this is just the point on which they differ from models: their role is not to account for our day-to-day experience, even if their founders meant them that way.[2] In fact—and on this point some ethnologists or sociologists show a better appraisal of the nature of the problem than many research workers in the field of the exact sciences—with regard to myths, it is necessary to wholeheartedly accept a quite different criterion; a criterion definitely based on the more or less intense feeling of participation in Being that the myth provides. In light of such a criterion, even the myth of Incarnation, for example, is, as Whitehead pointed out, one of those which could be considered trustworthy.[3]

---

[2] This, in fact, is a subject that is so vast and touches upon so many unanswered questions that statements of such a kind contain infinitely subtle shadings. Thus, for example, the quantitative science of nonequilibrium phenomena, dissipative structures, macromolecules, and so on seems to still be in its infancy. It hardly permits anything but frustratingly rough evaluations concerning the probability of the advent of complex living organisms in the universe. Hence, in the present state of our knowledge, it is somewhat risky to peremptorily deny any "explanatory" value to the myth of a divine love creative of all forms. Indeed, this is a sphere of problems in which we should reconcile ourselves to the idea of saying a few words that are quite often difficult to utter: "I do not know" or "I do not know yet."

[3] With regard to Christianity, it seems legitimate to describe it generally as follows: To start with, the set of all phenomena of consciousness, of sensations, pleasures, pains, and more generally of all emotions that seem to arise within mankind with the greatest intensity is considered. Let the set thus defined be given the name "heart of man." The divinity of Jesus is then the assumption according to which the "heart of man," as far as it is "good" (a notion which should be specified separately), constitutes an entity which exceeds the limits

It goes without saying that here such questions can only be touched upon in a highly schematic way. Besides, in this domain, a detailed analysis can hardly avoid arbitrariness. Presumably, it would therefore be less useful and pertinent than a view of the main outlines. The latter are summed up in the idea that the "faithful" one is probably right in the "realization" that he makes, in the same way that the pure technician is right about the very different realization that he attains. But it remains true that a thoughtful man—within the admittedly easy comfort of a realm outside of practical affairs—is not in the wrong in choosing a standpoint wherefrom the view is wider. From such a point of view, the objective descriptions of the different sciences are essentially models and those of religion are myths. Essentially, both are true according to their particular norms, or at least they could be so without contradiction.

If the abstractness of this conception is objectionable it at least has one concrete virtue: Without causing any harm to what is at the depth of the religious yearnings, it allows for a very strict condemnation of religious fanaticism which, as experience shows, unfortunately constitutes a natural twist of even the most authentic attitudes towards faith.

10.2 Animism

Religions and myths are almost all pervaded with spirituality, in other words, with references to consciousness. For this reason it is appropriate to compare them with another doctrine which also refers to the notion of consciousness. This is the theory that "all is sensitive," which has already been alluded to in the preceding chapters. This theory is very old. Leibniz, and in more recent times, to some extent, Whitehead, professed it, and it has received the endorsement of many poets. Those who compare it to religion sometimes distinguish the two by introducing the concepts of "higher" and "lower" spiritualism. While a description founded on "higher spiritualism" (the theism of Berkeley, for instance) strives to explain the phenomena through the operation of but one spirit who perceives things "from above," so to speak—the Demiurge of the second of the realistic conceptions analyzed in Chapter 9 bears some resemblance to such a God—the thesis of "lower spiritualism," the thesis of animism, or of the conception that "all is aware," assumes, on the contrary, that all facts—including the existence of human consciousness—can best be

---

of any individual man, "covers," so to speak, all of them and mysteriously rejoins Being. It is clear that such an assumption is not of the order of scientific hypotheses. It does not aim at explaining phenomena; even less at predicting them. It is, however, of a kind that is capable of providing man a (conjectural) glimpse of Being; a glimpse of Being which, enigmatic as it is, still helps man to clarify his own status with respect to it, and can, to that extent, be considered revealing.

explained with the help of the hypothesis of the existence of a multitude of "souls of things."

In fact this method of considering religions and myths together while discussing animism separately is a procedure that calls for a comment. To be sure, one of the claims of both religions and myths has always been that they accounted for the phenomena; hence it is right to say that these doctrines aimed at explaining experience. But, again, this is the very point on which religions and myths seem obsolete today. In fact, compared to the power of coordination of contemporary science, that power which a religion or a myth claims seems quite illusory today. If the latter remain for us so important, it is for different reasons, pertaining, as we have seen, to the symbolic description of Being and to the relationship between it and ourselves that we hope to discover with the aid of religion and myth. In other words, it is through a kind of sublimation of their content that the religions remain legitimately alive. On the contrary, while it is true that the thesis that "all is aware" was also sublimated by some poets, the latter were never numerous, and in fact this thesis is popular because it claims to explain some specific phenomena. Therefore, it is these claims that should be scrutinized.

The question is momentous. Here it can only be quickly surveyed. But even in a summary analysis, two different versions of the thesis must be clearly distinguished.

The most popular version is a doctrine of near realism. Every electron (and, more generally, every elementary particle) has a "soul" or a "consciousness" sometimes called its "inside" in order to enhance our feeling that the theory is indeed profound. The "materiality" of the electron, or its external appearance (as a rule, the supporters of the doctrine do not distinguish between matter and appearance) is then called its "outside" (of course, in general, it is either stated or suggested that the "inside" of a particle has a deeper reality than the "outside," or even that it has somehow a higher value). Proceeding along this line of thought, it is a simple matter to derive practically anything. If a particle of a certain type attracts particles of another type, this phenomenon will be described as the existence of some "love" between them, and so on. More generally, those "philosophers" who have chosen this point of view as a guideline for their thinking have an easy time gleaning in physics, in biology, or elsewhere phenomena that they declare to be mysterious and to which—in their elementary spiritualistic language—they provide a qualitative explanation which, to them, seems to be of dazzling clarity. In almost all these cases it so happens, of course, that the phenomena in question can actually be explained quite satisfactorily by physics, or by another science which, in principle, has its roots in physics. It is even quite often found that physics can calculate, and thus predict, their development. But, to be sure, this sometimes must be accomplished according to the rules of quantum theory, that is to say (within the conventional interpretation of the latter), according to a positivistic epistemology. In this regard, and in this regard only, these phenomena could indeed be considered to have something mysterious about them, at least in the eyes of a realist. But if this latter observation were made explicitly, it would imply, or at least suggest, that realism—a view which enjoys the spontaneous favor of all uniformed members of the public—should be abandoned. Therefore, the most clever among these thinkers refrain from doing so. Instead, they indulge in long qualitative discourses on mind, love, participation, and related topics. In a way, this version of animism proves to be the exact antithesis to the conception of naive scientism criticized in Chapter 6. But, in certain regards, its value is even smaller, for this animism is no more consistent and even less usable.

The other version of "animism," compared to the first one, is more interesting because it does not indulge in verbosity and is not concerned with false problems. The problem it tries to solve is quite real, for it is nothing but the problem of the collapse of the wave function (or of the mathematical entity that stands for it) during a measurement. It will be remembered that this problem is essential in any conception that is explicitly realistic and that, at the same time, is unwilling to take into consideration either nonlocal hidden variables or the splitting of the observer between macroscopically different states, and which, nevertheless, maintains that quantum theory should be applicable to any atomic system, be it large or small. In fact such conditions are, strictly speaking, too restrictive, since it can be shown[4] that they prohibit any solution. Therefore, the conception under study mitigates them to some extent. But it does so in a way that its supporters consider to be, after all, the least arbitrary one, when due account is taken of the observed facts. They point out, on the one hand, that no human being was ever conscious of being split as described above and, on the other hand, that quantum theory strictly applies, nevertheless, to all the cases in which it is possible to put it to an experimental test, including some cases in which the observed system is macroscopic (though not conscious). These facts are believed to constitute a serious indication in favor of the hypothesis according to which conscious beings, and they alone, could in certain cases violate quantum theory by "collapsing" the wave function of a system that includes them.

A hypothesis like this is still not precise enough. What are in fact those conscious physical systems? As everyone knows, it is impossible to give a scientific answer (that is, an answer based on experience) to this question. Indeed, any reaction to a stimulus can always be interpreted as the effect of an unconscious automatism, and this remains true with regard to very complex reactions to complicated stimuli (we could think here of computers). Hence, strictly speaking, all I know for sure is that *I* am a conscious being. It seems to me most likely that other human beings are conscious

---

[4] Cf., for example, B. d'Espagnat, *Conceptual Foundations of Quantum Mechanics*, 2nd edition, Addison Wesley, Benjamin, Reading, MA, 1976.

too, and even the animals (with Descartes's leave!). An apparently very reasonable criterion then comes to mind: All physical systems possessing a nervous system of a given complexity (which can be specified), and those alone, are conscious. Of course, such a restrictive hypothesis is still quite far from animism. Moreover, it must be granted that it does not match the previously mentioned considerations which are derived from the collapse of the wave function. In a realistic conception with no hidden variables, the wave function must be considered to be universal reality. How could we accept that it is "collapsed" only by the nervous systems of some species of animals, which exist only on one or a few celestial bodies such as our Earth? Thus, once engaged along these lines, we are led to generalize the hypothesis and to take the idea of a consciousness abiding in things seriously. But then difficulties arise at the microscopic level. The wave function of an unobserved electron is not reduced. Am I not in danger of contradicting this elementary fact (and this fact has been established by experiment!) if I attribute a consciousness to the electron? In Young's two-slit experiment, is it possible that an electron which knows through which slit it passes should still be able to contribute to the construction of the interference patterns that are observed on the screen? Answers to questions of this kind are unavoidably somewhat arbitrary since the questions themselves are ambiguous. What do we mean exactly when we speak of the consciousness of an electron? It is not *inconceivable* that in the future a theory will be constructed in which the notion of consciousness will be precisely defined and which will—in a consistent way—attribute to physical systems a consciousness—although a very hazy one for very small systems. It is not impossible that such a theory, when fully developed, will prove to constitute a real advance in our systematic explanation of the phenomena in microphysics. But all that can be said at this time is that these are extremely hazardous anticipations. Such a theory does not exist, not because no physicist has ever had such ideas, but because of several technical reasons (whose details would be tedious to explain) which make its construction extremely difficult (and perhaps even impossible if arbitrariness is to be avoided).

Under these conditions we must adhere to general considerations which unfortunately must remain somewhat ambiguous. In fact, in the present case, there exists a qualitative equilibrium between those arguments in favor of the idea that microsystems could be considered animate and those that favor the opposite view. Among those of the first category, we find, first of all, of course, the argument already mentioned above; namely the nonexistence of a definite separation between nonliving and living beings, on the one hand, and, among the latter, between unconscious and conscious beings, on the other hand. The argument then proceeds by stressing the arbitrariness of any hypothesis restricting to a special category of physical systems the attribution of a quality—consciousness—that is otherwise known to be irreducible to the phenomena studied in physics. Although the basic idea of this argument does not depend on the detailed structures of the physical theory considered, it has nevertheless been stressed in Chapter 9 that the failure of the multitudinistic conception that is so typical of classical physics reinforces its strength. In fact, that failure obliges us either to base science on *weak* objectivity only (thus attributing, in the scientific description, an essential role to such *facts of consciousness* as the preparation of the state and the observation of physical quantities) *or* at least to give up the view that particles and fields are distinct localizable simple self-supporting realities, such that the facts of consciousness should naturally be interpreted to be transient emanations of temporary aggregates of them. Nonseparability shows that such a description is naive. And then, the fact that consciousness exists is no longer obviously secondary with regard to the existence of the particles, especially since the latter are themselves only simple properties (illusively localized) of a nonspatial reality.

On the other hand, if I attribute individual consciousness to microsystems, or at least to a great many small localized physical systems (large molecules, microcrystals, etc.), and if I assume that, in one way or another, these small individual consciousnesses can induce a collapse of the wave function which is itself considered to be objective (in the strong sense), then admittedly I account in a simple way for some specific features of present microphysics, but I have not thereby clarified all its aspects. From such a view of the world, nonseparability remains enigmatic, for the least that can be said is that it does not follow from such a view and that is not even *a priori* suggested by it. In fact, nonseparability should incite those who wish to attribute a prominent role to consciousness within the realm of physical phenomena to choose the notion of a cosmic consciousness of which individual consciousnesses are but mere emanations.

Another qualitative argument in favor of the theory of animism can be described as follows. There exists no conscious being that does not have its own activity. Such an activity—however difficult the definition of such a concept may be—could thus, in some way, qualify as a specific feature for the existence of a consciousness. On the other hand, as soon as it "really" exists, the microsystem, too, is in a certain way active. Without being unfaithful to the Copenhagen school, one could in fact say that a quantum system—an electron, for example—does not actually exist except when it interacts with a measuring apparatus.[5] In the case of microphysics, as in that of an animate system, existence is thus fundamentally linked to inter*action* with the environment.

Moreover, both types of systems arise as organized "wholes". Intuitively, the analogy is striking. For example, different excited states of the same atom differ qualitatively through the form of their orbitals, and intermediate configurations cannot exist. This fact may well remind us of

---

[5] C. N. Villars, *An Organic View of Nature* (unpublished).

the qualitative differences which exist between living species. But it may also remind us of the differences which exist between crystals, between harmonics of the same sound, and so on. Here we recognize the danger of analogies. More generally, the analogy based on the fact that the microsystem and the animate being both behave as unseparable entities obviously does not in itself constitute a serious argument in favor of the thesis that "all is sensitive." The same must be said with regard to the argument given above, concerning the "activity" of microsystems. The analogy exists, but is it more than an analogy?

In view of the preceding discussion, it seems that the idea that "all is sensitive" can be neither refuted categorically nor accepted without considerable reservations. What is certain is that it cannot—or not yet—be considered to be a well-grounded scientific theory. We should therefore refrain from hastily referring to it in order to explain experimental facts. The publicity given to parapsychic phenomena could certainly constitute such a temptation and even more so, since the real existence of these phenomena is considered to be indubitable by a minority of reliable persons. But, on the other hand, it must be kept in mind that, except for these few individuals, most of the believers are definitely uncritical. This should make us especially wary, particularly in view of the fact that at present any theoretical attempt to account for such (potential) phenomena ultimately belongs to the realm of speculation. On these matters, any rough draft of a theory or model is unavoidably distorted by powerful and aggressive popularizing media. Under these conditions, a theorist is entitled to consider that the safest way in which he can hope to contribute to general knowledge is to turn to other topics. Or, if he nevertheless chooses to be concerned with such matters, he at least should remain very cautious about what he says on these matters (at least up to a time when, having surpassed the considerable difficulties to be found there, he can produce a theory that is exact, precise, and verifiable by a large number of known facts, and that, moreover, fits satisfactorily within the body of presently existing science).

On the other hand, there is no great harm in considering the "all is sensitive" doctrine to be a great and beautiful myth, rich with hidden meaning. If a wise man, after lifelong meditation, has evolved a firm belief in animism, he should know that even a scientist can understand his viewpoint, at least within an interpretation of a certain kind, and that such a scientist may even consider this understanding to be enriching in a kind of roundabout way to his personal view of the world. Then, for both of them, the matter is no longer to master such facts as levitation or bending iron bars! What is really at stake is the possibility of gaining some insight into those relationships between human mind and the ultimate reality that are *not* merely rules for action.

CHAPTER 11

Science and Philosophy

The great outlines of what, for lack of a better word, I must call my "philosophy" (or—even worse!—my "conception of the world") were described in Chapter 9. The expression "philosophy of veiled reality" summarizes it adequately. Though not based exclusively on considerations derived from contemporary physics, it still seriously takes into account the constraints imposed by some basic physical facts (as the chapters dealing with nonseparability, the philosophy of experience, and Einstein's unsuccessful attempts to restore a purely physical realism founded on locality have shown). As we have seen, these constraints lead us quite naturally—if we only bar the unlikely appearance of some very subtle counterargument—to the conclusion that some sort of nonphysical realism seems, after all, to be the only conception presently compatible with available data.

Regarding that view and the analysis leading to it, reservations might however be made, and with some apparent justification, by individuals with various sorts of training. Thus, some philosophers may object to the general method used here; they may put forward the idea that it was not at all necessary to argue from experimental data and great contemporary physical theories in order to get results which, according to them, could have been obtained directly by a mere *a priori* analysis that would have brought out the intrinsic inconsistency of any "scientific realism." But, at the other extreme, many scientists may well criticize what they might call the schematic and qualitative nature of the same argument, and this may lead them to question my reservations concerning physical realism. In daily life, they may well stress, analyses of this type generally suffice to lead to correct conclusions, since the concepts that these analyses implicitly entail are preadapted (having been elaborated in view of daily life, either by the children we were or by the vast series of our ancestors, or by both, as already stated). But when we are analyzing the innermost structure of matter (a domain inaccessible both to the child and to our ancestors, for lack of motivation and appropriate instruments), all is new, even the concepts. And under these conditions the qualitative methods of natural thinking are probably inadequate. Such critics would therefore stress that such matters must in fact be analyzed much more precisely and quantitatively than can be done in a book intended for nonphysicists. And, more precisely, they would stress that these analyses must take the whole artillery of contemporary physical theories into account. It is only by such methods—they would argue—that it is possible to ensure the nonexistence of the "subtle counterargument" alluded to above, that is, of an argument that could invalidate the conclusions to which our mere "qualitative" argument naturally leads.

It is quite natural—nay, it is even essential—that such reservations be expressed. This chapter, which is somewhat more technical than the previous ones, aims to examine them and to indicate, at least in general terms, the reasons for which, in my opinion, they disprove neither the general conclusions under study nor the procedure of analysis that led to them.

11.1 The Macroscopic Diversion

Let us first consider the kind of reticence attributed above to scientists. Many among them would like to reconcile physical realism with what we know about the facts. And, for that reason, they cherish the hope that some day some nonelementary argument (or even some *subtle* one, if we care to use that epithet) will appear that will offer a way of reconciling physical realism with quantum theory (which describes so many important facts). In this field there is an idea which nowadays meets with almost unanimous assent. It is that to the extent that such a hope could conceivably materialize, this should necessarily be due to having given proper consideration to the macroscopic nature of the instruments that are used for measuring physical quantities. In the foregoing statement, the subjunctive tense is justified by the fact that up until now the experts in such matters have failed to reach a complete agreement on whether this condition is sufficient.[1,2]

Attempts at making such an idea more definite meet with a difficulty related both to the general conception we have of objects and to the definition of the words used. Macroscopic objects are extended in space. This means that it is possible to conceive of them as made of parts, each of which occupies a definite region of space, the union of all these regions being the total extension of the object. Ideally these parts can be similarly

---

[1] It can be said again and again that on purely mathematical questions, the experts—by definition—always agree! Hence, the absence of general agreement on the question considered here is in itself an interesting piece of information. It shows that it is a problem which is intrinsically quite difficult and which cannot be solved simply by manipulating mathematical symbols, although such manipulations necessarily play an important role in its study.

[2] While the matters introduced below are quite essential elements of any thorough discussion of the present problem, they have only a limited impact on the general ideas. Our attempt to explore systematically what can be said of the latter in the light of modern physics continues in Chapter 13.

partitioned, so that it is extremely hard to think of a macroscopic object without considering its "microscopic" components. In fact, not to think in this way is quite impossible, considering conventional physics, since the latter shows, by means of its most well-known experimental and deductive methods, that indeed the macroscopic bodies—the "objects"—do appear to us to be comprised of components. Physics even specifies the nature—molecules, atoms, electrons, nucleons—of the microscopic components in question.

But if, on the other hand, I candidly embark upon such a course, what is it that I shall call a "macroscopic" object (or body)? Most certainly it cannot be a physical system composed of two or three particles (or atoms). In fact, experimental data show with certainty that such small systems still obey the laws of quantum theory (for example, they can be diffracted, just as their components can). They also show that measurements can be performed on such systems, whose results, according to quantum theory, cannot be reconciled with the assumption that such systems possess, on any occasion and at any time, well-defined—or at least macroscopically well-defined—positions. However, for a possible reconciliation of physical realism with quantum theory to be achieved, it would be necessary that such an assumption be tenable at least with regard to the various parts (pointer, dial, etc.) of the instruments. But, then, what, in terms of the number of microcomponents, is the minimal complexity an object should have in order that the assumption in question be valid? Is that number equal to thirty seven, seventy five, or to forty billion? Clearly it is impossible for any such answer to be correct, for such a choice is arbitrary. Nowadays, in fact, the theorists who think the reconciliation is to be achieved along these lines almost all agree (on the basis, again, of elaborate calculations) that the number in question must necessarily be infinite. What this means is that in order to consider that a given complex physical system possesses—at any time and under any conditions—intrinsic properties (such as an approximately defined center of mass position, an approximate velocity, etc.), a necessary condition is that the number of components of this system be infinitely extended in all directions in space. According to some authors, it must also be assumed that, apart from a few simple macroscopic ones, the quantities that on such a system are observable in principle (and to whose mathematical expressions a physical meaning must therefore be attached) can only depend on a *finite* number of elementary components of the system or, at best, on a number of elementary components that, if it is infinite, is nevertheless a fraction (strictly smaller than unity) of the total number of such components and which must obey other suitable constraints. Moreover, other conditions must be satisfied, which we need not review here.

That such a set of conditions at best describes only an idealization is a fact on which everybody agrees, and, first of all, the promoters of these conditions! But they claim that such an idealization is justified. To be sure, the macroscopic physical systems are not infinite. But, nevertheless, they are extremely large compared to the dimensions of atoms and molecules. To discuss them as if they were infinite is, according to these promoters, no more objectionable than to consider as completely isolated a system that is so only to some good approximation (a very common practice to which nobody really objects). Moreover, they point out, the idealization in question has proven to be useful. In fact, it is by applying a very similar procedure that the physicists could, for example, construct the theory of phase changes. And finally, they say, the reconciliation aimed at here (between quantum theory and physical realism) is somehow linked with that between the reversibility of the equations of microphysics and the irreversibility of the macroscopic world, which other investigations of a more classical nature could elaborate. On the basis of these arguments, the scientists in question assert that, after all, quantum theory and physical realism *can* be reconciled.

The arguments in question are quite strong, but, as we see, they are also quite subtle. Even when our mind has thoroughly understood them (at the price of a serious study of all their technical aspects), it finds it difficult to decide whether or not they really carry conviction. Indeed an opinion on this point must unavoidably depend on what we expect—sometimes implicitly—from science, and, more precisely, on the strength of our requirements regarding its explanatory power. Here I question the pertinency of the arguments in question, essentially on the basis of the observation that in the case in which the problem under study has to do with a search for knowledge of what "really *is*," the requirements in question should, in my opinion, be very different from what they would be in the case in which the problem is of a scientific nature.

Such an assertion calls for an explanation. The study of the phase changes of matter, alluded to above, is, I think, a good example of a problem of the second kind, for it deals only with phenomena. If, for the idealized model of an infinite physical system, I manage to construct a theory of the phenomena which is free of internal contradictions and which gives a correct qualitative account of the observed facts, I can be content with that, for I may quite naturally believe that there are no essential reasons for the case of finite, but large, systems to differ very much from the case of the idealized model, albeit the former is more difficult to study. And I may reasonably expect that the small differences unavoidably existing between the two cases are subtle enough to have escaped observation. My knowledge that such differences really do exist therefore does not disturb me in the least! And this, obviously, remains the case even if I begin to think that an especially well-equipped experimenter could—if he cared to—amplify the effects of the differences in question and thereby make them observable. I may even carry this further and imagine some demon provided with infinitely fine senses[3] and who

---

[3] This is intended to mean that he would be able to measure *any* of the entities that correspond to a combination of mathematical symbols of the type of those ("Hermitian operators") associated by the theory to physical quantities.

would directly perceive the differences existing between the observed data and the predictions of the idealized model. Admittedly, to this demon, the model would seem to be a poor one. But to us it is a good one, for we are not sensitive to its departures from (empirical) reality. And a scientific model that, like this one, correctly accounts for our observations, and furthermore makes it possible for us to predict what we shall observe if we study some other substance, is unquestionably a good model for the scientists.[4]

We just examined problems of the first kind, that is, problems that are, so to speak, internal to science. With regard to the problem of reconciling quantum theory and physical realism (henceforth called "the reconciliation problem," for short), the situation is very similar in some respects and quite different in others.

Let us first consider the similarities. One of them is that here, also, the only consistent existing theory of the instruments is based on the idealized model that considers macroscopic systems to be infinite. Another similarity is that the differences between the predictions of such a model and the factual data bearing on real macroscopic systems (such as instruments or parts thereof) are very difficult to detect (in practice, they are even entirely out of reach of our experimental procedures). A third similarity is that, nevertheless, the differences in question are real. If quantum theory is exact, and unless a specific *ad hoc* hypothesis (stated and discussed below) is made, the demon, if he were presented, for example, with two real (i.e., noninfinite) macroscopic systems having interacted in the past, could in general manage to observe some phenomena of the general type of interference phenomena, that is, phenomena that would be incompatible with the idea according to which the center of mass of each system is at any time macroscopically localized.[5]

Let us now inquire in what respect the situation in the "reconciliation problem" is different from that in the phase-change problem used as an example above. The answer is straightforward. The situation is different because—and *just* because—the differences, which exist in *both* cases between the factual data and the predictions of the model, must, in the case of the reconciliation problem, be considered by us—although they are not observable to us!—to be definitely incompatible with our requirements of physical realism, and are therefore unacceptable.

Here, as we see, the discussion becomes rather subtle. The point is that

---

[4] Similar remarks could be made with regard to irreversibility. Without entering into the details of this highly complex problem, we may indeed observe that, to the demon in question, the phenomenon of irreversibility would in some respects seem to be less clear-cut than it is to us, for here, also, it is out of the question to deny that complex correlations exist which the demon, unlike us, could observe and which would make the very notion of the irreversibility of such phenomena as the mixing of two fluids much less significant to him than it is to us.

[5] The quantum theory of measurement offers clear-cut examples of such a fact. The interested reader with some background in modern physics can find a quantitative discussion of this and, more generally, of the subject matter of the present section, together with references to the original articles in a previous book of mine already cited (page 117).

the demon can absolutely not accept the assertion—which to the upholders of physical realism is quite a basic one!—that in any case and at any
time any part of an instrument—any pointer, for example—either is totally in one suitably defined region of space (e.g., a graduation interval on
the scale) or is totally in some other region; for he knows that in some
cases *he* can perform experiments and measurements that will prove to
him that the assertion is certainly false. Hence, the thesis that the parts of
an instrument are always localized (in the sense just defined) cannot be
universally true.

"But," one may object, "your demon does not exist!" Certainly he does
not, but what matters here is that we can imagine him. An assertion
cannot be true when some consequences of it which could, in principle, be
verified turn out to be certainly false, and such an impossibility holds even
in cases in which none of these consequences can be verified in practice
because of an insufficiently advanced technology or for similar reasons,
which are indeed binding ones but only in reference to human capabilities.

The discussion can be continued with neither of the two opponents
acknowledging defeat. This, I believe, is not due to one of them being
illogical in his reasoning procedure, but is due to the fact that they envision reality differently. The one who stresses that the demon does not
exist, and who, more generally, bases his argumentation on some practical
limitations inherent to mankind, is thereby either explicitly or uncon-
sciously a Kantian. Heisenberg, for example, was explicitly a Kantian,
although he rejected Kant's metaphysical concept of the *a priori*. What a
follower of Heisenberg simply calls "reality" is thus, in fact, reality as
perceived *by man* (who else, he points out, could perceive it?); and this
coincides with what I called "empirical reality" above. Since such a
follower of Heisenberg is unwilling to consider any other conception of
reality to be meaningful (except perhaps a certain "potentiality"), he may
appropriately discard the objection that we explicated above in terms of a
demon or of experimenters endowed with superhuman craft. He can then
assert that the introduction of the notion of macroscopic objects *does*
solve the problem. But his opponent in the foregoing discussion can just as
legitimately—this is again the same old problem!—decline to consider as
final a conception of reality—such as this one—that is ultimately man-
centered. To such an opponent, the objection in question remains valid,
and to him, therefore, the problem of the reconciliation of quantum theory
with physical realism is *not* solved by the mere introduction of the concept
of macroscopic objects, no matter how fruitful this concept generally is in
physics. As far as I am concerned, since I defined reality to be independent of man, mere consistency forces me to embrace the second point of
view rather than the first.

Above, in order to avoid rambling off into digressions, I set aside an
assumption for further examination. This assumption, which I termed *ad
hoc*, should now be specified, and it should be shown that the assumption
cannot change the foregoing conclusion.

In fact this assumption has already been mentioned a few pages before.

It is the one which stipulates that the majority of observable physical quantities on a system can depend only on either a *finite* number of elementary components of that system or, at any rate, on a number of such components subject to special restrictive conditions. Some of the physicists who think the reconciliation problem can be solved along the lines described here rely especially upon this assumption. I fear, however, that its use in this connection only seems plausible because of some looseness of its very formulation. What, in fact, is the exact meaning of the word "observable" in the foregoing statement of the assumption? If it merely means "observable by the human beings of today, account being duly taken of the practical limitations of their technology," then of course nothing is changed in the argument summarized above. If it means "observable even in principle," then admittedly the objection against reconciliation is no longer valid in the form given above, since, then, even the demon could not check the difference between the prediction of quantum theory and those based on the universal quasilocality (localization within given domains) of instruments and parts of instruments in any experiment. I maintain, however, that the objection (which, again, is only an objection to the possibility of a solution of the reconciliation problem *within the realm of physical realism,* i.e., within the realm of a non-Kantian and non-Heisenbergian realism) then reappears in a new form. With regard to real systems, and within present-day quantum theory, there does not seem to exist any rational method for splitting the set of mathematical entities ("Hermitian operators") *a priori* acceptable for describing physical quantities into two subsets, the elements of one of them corresponding to quantities that are observable in principle and those of the other having no such correspondence. Or, more precisely, there does not seem to exist any rational method for accomplishing this split in such a manner as to open the way to a realistic description of the measurement problem in its most general aspects. The profundity of the problem—into whose technical aspects there can be no question of entering here—is essentially due on the one hand to the fact that it concerns real—and hence noninfinite— systems and on the other hand to its *yes–no* nature. Either a given mathematical entity *does* correspond to a physical quantity that really exists (and that therefore can be observed by the demon) or it does *not*. No intermediate case exists in our conceptual apparatus.

The foregoing discussion may well seem recondite, yet it is far from reflecting the actual complexity of the problem. Thus, for example, even under the assumption that a consistent reconciliation could, after all, have been achieved between quantum theory and the principle of the universal quasilocality of parts of instruments (e.g., pointers), even then some addition to the theory in question would have been necessary in order to reconcile it completely with physical realism. This addition is that of new variables, supplementing the wave functions of these instrument parts and labelling the actual position taken by any of the latter after a measurement on a quantum system has been performed; for indeed, in general, such positions are not predetermined. They are specified neither by the initial

wave functions nor by the final wave function of the composite object
constituted by the system and the measuring instrument. In this sense,
they thus appear as variables taking precise values only when the measurements are performed. The unavoidable—even if nonphysical—
question of knowing what minimal degree of instrumental complexity
would bring forth the appearance of such new variables represents just
another facet of the conceptual difficulties described above.

For solving such problems, use of the notion of irreversibility has often
been suggested. But this can only shift the difficulty. The point becomes
clear when due account is taken of the considerable problems—which,
moreover, bear a strong similarity to the ones already described—
encountered by any attempt to define what is meant by "an irreversible
phenomenon," in a "strongly objective" sense particularly when it is requested that this definition apply to actual systems and not exclusively to
systems idealized in the manner described above. Finally, it may be noted
(a) that a somewhat promising approach to the difficulties studied here is
to try to make use of the fact that, in practice, macroscopic systems are
never isolated well enough to really fully justify the application of quantum theory to them, but (b) that a systematic study of this approach raises
anew some of the subtleties and unsolved problems we have already
encountered above.

Up to this point, I have explained that having once defined reality to be
independent of man, a mere consistency requirement forces me to agree
with the view according to which the mere consideration of the macroscopic nature of the instruments is not sufficient for reconciling quantum
theory with the postulate of physical realism. In the preceding chapters,
the point was even made—albeit in a more succinct way—that, more
generally, there does not, in my opinion, exist any general nonarbitrary
conception that would make such a reconciliation possible. I must therefore now stress the fact—which may at first sight look paradoxical—that
in spite of this, I consider some of theoretical developments which seem to
aim at such a reconciliation to be extremely interesting and instructive.[6]
As a matter of fact, this is *not* paradoxical, since most of the authors of
these developments declare that they fall more or less in line with Heisenberg; for indeed their problem (a well-formulated but highly complex one)
then merely bears upon the relationship between *empirical* reality and
man. Unavoidably man (just like the animals, presumably) feels he abides
in space, and that reality, space, empirical as it may be, still is, to him,
infinitely "real." Similarly real also, to him, is the irreversibility of time,
since he feels time elapsing. Even though irreversibility is not the subject of
this book (no one should aim at discussing every problem!), it is fascinating
to study the detailed connections and "feedbacks" that seem to exist between, on the one hand, the microphysical objects as *perceived* by man

[6] See, e.g., I. Prigogine, in *Connaissance et Philosophie,* Pub. Académie Royale de
Belgique. This text contains references to other works by the same author. See, also, I.
Prigogine and I. Stengers, *La Nouvelle Alliance,* Gallimard, Paris, 1979.

and, on the other hand, the "natural" propensity of these objects to combine into irreversible and/or organic macroscopic objects, the influence of such a building-up process on the structures of *thought* (arising in some such objects), and finally—closing the loop!—the effect that these thought structures *themselves* have on man's possible means of perceiving microphysical objects. The quantitative results of these investigations—aside from any arbitrary speculation—yield a glimpse at a few interesting truths concerning the way in which, for example, what we living beings call "order" can progressively appear within "disorder" without violating the physical laws, and concerning other similar subjects.

Together with the obvious fact that, by definition, human beings can directly perceive nothing but *empirical* reality, the fact that discoveries such as the ones mentioned above could be made with operational physics only—i.e., without having recourse to any *a priori* option concerning Being—could easily generate the idea that, after all, the only reality that matters—the only reality that can have a meaning for man—is empirical reality. Hence, it is quite understandable that such a view—which, for example, is embraced by Wolfgang Pauli in the quotation from his letters given in Chapter 3—should be explicitly taken by many theoretical physicists. But, on the other hand, even when we acknowledge the earnestness and weight of some arguments in favor of a given conception, we may of course legitimately take the opposite point of view if, after close examination, we feel that the arguments in favor of this view are even more convincing. This is precisely the case for me with regard to this problem, as I have already pointed out. The arguments that, in my opinion, thus turn the scales have been thoroughly described in the foregoing chapters, but here they can be briefly summarized by two main ideas. One of these, admittedly, is *a priori*: I can agree *neither* with the—in my eyes presumptuous—thesis that all of reality is man-centered, *nor* with the (to my mind, overly pessimistic) view that man, whatever he attempts, can never have access to anything more than mere semblances! The other idea is *a posteriori*. It is based on the ascertainment of the fact that nonseparability is not only a feature of independent reality, but can also be checked by experiment. The second of these two statements has been proven in Chapter 4; the first will be justified explicitly in the next chapter. Obviously, when taken together, these ideas to some extent permit the notion of independent reality to come down from the heavens of great metaphysical ideas, so that even such down-to-earth individuals as scientists can again begin to consider it.

11.2 The Philosopher's Beeline

Above I examined the objections to my conception of a nonphysical realism that could arise in the minds of contemporary scientists. I must now consider those that could come from philosophers. In fact these objections do not bear on the conception itself, but rather on the method used here to establish its truth. The philosophers I have in mind are those who—like F. Alquié[7]—assert (if I may schematize their views) that the physical realism defined above is *a priori* absurd and that, nevertheless, the concept of Being is meaningful, whence a nonphysical realism or something similar to it. My purpose here is to try to show that the method these philosophers use for establishing this—the method that enables them to make a beeline for the conclusion without introducing any specific information about the actual structure of physics as revealed by experiment—while it has the merit of being expeditious, nevertheless is less reliable than my own, which, on the contrary, is based on such "details." At any rate let me explicate my opinions in this respect and thereby reconcile the two points of view, or, at least, bring them closer together.

As will be remembered, the thesis of physical realism is, schematically, the idea that nature possesses some objective reality independent of our perceptions and our means of investigation but nevertheless describable, in principle, by physics. Whoever accepts such a thesis is thereby more or less unavoidably prompted to take two steps. One of them is to define physical reality to be composed of the set of all objects that are, in principle, within reach of man's experimental knowledge (directly or through the medium of theories). The other step is to assume that reality is prior to mind, since the notion of nature includes all that exists, including the mind. The objection of the philosophers in question is directed toward the upholders of such a view. It goes as follows: It is self-contradictory, they say, to assert the primacy of physical reality over mind and at the same time to define that very physical reality "at the level of the scientific object, that is, precisely, as a construct of human mind."[8] The conclusion is that any so-called "scientific objectivism," that is, any philosophy defining matter at the level of scientific object (this is, in particular, the case of Lenin's doctrine, and also that of many "materialists" who claim to think scientifically) is simply an idealism unaware of its own nature.

What is the value of this argument? If it holds, how can we explain that it escaped the attention of so many intelligent persons. If it does not, where is the mistake?

For my part, I think that the argument must be considered to be correct by anyone who demands that science be *certain*. Indeed, strictly speaking, nothing is really certain to us except our operations. If science is required to be certain, then it can make only operational statements. However, operational assertions have no meaning except in reference to the community of the operators. For example, the assertion that each of the particles called electrons exists independently on the grounds that it was possible to operationally discover some experimental regularities that the notion of such individual particles helps to describe amounts to a statement that is of uncertain nature and goes far beyond what science can strictly assert. And

---

[7] See, e.g., F. Alquié, *La nostalgie de l'être* P.U.F.
[8] See footnote 7.

the same is true of everything else. If I demand that science be certain, then the notion of any scientific object whatsoever reduces completely and is totally exhausted by the notion of a given set of operations that *we* perform and of the results that *our* mind can perceive. For science, there is nothing—there can be nothing—underlying this, for whatever it would be, it would be uncertain. Any assertion would be perhaps true, perhaps false, and perhaps also meaningless. So the philosophers are quite right; and even though the example of the electron helps us to understand their argument more easily (especially if we know some modern physics), it is by no means essential. Strictly speaking, the argument is *a priori*; in other words, it is completely independent of the actual experimental data and theoretical structures of physics.

But, on the other hand, this conclusion cannot be considered to be final because nothing forces us to demand that science be *certain*. Is not a quasicertainty sufficient? Indeed it *must* be, for the epistemologists have known for quite a long time now that in reality *radical* empiricism is fruitless, that any absolutely strict operationalism would in fact be useless to science. To make generalization possible, to lay the groundwork for the notion of universal laws, it is necessary to go somewhat beyond pure operationalism.[9] Through this loophole, some uncertainty, to be sure, arises in principle with regard to the validity of scientific statements. But fortunately that very same science has taught us that there exist cases in nature in which uncertainty of an assertion is so minimal that, in practice, the assertion is tantamount to a certainty.

As everybody knows, the probability is not zero that if we place a kettle on a fire its contents will freeze instead of boil. But that probability is so small that we can neglect it completely. In the predictions of science—and even more so in its interpretations—we therefore find it natural that a small degree of uncertainty should exist.

Now this is sufficient to drastically change the elements of our problem. To see this clearly, let us imagine a world admittedly quite different from ours but nevertheless conceivable: a world—an "independent reality"—in which Newtonian mechanics is exact, a world similar to the one that d'Alembert, Laplace, Lagrange, and, more generally, most of the theorists active at the end of the eighteenth century and at the beginning of the nineteenth seem to have imagined. In this world all the phenomena could be accounted for by the Newtonian mechanics of the point-particles submitted to forces themselves due to such particles. When I assert that such a world is conceivable, I do not claim that it could actually exist. Quite possibly it could be shown that Laplace was *a priori* wrong and that actually no structured solid, no organism, and hence no brain could form in such a world. But such a proof, assuming it is possible, does not belong to the realm of that which is immediately clear, since it escaped the attention of the greatest minds of that time. This is all I mean when I claim that a Newtonian world is conceivable. Now, if I lived in such a

---

[9] See Chapter 12.

world, and if I were engaged in constructing its physics, I would most certainly introduce the relevant concepts by a mental operation based on my day-to-day experience of my possibilities of action, just as was done, in the real world, by the physicists who constructed *our* physics. At this stage, therefore, the philosopher is still right: even within such a simple elementary universe, the "scientific object" would, strictly speaking, be nothing other than a construct of our mind. And if the physicist wanted to be able to consider his science to be a set of certainties, he would have to acknowledge—in this universe, just as in ours—that the certainties in question bear exclusively on what the set of all living, thinking, communicating beings do, feel, write, read, and so on, and *not* on independent reality. But if the physicists of this Newtonian world were, as in ours, satisfied with quasicertainties, then they could, I think, quite legitimately refer to the principle that in a case in which there is only one simple consistent explanation of a whole set of facts, the probability that this explanation is true is extremely great. They could then easily maintain that the *constructs* "particles" and "forces" faithfully reflect structural elements of the independent reality, for they would correctly point out that such an idea is by far the simplest and the most consistent explanation of the observed regularities and indeed of the whole of knowledge. By applying the principle just formulated, they would then infer—quite appropriately I think!—that in all probability the idea in question is true and that the so-called "scientific objectivism" defined above is therefore, after all, a meaningful and true doctrine. And we—who know the ultimate truth of this matter because we constructed the whole scheme—know that indeed these claims would be completely valid.

By the preceding argument, I hope I have shown that unless an absolute certainty were demanded (and it is not), it is not possible to disprove the doctrine of physical realism by merely making use of the *a priori* argument of the philosophers.[10] For this purpose, it is necessary to take into account the actual content of physics, as has been done in the preceding chapters. To summarize, the set of notions and principles progressively built up by common experience, refined by thought, and found applicable to physics is admittedly a set of *constructs* which could finally be arranged into a consistent universal theory, but, in my opinion, it is *only* because the elements of this set cannot all be interpreted in a unique—hence nonarbitrary—strongly objective way that physical realism ought to be discarded.

---

[10] I am well aware of the fact that the philosophers can put forward quite serious arguments against my use of the concept of probability. Indeed this concept is based on induction; it should therefore be applied only to reproducible phenomena. This is what justifies the philosophers' distrust for anything that is merely *likely*. And that is what should make respectable (in the eyes of scientists) the demand for certainty that has buoyed them up since Descartes's time. But, alas, certainty can never be achieved. Hence, to tolerate mere likelihood is not so foolish as they think.

CHAPTER 12

Nonseparability and Counterfactuality

Previously (see Chapter 4) nonseparability was proven on the basis of experimental data. As may be remembered, this proof made use of a similarity between quantum measurement and examination tests. Up to some reservations concerning technical details, the proof in question was understood to call for no preliminary assumptions.

On the other hand, the analyses that followed, those of Chapters 5–7 in particular, have shown that, quite generally, the human mind is spontaneously overconfident on such matters. In particular, it too frequently raises ideas that look "clear and distinct" to the level of absolute truths. It sometimes fails to note the cases in which the notions in question are, in fact, of questionable validity or are relevant merely within some limited context. As we have already pointed out, this deficiency of the human mind implies that in any study of the foundations of physics (and in the present one in particular), it is extremely important to systematically search for any implicit notions or assumptions that might conceivably have crept into the argument. Sometimes this search turns out to be fruitless. This should be considered most satisfactory, for it shows that the argument under study is generally valid. In other instances, the search eventually discloses the presence of a notion or an assumption which we could, after all, conceive as possibly erroneous or meaningless. Under such conditions, it is of course necessary to consider the notion or the assumption in question as a premise of the argument. We then have a choice between two possibilities: either we accept the notion or the assumption—together with the previously considered ones—and then the conclusions of the argument follow, or we wish to escape these conclusions. This we can now do, but we know that we must then consider the new assumption to be false or meaningless. This provides a supplementary piece of information, and it does so even in the cases in which the new assumption or notion is intuitively so "obviously" correct that, as a last resort, our minds prefer to bow to the conclusions under discussion rather than to reconcile itself to the idea of giving up the assumption or the notion.

In a book intended for the general public, such discussions would be out of place. But it is likely that the present work will, in some cases, fall into the hands of individuals who have both some time available for reflection and some natural inclination towards the investigation of such matters.

For them, and for them only, the present chapter—boring for others!—is meant. Compared to the questions studied in the preceding pages, those taken up here are, on the whole, secondary ones. So the hurried reader will lose little information if he skips over the remaining part of this chapter and turns directly to the next one.

Since any even so slightly technical analysis should preferably be concise, there would be no point in trying to explicitly motivate the order of the following items. Its justification will become progressively clear as the arguments develop.

12.1 Epistemological Difficulties Concerning the Problem of Defining Dispositional Terms

Such difficulties appeared, and proposals for solving them were put forward, a long time ago. The epistemologists give the name "dispositional term" to any word that, instead of qualifying a property (of a physical system) that can be directly observed (assuming such properties exist!), labels, on the contrary, the *disposition* of a system to a given response P'' under specified conditions P'.[1] The word "magnetic" can be used as an example, for, most often, the intention is to define (in an operational way) the property (call it Qx) of being magnetic possessed by an object x as being such a *disposition*. For example, we seek a way of defining Qx by referring to the fact $(P''x)$ that x attracts small iron specks when $(P'x)$ such specks happen to lie in its vicinity. It is quite clear that there are many dispositional terms within the empirical sciences and that other examples are therefore easily found. In fact, since, strictly speaking, the properties of reality are never directly knowable, the difficult problem would be to discover epithets that are not ultimately just dispositional terms!

In any case, the scheme sketched above for a definition of dispositional terms is still quite vague and must be made more precise. But at this stage difficulties appear. Indeed, the first idea that occurs to us is to write (using the language of formal logic):

$$Qx =_{\text{def}} (P'x \supset P''x) \tag{1}$$

that is,

"x is magnetic" $=_{\text{definition}}$: "if iron specks lie in the vicinity of x then they are attracted."[2]   (1')

---

[1] Substantially, the description given here of the problem is the one put forward by C. G. Hempel in *International Encyclopedia of Unified Science,* University of Chicago Press, Chicago, 1953; albeit the solution proposed here is not the one that is favored by the moderately operationalist standpoint chosen by this author.

[2] The definition is purposely simplified with respect to quantitative details that are irrelevant here. In particular, it should be clear that an object can be magnetic at some times and not at other times.

However, in formal logic, the symbol . . . ⊃ _____ which reads "if . . . then _____" is always meant to represent the so-called "material implication." That is, it is supposed to mean "either not . . . or _____." Can this meaning be retained here? Obviously not, for then the right-hand side of equality (1) [or (1')] would be satisfied (would have "yes" as its truth value) not only in the cases in which iron specks lie nearby *and* are attracted, but also in all cases in which *no* iron specks lie in the vicinity of x. The definition (1) [or (1')] would thus imply, in particular, that any object x in the vicinity of which no iron specks are lying is *ipso facto* magnetic; but clearly this is not the idea that the definition we are looking for is expected to convey!

But, after all, what is the idea in question? Clearly, it is better approached by a phrase constructed in the subjunctive tense, such as:

"x is magnetic" = definition: "if iron specks *were* lying in the vicinity of x, then they *would* be attracted."   (2')

For this, however, it is still necessary to make the meaning of this phrase (2') completely explicit, and to do so in such a way that this meaning should really coincide with the idea we actually have in mind when we think of a magnetic object. But it seems that this idea contains a judgement bearing on the consequences of a premise that is contrary to facts, something whose expression involves an apparent contradiction, such as the sentence, "Even in the cases in which there are no iron specks nearby, if there were, they would be attracted."

Such judgements are said to be "counterfactual." It must be granted that they look quite strange as soon as they are stated explicitly. Admittedly, moreover, there are cases in which they are somewhat ambiguous. For these reasons, the logicians hold them in suspicion to some extent, so that even with regard to the problem of defining dispositional terms, some epistemologists have tried to manage *without* these counterfactual assertions. For example, Carnap proposed replacing definition (1) and (1') by what he calls "partial definitions," formulated by means of "reduction sentences." A "reduction sentence" which provides a "partial definition" of the expression "x is magnetic" is of the type:

"If x is subjected to the test which consists of placing iron specks in its vicinity, then it is called magnetic if and only if the specks are attracted."   (3')

Or, symbolically,

$$P'x \supset (Qx \equiv P''x) \qquad (3)$$

(if $P'x$, then Qx if and only if $P''x$: the symbol $\equiv$ indeed reads "if and only if").

Hence, we see that the partial definition (3') can be translated into the language of conventional formal logic, or, in other words, that it can be formulated exclusively using the symbols of logic. This was not the case with definition (2'). Moreover, it is easily checked that the objection against definition (1) and (1') cannot be made against (3) and (3').

On the other hand, the range of definition (3′) is obviously much smaller than that of definition (2′). This is due to the fact that (3′) yields no interpretation for a statement such as "object x is magnetic and there is no iron speck in its vicinity."

Some epistemologists tend to think that this limitation is not a very serious one, and that, at least, it is not redhibitory. They even stress that it saves a kind of "openness," which turns out to be useful with regard to the meaning of scientific terms. With respect to this, they point out that one and the same term can be given several different partial definitions covering a whole range of cases [such as a definition like (3) but in which $P'x$ means "x travels along the axis of a solenoid whose wiring is closed and unconnected to any generator," and $P''x$ means "an electric current traverses the solenoid"]. Other epistemologists—and I sympathize with them—assert, on the contrary, that the formal gain derived from the use of sets of partial definitions does not compensate for the lack of generality of the latter.[3] They consider it utterly unacceptable that once a finite set of N partial definitions has been stated, such a clear statement as, for example, "x is magnetic, travels through no solenoid, has no iron specks in its vicinity, and so on" (N terms) should, to a logician, remain incomprehensible and even meaningless!

But, if this standpoint is taken, then it seems clear that one way or another the limits of traditional formal logic must be transgressed, for example by using counterfactual sentences within the definition of the dispositional terms. Along these lines, we are led to confer a meaning to the following definition:

"x is magnetic" $=$ definition: "in the cases in which iron specks are present near x, they are attracted, and in the cases in which there are actually none, if there were some, they would be attracted." (4′)

From now on, the statements of the type of the right-hand side of this equation will be called "conditional implications." For short, we shall even take the liberty of translating definition (4′) into a symbolic language, as

$$QX = {}_{\text{def}}(P'x > P''x), \tag{4}$$

where Qx, $P'x$, $P''x$ have the meanings stated above and where the symbol $\ldots > -$ means "if $\ldots$ is true then $-$ is true, and if $non \ldots$ is true, then if $\ldots$ were true $-$ would be true." Again, this meaning is strange and apparently paradoxical; in short, it is "counterfactual," but by this it merely reflects, as we have seen, the true features of the *dispositional*

---

[3] The objection is even more relevant in quantum mechanics, where an attribute is definable by an infinite number of measurements that, strictly speaking, are all essentially different from one another (H. Stein, *Paradigms and Paradoxes*, Vol. 5, University of Pittsburgh Press, Pittsburgh, 1972). In principle, the method implies that all of them should be included!

term concept, as conceived by the mind. It is unnecessary to stress that the "symbol of conditional implication" used in (4) does not belong to conventional (i.e., nonmodal) formal logic.

12.2 Link with the Concept of Physical Laws

For a long time, the empiricists thought that the (quite often stressed) universality of the physical laws was due to the fact that they are of the form "whenever conditions A are satisfied, facts B are observed." But recent epistemological investigations have stressed the fact that not all statements having that form are of the nature of scientific laws. G. Hempel[4] mentions, as a counterexample, the statement "in all the cases in which an object is constituted of pure gold, it is observed that its mass is smaller than 100 000 kg." Unquestionably, this statement is literally true and has the considered form. However, nobody would identify it with a natural law. We all regard it to be of a "contingent" or "accidental" nature. Such a counterexample is sufficient for showing that a scientific law is something more than just a true statement having a universal form (in the sense of the above counterexample).

But then what differentiates the true scientific laws from mere accidental generalizations? According to a number of epistemologists, the answer is as follows: Unlike an accidental generalization, a law can be used to corroborate a counterfactual assertion. For example, let us consider the assertion "if the sugar lump I hold in my hand had been immersed in water for a sufficiently long time, it would have dissolved." The assertion is counterfactual since the premise it entails did not take place. However, I know the assertion to be true because I know the law (established either deductively or empirically or both—the point is irrelevant here) according to which crystals of sugar are soluble in water. The law is thus differentiated from an accidental generalization like "all the sugar in Martinique is cane sugar," for even if this assertion accidentally happens to be true today, it cannot be used for corroborating the counterfactual assertion "if the sugar lump that I am holding in my hand were on Martinique, it would be a lump of cane sugar."

It is conceivable that eventually the concept of physical laws will become obsolete, as has been the case for many others. It is unlikely that this will take place due to a mere return to the notion of accidental generalizations. But, then, if the distinction is to persist, and if the analysis summarized above is correct, it should be concluded that, in conformance with what intuition indicates and in spite of the difficulties mentioned above, not all counterfactual assertions are necessarily meaningless.

---

[4] G. Hempel, *Philosophy of Natural Science*, Prentice Hall, Englewood Cliffs, NJ, 1966.

12.3 Connection with Physical Realism as Applied to Objects

To every human mind, definition (4')—which involves a conditional implication—suggests its own interpretation; an interpretation which, indeed, is so obvious that it seems almost necessary and which consists of calling forth the notion of properties *possessed* by a physical system. The right-hand side of (4') is meaningful—and true—because *x possesses in itself* a certain property, and it is this property that, according to definition (4'), we agree to express by means of the word "magnetic." This could easily be carried over to other notions such as that of the hardness of a flint, and so on. The philosophy (implicit in almost every human mind) that could be called "objectivist realism" or "realism of the properties" thus appears to be closely linked with the ability of the human mind to consider the conditional implication meaningful, in spite of the fact that it involves a counterfactual assertion. This ability is so widespread that it is only through more careful thought that its surprising (not to say para-doxical) nature is revealed. And we should even say that it looks surpris-ing only to individuals whose thinking is influenced by the philosophy of experience, for, with regard to others, those whose thinking is based on the postulate of objectivist realism, the ability in question only reflects their presupposition that there are objects which possess properties. Since—by assumption—the objectivist realist considers that he knows this, he is fully justified in trying to determine the identity of these things and their properties. To this end, he strives to discover regularities in human ex-perience, and he asserts that the corresponding things and properties exist. To give names to the latter, definitions of the type (4') are, to him, the obvious ones to be used, and contain no mystery.

This is the appropriate place to point out that such definitions [defini-tions of type (4')] are, in particular, used by the objectivist realists in order to define what they mean by the statement that a physical quantity A has value a on an object x. Symbolically:

$$\text{"A has value } a \text{ on } x\text{"} =_{\text{def}} (P'x > P''x), \tag{5}$$

where $P'x$ means "the physical operations corresponding to a measure-ment of A are (would be) made on x" and where $P''x$ means "the value a is (would be) found." Here, again, the presence of the sign $>$ [to be defined as in (4')] implies the emergence of the realistic idea according to which x has in itself the property that, on it, A has the value a, quite independent of whether or not any human being cares to, or does, measure it.

12.4 Counterfactuality and Separability

The purpose of this chapter is—as will be remembered—to inquire about the precise nature of the assumptions that might conceivably be necessary in order to ensure that the proof of nonseparability presented in Chapter 4—on the basis of experimental data—be rigorous.

Constructed using the example of the twins, this proof is based on the fact that—account being taken of the strict correlations observed during all the preceding years in the university under consideration—if one of the twins has just passed a test in a given subject, it is certain that his brother possesses the aptitude for success in the same subject. Thus, it is unnecessary that he should take that test, and he is actually submitted to a different one. It is quite clear that the proof rests on the validity of some counterfactual assertions that come into play in conditional implications. I know that Peter's twin brother has passed the Greek test. In the case in which Peter himself is to take that same Greek examination, I know (by induction) that he will succeed. In a straightforward way, I interpret this in the realistic manner, namely I speak of Peter's *aptitude* for passing the Greek test and I consider this aptitude to be a property possessed by this individual. I am thus led to attribute a meaning to—and to consider true—the counterfactual assertion which, concerning precisely this individual called Peter, stipulates that his aptitude for success in the Greek test would have existed even if his brother had not taken a test and even if he himself had finally given up his intention of taking it. Together with a locality assumption, these considerations lead—as shown in Chapter 4—to the conclusion that the strict correlations between the twins imply the existence, at any time and concerning each student separately, of well-defined positive or negative aptitudes relative to three (or more) types of examinations. The Bell inequalities follow.

The conclusion of the foregoing analysis must therefore be that, quite generally, the Bell inequalities cannot be derived from the locality assumption alone (no "influences" travelling with infinite velocity), but only from the union of that assumption with another one, namely the one according to which counterfactual assertions are meaningful at least in some well-defined cases, which, again, are the cases in which these assertions appear in conditional implications.

With regard to the problem raised by the violation of the Bell inequalities, we thus see some indications taking shape (whether or not they will materialize is not yet known) pointing to the possibility of a solution that would differ from the one investigated in this book; for it would not hinge on nonseparability (i.e., on the violation of the locality assumption), but on the denial that any counterfactual extrapolation of a meaningful factual statement can itself be meaningful.

Again, counterfactual assertions are somehow held in suspicion by the experts in formal logic; from this point of view, the idea of a solution based on the view that these assertions are meaningless is therefore rather attractive at first sight. In particular, we could then do without the symbol >, by means of which we summarized such assertions above and which is not an element of the conventional "calculus of propositions." If we were to follow this procedure, then, with regard to the problem of defining the value of a physical quantity at a given time, we would give up the type (5) definition—which makes use of this symbol—and, following Carnap's idea, we would confine ourselves to *partial definitions* of the general type

(3) or (3′). In other words, instead of (5), we would be led to write

$$P'x \supset (\text{"the value of } A \text{ on } x \text{ is } a\text{"} \equiv P''x),\tag{6}$$

where $P'x$ means "A is (directly or indirectly) measured on x" and $P''x$ means "a is found."

Within the realm of a definition such as (6), we would have to assert [if (6) is the only partial definition expressed] "it is only when the measuring instrument intended for measuring A is present that the statement 'the value of A on x is a' is meaningful." Similarly, in the case of the example involving the students, it is only when an examiner in Greek has examined or, at least, is on the verge of examining Peter's brother, or Peter himself, that the statement "Peter possesses the aptitude for passing the Greek test" may have any meaning whatsoever. If we turn back to Chapter 4, we then easily observe that, under such conditions, the proof of the Bell inequalities described there no longer holds, for the transition from one sample to another is no longer possible. Therefore, we see that this approach offers a formally sound way of accounting for the fact that, in some cases, these inequalities are violated both by the set of experimental data and by the predictions from the general quantum-mechanical formalism.

Such considerations look somewhat similar to Bohr's theses. Can we go as far as to say that they throw some light on their content? This question is somewhat subjective, since some physicists assert that Bohr's writings are clear enough and therefore do not need any explanation. On the other hand, there are others who—without denying Bohr's depth of vision—nevertheless consider some of the features of his writings to be, to some extent, rather obscure. It is to them that an explanation of one of those aspects is offered here, an explanation based on the foregoing considerations.

The point to be studied is the argument by means of which Bohr disproves the reasoning of Einstein *et al.* that aims at showing the incompleteness of quantum mechanics. Bohr's argument is based on the idea that the whole experimental set-up must be taken into account. It emphasizes the essential role of the latter in the very definition of the phenomenon. Whatever the set-up (and, of course, it may have an arbitrarily large spatial extension), Bohr[5] asserts the following with respect to the influences that its parts may exert: "Of course there can be no question of a mechanical influence" (that might violate locality if the set-up is extended) but "there is essentially the question of an influence on the very conditions that define the possible types of predictions concerning the future behavior" of the considered system.

To those scientists who consider the terms used here by Bohr to be somewhat cryptic, we propose an interpretation of them. This amounts to

---

[5] N. Bohr, *Phys. Rev.* **48**, 696 (1935).

identifying their content with the above-considered solution of the problem raised by the violation of the Bell inequalities. Within this interpretation, the statement cited above would substantially mean "the statement 'the value of A on x is a' has a nonambiguous meaning only in the cases in which, due to the presence of appropriate measurement instruments, the conditions are fixed that define some given types of possible prediction concerning the future behavior of the system." In other words, Bohr's statement would simply mean that, with regard to the systems of interest in microphysics, the definition of the value a physical quantity on a given system should, in every case, be but *a partial definition*, that is, a definition of type (6). If the students were such systems, then the statement "Peter has the aptitude for passing the Greek examination" would indeed be meaningful only in the cases in which an examiner in Greek is on the verge of testing Peter's brother or Peter himself (or in other cases, also specifying partial definitions).

Formally, such a solution is admittedly correct. But it must be stressed that in view of the great generality of the principle on which it is based (the principle of accepting no counterfactual statement whatsoever), it raises serious difficulties to any upholder of strict physical realism. For, indeed, if the principle in question is to apply only to "small" systems—those for which quantum theory turns out to be appropriate and convenient—then it is necessary to specify quite precisely the criteria for classifying a system as "small"; and the difficulties in discriminating between microsystems and macrosystems then reappear. Conversely, if the principle is taken to be completely general, if, in other words, it is asserted that no counterfactual statement may be accepted, not even in macroscopic physics, then, as we have seen, considerable difficulties arise with regard to the problem of specifying the distinction—which undoubtedly must be made!—between scientific laws and mere accidental generalizations. Moreover, let us again consider a test of the type we called A on page 68. Assuming a psychologist has repeated the test on a great many individuals and has found, in every case, that the latter repeat their first answer, would he not conclude that each individual, after just one positive answer, possesses the *aptitude* for giving that answer again? An aptitude which is more than a mere piece of information about the past and which, on the other hand, is quite independent of whether or not any plan to repeat the test exists?

This is so strictly true that if the Bell inequalities turned out to be violated in a case such as the one imagined in Chapter 4 (strictly correlated twins) or in Chapter 7 (males and females strictly correlated within pairs, in several tests), neither the president of the university nor the psychologist in charge of the test would ever dream—for accounting for these violations—of resorting to such a radical assumption as that of the violation of conditional implications or (what amounts to the same) to a general criticism of the commonly accepted meaning of the dispositional terms. This is all the more certain since these authorities would have at their disposal the possibility of resorting to a mode of explanation which, after all, is much more conservative and which consists of admitting the possibility that distant influences may operate between, say, the examiner of a given student and the latter's brother, who is in another room (or between the assistant in charge of the test given to the male and the latter's female counterpart, who is somewhere else). This simpler mode of explanation, which is compatible with the realistic viewpoint, leads to what I called nonseparability above.

12.5 Discussion

Thus, one conclusion of the present study is that, strictly speaking, it is impossible to derive the Bell inequalities just from a locality assumption, that is, merely from the idea that some distant influences violating certain general conditions do not exist. To build up a strict derivation along the present lines, it is necessary to assume, in addition, that some counterfactual assertions—and, in particular, some definitions of attributes that are based on such assertions—are meaningful. On this question, however, it must be noted that in order for the proof described in Chapter 4 to be valid, it is not at all necessary that *any* counterfactual statement whatsoever should be attributed a meaning. In particular, the proof in question does not consider the case in which Peter and Paul are two students in *partial* correlation (let us say, they are not twins) who are tested in two separate rooms. Unlike other attempts to derive the Bell inequalities, the proof discussed here does not therefore rest on the idea that—assuming Paul to have succeeded—the counterfactual statement "if Peter had taken another examination, Paul would nevertheless have succeeded" is also correct in the case considered. Now it is fortunate that the proof does not rest on that idea, for such a counterfactual statement is of somewhat dubious validity, even to a realist. This is a result of the fact that, in the case considered here, we cannot exclude the assumption that Paul answered partly haphazardly and did not entirely owe his success to a preexisting aptitude. It is then not clear that he *could* not (hypothetically) have given some other answer even if he had been placed in the same circumstances.

Again, the proof in Chapter 4 is free from such a criticism. The counterfactual statements on the meaningfulness on which it rests are just those that are present in the conditional implications. Hence, all of them belong to the category of those of which *the logic used in everyday life demands* that they be considered meaningful. Substantially, in this respect, they may be compared to the statement "if iron specks were lying near enough to a magnet, and if they were not fastened to any support, they would be attracted."

Nevertheless, it remains true that the assumption according to which the counterfactual statements belonging to this category are universally valid may also be rejected, as we have seen. This is the standpoint taken by Niels Bohr. On this assumption, the Bell inequalities can no longer be derived.

Should we conclude that the violation of these inequalities can be accounted for without resorting to the concept of nonseparability? Let us stress once more that a *realist*, at any rate, cannot consistently do this because, *to him*, the alternative explanation, the one based on the standpoint chosen by Bohr, *also* calls on nonseparability, albeit in a round-about way, or at least on the notion, which is philosophically equivalent, of an indivisible whole constituted by the system together with the measuring instruments.[6]

The experimental corroboration of nonseparability (or of indivisibility *à la* Bohr, which essentially amounts to the same) quite obviously constitutes a strong argument against the hypothesis of objectivist realism as applied to microscopic objects and even—for the reasons described above[7]—against that of objectivist realism as applied to macroscopic objects only.

We could even be tempted to assert more bluntly that the corroboration in question constitutes a strong argument against the hypothesis of realism; that is, that it favors a kind of idealism reflected by the operationalistic attitude of most present-day theoretical physicists. But, on the other hand, we must also consider the fact that an experimental study *is* possible that specifically involves the notion of an independent reality, together with the general properties attributable to that reality. This very fact implies, as a consequence, that the notion in question can no longer be considered to be totally devoid of any conceivable relationship with human experience. Therefore, the idea of completely discarding such a notion by styling it as metaphysical and meaningless becomes considerably less cogent. It is appropriate, though somewhat paradoxical, to assert that, in view of this, a certain pre-Kantian realism becomes—even in physics—respectable again, to some extent.

---

[6] Carnap, Hempel, and other epistemologists did, in fact, consider the case of "dispositional terms" depending on time. Thus, for example, an object can be magnetic at some times and nonmagnetic at others. The "partial definition" concept introduced by these authors fully applies to dispositions that are time dependent. However, in the case studied here, we witness the appearance of a particular circumstance, which is that the conditions $P'x$ are constituted by an event which can be separated by a spacelike interval from the event (Qx): "the object under consideration has the property defined by the dispositional term." It does not seem that these epistemologists have discussed the possibility that such a circumstance should have to be considered. The circumstance in question entails (through the coexistence of several partial definitions of one and the same property, as described in Section 12.1) the appearance of "particular laws" that here are of a nonlocal nature. For the Bell inequalities to be violated, it then is necessary for such "laws" to be irreducible to *effects* of local *causes* (such as correlations established at the source). It is an idea of this kind that the expression "indivisible whole" is meant to convey.

[7] Nonexistence of a sharp boundary (see Chapter 11).

12.6 Nonseparability and New Logics

A priori we might also wonder whether the proof of the Bell inequalities, described in Chapter 4, does not also implicitly depend upon still another assumption, namely that of the validity of conventional (also called two-valued) logic. The question may seem relevant, for indeed the proof of Lemma A in Chapter 4 implicitly depends on this assumption since it contains the assertion "(any young woman) necessarily belongs either to the class of female smokers or to that of young nonsmokers." Transposed into the field of particle physics, such a statement is necessarily true only if the *properties* of the particles are describable by means of propositions which obey the rules of conventional two-valued logic. However, there exist some formulations of quantum mechanics in which the propositions that are considered applicable to the properties of the particles do not obey this logic but another kind, which is called "quantum logic." Lemma A is not generally true in this logic. This also holds with regard to Lemma B, as formulated on page 2, where, just like Lemma A, it bears upon *properties*.

However, the derivation of the Bell inequalities described in Chapter 4 is not based on the consideration of properties hypothetically possessed by the systems: it is based on measurement results. Now, it is quite certain that the propositions bearing upon measurement results *do* obey conventional logic. With only the help of the assumptions of locality and realism (or, otherwise stated, with only the locality assumption associated with the use of the "conditional implication" for defining dispositional terms), the derivation in question *proves* that, at least in the cases in which a strict correlation certainly exists (this certainty being induced from past observations on similarly prepared systems), any particle belonging to one of the considered pairs *possesses either* the property of yielding a certain well-defined experimental result if made to interact with an appropriate measuring instrument *or* the property of yielding, under the same conditions, the opposite measurement result.[8] Moreover, the derivation in question proves this not only with regard to *one* type of measurement, but with regard to several types (actually, it is enough to consider three of them). In other words, before arriving at a Bell inequality, the derivation shows, in an intermediate step (and only in the special case of strictly correlated particle pairs; but this is enough for this purpose), that there exist properties possessed by the particles and that obey two-valued logic (even if these properties are not specifically knowable). It is thus quite clear that for this derivation to succeed, there is no need to postulate *a priori* the existence of such properties as a supplementary assumption. Otherwise stated, regardless of the interest attached to the consideration

---

[8] The proof is described in section 4.3. (Recall that the term "property" is translated from "aptitude" in the example of Chapter 4.)

of quantum logic (and this interest is quite great), it must be denied that the observed violation of the Bell inequalities can be accounted for by such a consideration. If some individual believed both in locality and in realism (or in locality and in the validity of conditional implications), the observed violation would remain inexplicable to him, even after he had decided to enlarge logic in the manner considered here. On the contrary, for an individual who accepts the notion of nonseparability or that of an indivisible whole, as specified above,[9] the violation in question becomes explainable, even without modifying logic.

---

[9] See footnote 6 on p. 143.

Chapter 13

Glances

As long as an "expert"—an art critic, a biologist, a physicist—deals with his own field of research, we willingly note the facts he informs us of and the opinions he expresses. As soon as the same "expert" aspires to discover some links between such facts or opinions and more general conceptions, our natural tendency is to doubt his statements, for we consider—and, admittedly, rightly so—that on going beyond his own particular field, he loses his special qualifications. It is therefore with an *a priori* skeptical eye that we see him entering a domain of thought in which we believe we are just as learned and wise as he is, and perhaps even wiser! For is there not an appreciable chance that his specialized studies blind him in the field of general ideas? Moreover, does not experience show that on general problems the conceptions of the experts are more often than not both short-sighted and oversimple?

To be sure, the conceptions of the philosophers are more sophisticated in their form—but there, alas, some distortions of subtleness, such as preciosity, verbosity, plays upon words, are quite frequent—but admittedly they are also so with regard to their content. This fact would seem to indicate that, after all, the field of general ideas is just another speciality, in which it is necessary to work steadily and exclusively in order to gain competence. We would then be tempted to define the philosopher as an "expert in general ideas."

At this point, however, a certain—at least apparent—inconsistency becomes manifest and somewhat embarrassing. Is it at all possible to conceive of a radical "expert in general ideas," that is, a thinker, who would never refer, not even implicitly, to discoveries in particular branches of research? This appears unlikely. And if such a thinker exists, is there not a danger that he would simply "reflect the vacuum"? Or, alternatively, that he should let himself be lured by at least a few of the apparently obvious "truths" (bearing upon, for example, time, space, or life) that the "experts" in the various branches of science—biology, physics, etc.— have long since shown to be errors? Finally, since such a thinker has no possibility of testing his personal conclusions against any experiment whatsoever, it may be asked whether he is sufficiently aware of the risks of arbitrariness (and, hence, of errors) run by even the brightest mind in any field that lies far away from the realms of everyday life and human action.

These few remarks (more could be added) lead us to consider that while, admittedly, it is unduly naive to expect the answers to the essential questions to come exclusively from scientists, it would presumably be just as naive, in the domain of general ideas, to trust only "specialists in generalities," that is, professional philosophers. They are not as exclusively competent on such matters as some of them would like us to believe. But then, what should we do? Whom should we trust?

To the latter question, the obvious answer is, of course, "nobody." Each of us must build up his own appreciation. But in order to make it sensible, we should base it on all the serious information available. To be sure, we must know of the work of the pure philosophers, which constitutes a most valuable fund of possible views. But among all these possibilities—which often contradict one another—a choice must be made. And science can help us to make a choice, by diminishing the risks of subjectivity and arbitrariness. Or, at least, it can help those of us who know it well enough to be able to find their way among its data. Hence, it is *also* profitable to be informed of the general ideas that some experts in particular fields dare suggest to infer from the descriptions they give us of their own domain of research.

If the validity of the latter proposition is granted, or if at least it is considered reasonable, then—for consistency and contrary to the first impulse described above—it is necessary not to disregard the 'obvious' truth that if somebody happens to concentrate on a given field, this does not by itself disquality him from elaborating general views. It is then, moreover, reasonable to assert that such an individual is, in a way, morally obliged to explicitly connect the description of his own field of research to the set of general ideas he considers as likely to be true in view of the results of his own investigations.

Of course, it is then appropriate to demand from such an individual that in communicating his general conclusions he should not express himself peremptorily, for a thesis about Being or on the nature of values cannot and should not be formulated as forcefully as a physical law or a theorem of geometry. In principle, therefore, his sentences should all begin with words such as "it seems to me that . . ." or "it seems most likely that . . . ." And such careful wording should not render his theses less believable than those of the philosophers, for it is quite clear that systematically we should mentally add such expressions to the statements of the latter.

This chapter is simply an attempt to respond to this obligation. However, since beginning every sentence with the words "it seems to me that" or "it seems most likely that" would make the text unacceptably ponderous, such expressions are almost everywhere omitted. It must nevertheless be understood that they are implied; they should be mentally inserted by the readers. Moreover (but this, presumably, is stating the obvious), no initiation to a *system* should be sought in this chapter. It has

been a long time since people have given up believing in such philosophical constructions, and scientists are even less tempted than others to take
an interest in them. Better than anybody else, they know how very slow
and uncertain progress is in the realm of certainties. They also know quite
well that such progress can be nothing but the result of a steady collective
endeavor. Here we are thus dealing only with rather simple partial views
which refer mainly to the possibility of applying some indications gathered
from science to an improvement of the conception human beings entertain
about the world and about their role in the world (i.e., about their values).

Presently the conception in question is neither definite nor—we all
agree—satisfactory. Schematically, it is a trivial observation that modern
man bows under the yoke of either misery, ideological repression, or con-
suming vainglory, and that these yokes, diverse as they are, all generate
infantilism, which in turn generates obscurantism. To be sure, it would be
an easy matter to criticize such an analysis by stressing its sketchy features. A mere reference to cultural activities and university research pro-
grams which exist in many advanced countries would seem to be enough
to disprove it. And, admittedly, it partly does, but only partly, for all these
remarkable activities, on the one hand, interact only to a very limited
extent with the innermost thinking of most of our contemporaries and, on
the other hand, by their very nature, are essentially fragmentary. They are
wonderful studies for works of art, but a completed painting is nowhere to
be found.

Such a state of affairs has given rise to many attempts at explanation.
Among these there is one which is seldom considered but which, apart
from the fact that by itself it is credible (at least as credible as any other),
is worth considering here in view of its relationship to the subject matter
of this book. Briefly and roughly, the explanation in question is that contemporary human beings—or at least Westerners—have willfully de-
prived themselves of any (real or alleged) connection with anything that
they might meaningfully call Being or—less ambitiously—"given external
reality."

To be sure, such an assertion can easily be distorted and exposed to
criticism. For example, it should not be interpreted to mean that the (true
or illusory) feeling of intimate contact with Being automatically aids man's
development. In fact, the history of civilization and beliefs up to rather
recent times testify to the opposite. Who is not aware of the various types
of oppression that the notion of Being, together with the related notion of
destiny, of fatality, of divine commandments, or even of natural laws (the
"nature of things") have imposed upon our ancestors? Who does not see
that these notions, stirred by some ostentatious ignoramus have sometimes
served to justify excesses of various kinds and perpetuate all sorts of
influences devoid of rationality? It has been said that the "Greek miracle"
was, in fact, an invention which consisted in raising the *joie de vivre* to the
level of an essential part of culture. In an admittedly just as biased but, at
the same time, somewhat similarly striking abridgement, it might also be

said that this celebrated miracle consisted of inventing intellectual free-dom towards Being (remember the myth of Prometheus), and, just as well, that both inventions were in fact the same!

Essentially, all of this is true. However, no healthy notion is to be found whose exclusive use is not, unavoidably, a misuse. Similarly, no auto-matic recipe exists, a routine use of which—always and on every problem—would necessarily lead to a better development of man. With due account being taken of the fact that a systematic rejection of the notion of Being in this century has been the leading idea of every vanguard movement—and has been so, indeed, in quite a general and, one could even say, quite a "mechanical" way—is it not appropriate to wonder whether this rejection is not somewhat excessive? Is it not a misuse symp-tomatic of our present problems? To be sure, at this point we must grant that although such an assumption is suggested to some extent by the proliferation of partial models in physics, it presents a daring aspect, so that a tendentious account of this assumption could easily change it into its opposite. And it runs counter to too many taboos for no one to be tempted to distort it so as to be able to reject it more easily. Moreover, this *also* must be acknowledged: Even impartial minds are in no way obliged to accept the assumption in question. Indeed, I myself do not know for certain that it is true; at least I have no proof that it is. So all I require is that it should be taken into consideration. This, however, I request quite forcefully, for in it I perceive a possible means for discovering, between the developments of this book and some more general problems, a rela-tionship whose very existence might help, although in a modest way, our presently evolving culture to become somewhat less fragmentary and less fruitless.

Having formulated this request, I am now—first of all—bound to formu-late somewhat more precisely the symptoms of the gradual renunciation of any reference to reality (or, otherwise stated, to Being) that, according to my thesis in this chapter, has characterized cultural evolution during this century. This preliminary task must be fulfilled even if it implies that we must temporarily deviate from physics.

Indeed, these symptoms are many. They are present in many different domains, and while some of them correspond to evolutions that seem to lead nowhere, others have positive aspects. Among the latter, I unhesitat-ingly include what I consider to be an important outcome of the current renunciation of any reference to basic reality, namely the increased free-dom of manners. The fact that manners and behavior have largely been freed from any reference to a moral code attributed to Being itself—or emanating directly from the latter—appears to me to be a positive devel-opment, since man is an evolutionary being, since potentiality is one of his main attributes, and since his basic nature involves change. Again, as Nietzsche and Garaudy put it, man is truly a "being of the horizons." And, nowadays, nobody asserts that these "horizons" should all be transcendent. With the sole reservation that no harm be done to others, the increased freedom of manners must be accepted without qualms, for it seems likely that real advantages are attached to it. There are, on the one hand, obvious practical ones, which are related to a change in our way of life. But if suitably performed, such a liberalization also entails some appreciable moral advances. In particular, it obviously cures a major defect of the morals that prevailed before its advent, namely the fact that the only primitive impulses whose gratifications were considered acceptable—and even bestowing increased glamor—were the aggressive or martial instincts. We all agree that the liberalization in question has, at least, suppressed that exclusiveness and has thereby opened new avenues for the blooming of desire and, hence, also, of subtleness. Of course, it should be the task of the intelligentsia, politicians, and the media which popularize their messages to see to it that these routes should actually be followed by the public in place of the old, fruitless, beaten tracks of violence and Manicheism. The case, alas, is quite far from being settled, but at least we have a glimpse of how it might be.

Should we feel as optimistic with regard to the fields that refer to beauty? With regard to poetry, say? It is a fact that many poets of the past aspired to describe Being. Lucretius was certainly not the only one who aimed at knowing the Nature of Things. Through some—conscious or unconscious—recourse to Platonic views, most poets identified the Beautiful with some transcendent form of Reality. It is also a fact that all these conceptions are now considered obsolete. The fact has already been noted that the contemporary poet primarily views himself as a craftsman. In other words, he considers himself to be an artisan whose raw material is language. His purpose is to fit words together in new and clever ways. He leaves to the reader the pleasure of deriving a meaning or a conceivable reference, or—even better!—*several* possible meanings or references, from the interplay of words. With very few exceptions, the contemporary poets thus set aside any reference to Reality, be it even an implicit one.

Along these lines, the poets of the early twentieth century created a great many beautiful poems. Still, the poets of today are, in a way, their successors, and their poems are hardly read. This may admittedly be due to some universal decline of the cultural sophistication of the public. The cause, however, is more likely to be more specific. Would it be preposterous to surmise that it is linked with the increasing artificiality of poetry and that this artificiality is itself, in fact, an inescapable consequence of the new path chosen by the poets? Indeed, how could it be avoided if novelty is the *unique* criterion? And how, actually, could novelty be prevented in practice from playing the role of *the* sole criterion of choice when all those that would bring the poet back—be it even without his knowledge—to the more or less Platonic notion of "beauty, essence of Reality" have been discarded? Again, I am simply asking the questions here. I do not mean to answer them, not even implicitly. But I ask that they be considered, instead of letting taboos decide for us, within the collective unconscious of our selected set of vanguard thinkers.

With regard to modern art, it is possible to formulate questions similar to these but even more impertinent, considering the weight of the interests involved, for, chiefly since the end of World War II, modern art has been exacerbating a desire for novelty which, by itself, is commendable, but which is no longer so when it annihilates everything else. And in many instances, this tendency has led its upholders to present novelty no longer as just *one* essential criterion but as *the* unique criterion of value, thus efficiently preventing art buyers and the public from exerting any personal choice. For the *novelty* criterion embodies a complete and stony objectivity that forbids any flight whatsoever, as Valéry has already noted. For example, in order to know whether or not particular (extraordinary or, on the contrary, trivial) objects have already been exhibited, a comprehensive set of exhibition catalogues is clearly both necessary *and sufficient*! But here I attack (superficially, because of lack of space) a stately stronghold in which greatness and authenticity intermingle with fraud. Therefore, we must continue to wait before we will know which parts of it time will spare.[1]

Psychoanalysis emptied several abbeys, and this fact is easily accounted for. To the man who lives within himself—to the friar of the Imitation of Jesus Christ—beyond proximate reality, which he finds misleading, the existence of God is fundamentally obvious. Beyond sensory data, even beyond reason, God speaks to him in silence. It may schematically be said that the heart of the monk is sustained by that "obvious fact." But psychoanalysis attacks that very innermost stronghold. "That God"—it says—"that you believe you hear is merely your own ego, or a voice of your unconscious, or, otherwise stated, a resurgence of a tiny part of the vast flow of hidden affective data that have been stored within your mind from your earliest years. These voices of yours are quite literally your own—unfortunately, for your faith, merely your own!" Through this assertion, modern psychology appreciably contributes to making references to Being difficult and uncomfortable.

Hence, it is no wonder that even within Christianity—or at least its "advanced" segment—there is a movement to deemphasize—this is the least that can be said—the traditional references to any Being surpassing man. For most of the churchmen of today, the reference to Jesus takes precedence over the reference to the Father. For many Catholic or Protestant theologians, the human (rather than the divine) nature of Christ is

---

[1] Will it be, for example, art characterized by boundless abstraction and barrenness (a totally white, black, or grey square) imitating the soberness of a mathematical theorem? Or, will the public come to notice—in the very name of novelty!—that, in such instances, the model, in which soberness is both essential and difficult to attain, is far more beautiful than the image, in which that very soberness is, apparently, finally obtained just as easily as arbitrarily?

important. And, to a few of them—who are very much respected, particularly within the intelligentsia—this human nature is in fact the only true one, for they consider the concept of God to be, after all, undefinable and abstruse. For these theologians, the parable of the good Samaritan ultimately incorporates the whole essence of Christian religion.

Yes, but—some will say—such a dismissal of the notion of God, which both psychological and theological research perform, each in its own way, does not really undermine man's practice of referring to an external reality. What it disposes of—and that is fortunate—is merely the practice of referring to an erroneous concept of the said reality, which consists of viewing the latter as external to nature and in attributing to it some anthropocentric features. On the other hand—the same persons will say—science is at our disposal, and science refers to a reality independent of man, so much so, indeed, that it describes it in detail. Hence, it should not be said that the notion of a reality external to man is disposed of by present-day thinking. It should merely be said that present-day thinking views it in scientific terms.

Such a statement brings us back to physics. A few decades ago it could have been expatiated—as I have shown—without any mental reservations, and therefore with full assurance, even by men having an up-to-date knowledge of the results of scientific researches of that time. But this is no longer the case, as can, for example, be ascertained by reading the previous chapters of this book. Schematically summarized, the objection that ruins such a beautiful view is the following one. To consider science to be the only correct description of reality is a view that can be upheld—against the charge of arbitrariness—only if science is consistent, and, considering the interplay of its various parts, this means it should be unified. But unified by what principles? In all probability, by those that govern *simple* objects and the interactions of the latter, whence, by combining, the behavior of the complex objects can be derived. This means that unless we make use of great intellectual virtuosity—in the process of which the notion of Being again runs a serious risk of vanishing!—we can hardly conceive of any genuine unification of science except in reference to the principles of physics (we can, for example, easily imagine that biology might be deducible from physics: could we, conversely, seriously imagine that the behavior of the stars might be deduced from biology?). But then, if science really does describe a reality independent of man, is it not necessary that the basic principles of physics be expressible without any reference to the limits of human abilities with regard to action and observation? But this very condition—the condition of strong objectivity—is presently *not* satisfied by the principles in question.

What is more, almost all current investigations which aim at a deeper understanding of the first principles of physics point in the opposite direction. Again, they lead us more and more to formulate the principles in question with reference to two "operations" that are thought of as being the irreducible basic elements of the theory: the "state-preparation procedure" and the "measurement procedure." To be sure, many physicists can be found (and not all of them minor ones) who, generally speaking, still believe in the strong objectivity of physics. But this is merely an expression of faith. More precisely, it is an expression of the faith that "somehow these difficulties are minor ones and will be solved in due time." The distinctive feature of faith is that its upholders shun any analysis; and the reason why—in my opinion, at least—the belief in question deserves such a name is that the physicists I am referring to are at the same time unwilling to take an interest in the problem (since they consider it to be "minor") and unable to produce any solution to it that would withstand critical examination.

Thus, it must finally be granted that, because of its need to make ever more explicit use of the operationalist philosophy within the formulation of its own basic principles, science is now quite far from supporting the idea of a reference to the notion of independent reality, and that, in fact, it has done much to discredit this notion, a refutation which we have found to be a common feature to all the intellectual endeavors of the past hundred years in all domains.

At this stage of our analysis, it seems appropriate to note, at least schematically, the consequences this universal trend of contemporary thinking may entail with regard to the ethical problem of the nature of *values*. Generally speaking, a basic rule of the operationalist philosophy is, as we have seen, that any acceptable hypothesis must lead to testable predictions. A theory of the values constructed according to the norms of that philosophy must therefore comply with this rule. Right from the start, this requirement dismisses the traditional—but obviously unverifiable— hypothesis according to which human values result from some commandments of God or, more generally, from some call from Being. Indeed, the rule in question obviously dismisses from the start any explanation of the existence of values that would attribute to them an ontological status, that is, a status making them transcend phenomena. Under such norms, devotion to some cause, aspiration to freedom, and so on, are thus easily found to be notions that cannot refer to any goal that would surpass man, nor even to any *future* the concept of which would extend beyond that of the mere process of survival and development of our species, such as the one provided by natural selection. For, indeed, if we scan the whole range of living beings, starting with the simplest of them and going on to mankind, and if in the spirit of operationalism (or "behaviorism"), we deny any meaning whatsoever to what is not observable, then what we see gradually developing is just a set of physical systems that are more and more self-regulated, that are therefore more and more autonomous and memorizing (in the sense of the theory of computers), and that react in more and more specific and complex manners to external stimuli. Within such an analysis, there is no place where it would be necessary to introduce anything other than mere biological phenomena. Hence, according to the operationalist standards, any reference to any other concept must be dismissed. Then, to be sure, it follows that the notion of values cannot refer to anything other than biological phenomena.

If such a conclusion were really certain, if it were true that there is no rational way to escape it, then, to be sure, we would have to reconcile ourselves to it. But how uninspiring it is!

Up to this point, in a manner that has been clearly schematic, I have reviewed the symptoms of the gradual abandonment of the reference to Reality, and I have examined some of its consequences. Some of them were found to be positive, but others seem somewhat debilitating. What is more, it seems that this route has by now been fully explored. In the arts and in poetry, as well as in physics, we are presently quite far from the wonder once inspired by the great discoveries that accompanied the lucid and active conversion of the human mind to these novel ways of thinking. By now, these ideas are no longer novel and seem rather worn. Something else seems to be required. The very logic of the rejection of the old notions, namely the fact that this process makes novelty the supreme good, thus leads to the conclusion that we need something else. To be sure, such great intellectual perspectives are not to be found easily. Indeed, their discovery is incredibly difficult and cannot therefore be obtained by mere willing. But, while it is true that will is insufficient in this matter, it may nevertheless be a necessary component of success. At the present time, an exploration of the possibilities in this respect is, I think, to be wished for.

In this connection, I suggest—as has been seen in the foregoing chapters—a partial return to realism. More precisely, I suggest a search for a realism that takes into account the essential limitations that our present-day knowledge imparts to any attempt that aims at identifying Reality too strictly with phenomena. In fact, as explained in Chapter 9, what I propound is my concept of a veiled reality.

This name means, as I have said, that the reality it refers to is not exhaustively knowable by physics. The questions thus arise: "Is it unknowable? Or is it knowable in parts? Can it be explored by procedures differing from those of physics?" At this stage we enter a domain in which not only deduction is forbidden, but even reasonable conjectures become difficult to make, and must much too often be replaced by vague plausibility arguments. However, since neither intuition, nor any Great Book, nor conventional philosophy offers us any more reliable clue, such arguments should not be disregarded. On the contrary, it is, I think, quite essential to keep them in mind as soon as we try to go beyond day-to-day experience and construct an up-to-date comprehensive view, instead of just trying to piece together shreds of tradition that do not fit with one another.

Once more—as we have already done in some of the previous chapters—we must therefore try to gather the essence of the few ideas that can serve as guidelines in this difficult problem of Reality. If we skip all expatiation and shades of meaning, what remains is, I think, the following.

First of all, contrary to what is asserted by the positivists, and more generally by all those people who claim that the concept of Being (or of a Reality independent of man) is meaningless, such a concept of Being is useful, nay, even necessary. Indeed any theory that dismisses it suffers from an obvious weakness. In such a theory it is quite difficult, or even impossible, to account in any satisfactory way for the regularities of the observed facts—that is (according to this theory), for the *regularities* of the *impressions* that each of us thinks he extracts from some external world (from a world that, again according to the theory, partakes of the realm of delusions). Hence, in such a theory it is forbidden to inquire into the general cause of all these observed regularities. Consequently, the induction principle—which its upholders make use of just as much as anyone else!—is in fact just a matter of faith. In the most systematic positivism, where the existence of general entities is denied, we have to take many things on faith, for in this positivism there can be no principle of "induction in general." Here what we take on faith must somehow be *renewed* each time a new induction is made and, when we think about it, this really seems quite arbitrary.

Similar criticisms can be directed against the theories that assert that independent reality is a thing-in-itself, whose structures are either nonexistent or totally disconnected from observed phenomena. Both types of theories can, to be sure, try to account for the regularities in question as reflections of the consciousness of the observer and the structure of the consciousness in question. To some extent, this amounts to constructing a "realism of consciousness." However, the intersubjective agreement— the agreement between several subjects with regard to what they observe together—then requires an explanation.

Therefore, we see that it makes sense to take seriously the idea of structured independent reality, whose permanent structures would be mapped, at least in part, in man's mind, thereby accounting for the physical regularities that man observes. Far from being empty and superfluous, as has often been asserted, such an idea is, on the contrary, a reasonable one. To be sure, it does not solve all the problems by itself. It should even be acknowledged that it is not as efficient in that respect as "common sense" might assume. (For example, it does not really *solve* the induction problem. What makes us believe that the natural laws will not suddenly change? If this belief is based on our past experience, on what other grounds are we allowed to extrapolate it to the future, except, again, by an act of faith?) However, it still can be maintained that the idea of structured independent reality renders somewhat less arbitrary the postulates that open the way for a solution. (For example, with regard to induction, the act of faith just considered can be made *only once*.) Finally, the idea in question is not subject to the criticisms directed against metaphysical realism by the philosophy of experience and that are based on extrapolations of Gödel's theorem; for indeed, as we have said, such criticisms consist of showing that the Reality postulated by metaphysical realism cannot be known with certainty, and this fact is not denied by the veiled realism propounded here.

But if we take the latter standpoint—which, again, differs just as much from popular scientism as from the physical realism of Einstein, and also from conventional positivism—then our complete apprehension of all the basic problems of today is modified and revivified. With this notion, the contemporary human being will not be reduced to the sad condition of a pure technician or a pure juggler—of a *Homo faber,* so to speak—to which modern culture has been on the verge of bringing him. Through this conception, his full nature as *Homo sapiens* is given back to him, in the sense that he is no longer forced to interpret the nature he observes to be a mere reflection of his own human restlessness. For him, it then becomes quite essential to once again seek the correspondences that may exist between independent reality and the views he holds, even if these correspondences are uncertain.

It goes without saying that in such a quest we may not forget what we know. A correspondence that seems at first sight to be true but that some investigations have shown to be false cannot be retained. But we should not demand the opposite either; that is, we should not demand *proofs* in the scientific sense of the word. In a domain in which no proof of precisely this kind is possible, it would be giving way to the idiosyncrasy which entails the denial of the existence of anything whose existence one cannot prove. (Although this idiosyncrasy is widespread, it is quite objectionable. To consider just one trivial and quite partial analogy, should we positively state that no oil exists in places where no drilling can be undertaken?) To somewhat better express the standpoint that we advocate, let us say that it amounts to indulging in some tolerance even towards somewhat vague and rough ideas; ideas that can be enforced only by mere plausibility arguments, but of which, on the other hand, there exists no coherent refutation. Again, on the part of scientists, it would be a true professional kink to demand—in this domain—the degree of exactness and strictness to which their researches have accustomed them in other fields.

Under these conditions, the exploration of the set of possibly sound correspondences can be undertaken by again reviewing the various forms taken by the general discredit of all the references to Being that, as I have pointed out, is a characteristic feature of the culture constructed by our fathers and grandfathers, and by trying to see whether, under the assumption of (be it even veiled) realism adopted here, some of these forms of discredit are not perhaps exaggerated or unwarranted. Such a process leads us to first study the criterion of beauty. And, in particular, since it is with respect to mathematics that the basis for argument is strongest, the criterion of mathematical beauty.

With regard to pure mathematics, we have already noted our disillusionment (see, for example, Chapter 3). Whereas our ancestors considered pure mathematics to be a faithful mapping of Being, we have some good reasons for interpreting it to be either pure tautology or mere reflections of the structure of our own mind. However, at this stage it may be noted that the idea that our mind itself is, in this respect, not a very unfaithful reflection of Reality cannot be excluded. This view would indirectly restore some weight to the traditional (Platonic, in a way) view of mathematics. Unfortunately, no very convincing argument can be put forward in favor of this assumption, so that only the tolerance alluded to above can induce us to consider it acceptable. Moreover, the latter must be pushed to the extreme.

On the other hand, the situation on the side of mathematics as applied to physics is, I think, appreciably more favorable. To be sure, the structure of quantum theory forbids us, as we have seen, to consider the mathematical descriptions of the theory in question to be ontological descriptions. This, as may be remembered, was our basic objection to "Pythagorism." In fact, the mathematical descriptions under study are, strictly speaking, mere descriptions of *rules*—rules that govern the predictions of experimental results. Hence, they refer not exclusively to Reality, but, to a great degree, to our minds as well.

To be sure, this is entirely true, and therefore I cannot assert that the basic equations of quantum theory describe independent Reality *as it truly is*. But from this should it be inferred that these equations describe *only* the structure of our own minds? Obviously not! Such a conclusion does not follow. From the fact that the rules explicated by these equations refer to our own minds, it would be wrong and unwarranted to infer that they refer only to the mind and not at all to independent Reality (the concept of which we here postulate to be meaningful). For example, the equation of the hydrogen atom admittedly does not describe to us the intrinsic reality of such an atom. It merely allows us to calculate the energy values that can be observed when its excitation energy is measured, together with the various probabilities of the results of such a measurement (or of others that could be made in place of it). Shall I say, for all this, that this equation refers only to me and to other human beings? This would obviously be absurd, for it is clear that in some way the equation refers also to an environment which resists us, which is distinct from us, and which is common to all men. Though it is vague and unfortunately cannot be made more precise, I am nevertheless led to acknowledge that the structures of mathematical physics constitute at least a meeting place for *Being* and *man*, and that, in this respect, they reveal to the latter some—admittedly vague and mysterious, but nonillusory—perspectives towards the former.

Now that I have a rather strong plausibility argument at my disposal, I can perhaps venture to conjecture that the result can be extrapolated. The association of the observation of nature with a conscious activity of the mind has nonvanishing chances of leading to results that, mysteriously and most imperfectly, open vistas towards Being. This, again, I cannot prove. But since I have chosen "tolerance," it is enough for me to be able to disprove any alleged proof of the opposite assertion and to be able to base my opinion on the fact that I could ascertain its likelihood in at least one instance, which here is the one described above, in which, within physics, experimentation and theory are associated. Hence, I may perhaps take the liberty of looking down upon the present-day condemners of the "heavenly poets." Their argument to the effect of proving the naivety of the eternal search for truth within perceived beauty actually proves nothing at all. And the same holds with regard to the arts. Presumably, it would be better for us to consider as mere gadgets the ponderous theses that, in this domain, the allegedly "vanguard" pedagogy of so many official organizations set forth. In fact the latter do nothing other than endlessly expatiate these two familiar dogmas; one being that observation should be dismissed altogether and the other that any attempt to search for an enigma behind things should be totally abandoned. Now these two dogmas, which were new and fruitful half a century ago, rest on an idea which, again, has by now been fully exploited and which (according to its own logic) is out of date for that reason. The enigma in question actually exists or, more precisely, the idea that it exists, far from being childish, is, on the contrary, more likely to be true than false. Hence, to an artist, the search for that ultimate secret becomes beautiful and significant again, even though it is true that the secret will not entirely give way and that the painter, sculptor, or writer must therefore feel he is in the same relationship to it as Newton saw himself in relation to the outside world; admittedly an interpreter of the hidden, like a child discovering a few glittering shells on the seashore, who is confronted by an unexplored and mysterious sea.

Among the important consequences of the present-day rejection of the concept of Being, we noted above the influence this rejection—backed by psychoanalysis—has had on the evolution of religious thinking, which, at least within Christianity, has gone so far as to focus essentially on one *man,* considered at the same time to be representative and ideal. We have also noted the result of that rejection on the general conception of *values.* Though connected, these two subjects are quite distinct. With regard to the former, it is quite clear that one consequence, at least, of the rejection in question seems to be final: the archaic notion that is conveyed by the words "Lord" and "Almighty" will presumably never recover its full efficiency for lulling the ontological qualms of mankind. For a religious mind, turning towards Being should therefore become a subtler endeavor than was the mere acceptance of the heavenly will stated in the Bible, formulated by the priests, and exhibited by miracles. "Subtler," however, does not mean "meaningless." If, as I hope I have shown, the rejection of the notion of Being is just a transient idea, which was brilliant for a time but has already faded to some extent, then, assuredly, the quest for Being must be viewed anew as *a priori* reasonable. This is quite a basic point. From it, it follows that (contrary to the assertions of a number of theologians who consider themselves up to date) the parable of the good Samaritan—even though it still remains quite essential—can no longer be considered to summarize the whole content of the religions and the entire vague hope that they convey.

The—temporary!—rejection of the notion of Being will also have had presumably permanent effects on the ideas that man will from now on be willing to accept concerning values. Of course, this would not be the proper place for any thorough examination of the theory of the latter; the subject has been very much discussed and, due to lack of space, it could be sketched here only in an extremely schematic manner. Without going very much astray from the general subject of this chapter, we may however recall some of the main points of the problem. They correspond to the answers that can be given to two basic questions, which are (a) "Is *good* an objective or a subjective notion?" and (b) "What is good?" "Good," Aristotle would probably have said, "is just another name for God, which is itself nothing other than that towards which everything tends." Such a definition makes Good an objective concept. It may nevertheless be maintained that—to some extent—it refers implicitly to human beings, the latter being assumed, also implicitly, to be more or less in line with the general tendency of nature and to enhance its qualities. In this sense it may be said that the objectivity of the definition partakes, to some extent, of the *weak objectivity* on which contemporary physics is based. Such an appreciation is further strengthened by the remark that the notion of "tendency" entails a qualitative distinction between past and future, a distinction which, as we know, is almost foreign to the basic laws of physics. We can therefore speak of "that towards which everything tends" only if we identify the subject "that" of this sentence with *empirical* reality, that is, with a concept of "reality" similar to what Kant seems to have meant by this word, in other words, a conception that does not make reality independent of man.

The hedonistic definition of Good identifies it, as we know, with pleasure, and more precisely with that which, on the whole, gives the greatest amount of pleasure to human beings, while, at the same time, not being excessively unfair to any particular man. If the word "pleasure" is taken in its wider sense—incorporating the discipline that man willingly imposes on himself in view of a goal he considers beautiful (such as climbing a mountain or caring for the lepers)[2]—then such "pleasure" is just that towards which every man tends, and the hedonistic definition thus differs from Aristotle's merely by its restriction of the "everything" to mankind only.

Both definitions are interesting and useful. Due, in part, to the suspicion that today falls upon any concept linked with absolute Being, they have largely supplanted—in the mentality of our times—the archaic notion of

---

[2] It goes without saying that the pleasures of vanity and of action (glory, responsibility, and so on) *are* genuine pleasures.

Good, identified with conformity to the commandments of the supreme Being. When we consider the abominations that in the past proceeded (and still do in some places) from the archaic notion of Good, we must rejoice in this evolution and must consider the rejection of the archaic conception to be a stable attainment. It is this very attainment that constitutes the permanent effect—alluded to above—of the temporary rejection of the notion of Being.[3]

But, on the other hand, the definition of Good attributed here to Aristotle presents a few difficulties that can render it absurd in some contexts. If "that towards which everything tends" is a universal conflagration, it seems quite difficult to identify it with good. Admittedly, we could attempt to dismiss this objection by replacing "tend" by "yearn towards." But the element of subjectivity—and more precisely of desire—that is thereby attributed to the "everything" of Aristotle implies that a major postulate is then implicitly made with regard to the existence of a subjectivity of the whole universe, a subjectivity somehow similar to our own. If what is at stake is the universe as identified with empirical reality—and this, as we have seen, is the case—the least that can be said is that such universal subjectivity does not manifest itself in the combined data of physics and astrophysics.

With regard to the hedonistic definition, it is much less vulnerable than we commonly believe. To underestimate it would be a mistake. Quite impartially, however, we must note the fact that it is the object of a natural attitude of reservation (and sometimes even of aversion, but this then is quite often due simply to misunderstanding) on the part of a large number of serious men. If we try to analyze the causes of this attitude, we are led to acknowledge that indeed the hedonistic definition of Good, even when correctly understood, leaves some emptiness in the human soul. Such dissatisfaction can obviously be traced back to the fact that man is a "being of the horizons"; a fact, indeed, that must absolutely be kept in mind whenever mankind is studied. Somewhat more precisely, it seems that this dissatisfaction is presumably related in some way to the great frustration that man feels because of his confinement to time and because of the fact that, apparently at least, such confinement is absolute. Above, for example, the contemporary increased freedom of behavior was mentioned, which is a very direct result of the renunciation of the archaic definition of Good and the choice of the hedonistic one. Such an increase in freedom is, as we have stressed, quite positive. But all pleasures come to an end; and the trouble with any liberation is that no one frees us from the grip of time. Similarly, dedication to the welfare of other people does

---

[3] Dedication to some cause is a good thing if and only if the cause itself is good. In the hedonistic conception, dedication to the material and spiritual welfare of other people is therefore good. In the conception that identifies Good with submission to certain commandments, dedication to a cause is good only if the cause is in accordance with these commandments. Hence, the notion of dedication to a cause cannot alone constitute a basis for a definition of the Good.

not free us from time, since old age makes such dedication impossible. Hence, it is, in a way, a subtle refinement of hedonism to think about eternal Being and to live by such a notion. The priest, the monk, the anchorite, and others who dedicate themselves wholly to Being are, within our culture, the only people who—at least ideally—can laugh at time. However, their position cannot be considered to be merely an extension of the hedonistic philosophy, since in order to be effective, the reference to Being must go together with a genuine acknowledgment of its existence and preeminence. Good can then be defined only by reference to Being.

Ostensibly, we have moved far from physics. But can we really be removed from physics if it is truly as universal as we contend? In fact this science has a great deal to say on the concept of Being, as the foregoing chapters have shown. We have shown, in particular, that the only realist philosophies that are acceptable are far realisms; that is, conceptions in which independent reality escapes description by means of our usual categories and our familiar concepts. In particular the fact of the passing of time, which to us is quite familiar and which we tend almost unavoidably to consider as a basic reality, becomes, in the conception in question, a relative one that refers to the phenomena and not to reality itself.

If this is so, then there exist some assumptions that the physicist, even if he views them—according to his own criteria—as risky, cannot consider *absurd*. One of them is that every human being would have a possibility of establishing some kind of a link with Being. It is then up to him to discover the nature of that link. More precisely, it cannot be excluded that between every particular man and Being itself there exists a relationship that, while ineffable, is still describable in the least inappropriate way by the expression "a call from Being to man." If such a call exists, it is presumably naive—although hardly avoidable—to interpret it as a call to action, or to a task, or, more simply, as a call for accomplishment. In this, our naiveté may be comparable only to that of Thales when, lacking the adequate concept and even the adequate word, he pathetically identified (as we know) as plain *water* the physical reality—obeying general laws—of which he had introduced the abstract concept into human thought (thus founding science). For indeed, when we think of such "calls," we interpret our relationship with Being as embedded in time, whereas, like everything that relates to independent reality—or Being—such a relationship should in fact transcend time, at least in some respects.

Again, such assumptions are—this goes without saying—highly speculative. It seems quite impossible to prove that the (universally encountered) intuitions that, *a priori*, could be identifiable as such calls are not simply ascribable to genetic or psychological phenomena. The most we can claim is that, considering the necessity of taking the notion of far reality seriously—a reality existing beyond the frameworks of space and time, and prior to the object–subject separation—the assumptions in question are not absurd. No truly convincing argument exists that could prove their falsehood nor even—since we have discarded the positivist criteria—their meaninglessness. If they are true (tolerance principle), then they open the way to a third definition of the concept of Good and of values, this time based on strong objectivity, namely on submission to these "calls."

No immoderate use should be made of such a definition. It could too easily be used as a pretext for all kinds of arbitrary actions, and the authors of the latter could even quite candidly justify them in their own eyes by means of this definition. Therefore it seems inappropriate to make it a basis for a new scale of values, differing altogether from the one resulting, for example, from the hedonistic definition. The definition under study here should preferably be saved for contemplation or, otherwise stated, for the sublime, which implies that, without using it for appreciably modifying our preexistent set of values, we are free to read into it—without any risk of being validly contradicted—the true basis of these values. On this matter, as on many others, the positivist grin would be misplaced. Far from being immaterial, the choice of the general viewpoint on which we choose to base our accepted set of values is, on the contrary, quite essential. In fact, the emotional shades, and therefore the earnestness as well, that we attach to these values depend on such a choice, and therefore so does the degree of equanimity and even happiness that we can find in existence. As St. Francis first discovered!

It is on far realism that, as we have seen, any consistent realistic standpoint must be based. In the preceding pages, we noted the quite important changes that are brought about by the choice of such a standpoint in relation to the mentality that has today become the most widespread and which, in its depths, is associated with the rejection of the notion of Being. Conversely, if we seek plausible criteria that would make it possible to believe that a certain intuition, or a certain discovery, opens up (more fully than some others) vistas on Being, then it is natural to refer these criteria to the changes in question. A feeling, an idea, that awakens in me the same echo whether or not I have in mind the notion of an essentially *far* Being (far, I mean, with respect to our usual modes of thinking) has, according to these present views, only a faint chance of bearing upon anything beyond mere phenomena. This is the most general case, and, in particular, all positive science falls into this realm. It is only from a feeling or an idea that "sounds" quite different to me, according to whether or not I am attentive to the notion of such a Being, that I can expect that it will—perhaps—half-open a few perspectives on the latter.

If such a standpoint is adopted, then mathematical beauty—so often praised by the great mathematicians and by the great theoretical physicists—remains, in this respect, a highly valid criterion, notwithstanding the previously described shortcomings of Pythagorism. Indeed, as long as I merely strive to summarize (through appropriate mathematical formulae) a number of phenomena, the simplicity of the equations that

I may obtain will be quite unable to awaken in my mind an echo of the same intensity as the one that will arise if I consider that I can, by means of them, more closely approach a true knowledge of Reality as it is; or even if I merely feel I can hope to describe, in this way, relationships between *It* and man, in which *It* is mapped with some faithfulness!

But, here again, there is no reason to retain only *mathematical* beauty as a valid criterion. In fact, most human beings have many opportunities to apprehend natural or living objects which, at the level of the positive phenomena, have nothing special that qualitatively distinguishes them from things that are quite similar, but whose appearances nevertheless turn out to be "graceful"; graceful to the extent that if these spectators are ever so slightly familiar with the concept of Being and if no prejudice impedes them (such, for example, is the case of fresh minds not yet polluted by the media or by teaching), they feel bound to acknowledge that, indeed, under strange guises, an element of Reality lies hidden there. Here again, to be sure, many biological explanations are available which relate such an attitude of mind to the structure of *our* genes, hence, of *our* brains. But if the views described above are sound, there is no absurdity in the alternative standpoint that consists of seeing a genuine "recognition" of a Being hidden beneath things, or at least a reflection of it. Both views can be reconciled by adopting the theory of the microcosm. As we know, according to this theory, the brain and the human mind, which are among the most complex compounds in the universe, have preserved some structures that map those of independent reality (from which they stem) rather faithfully. The assumption is unprovable. It is nevertheless plausible to the extent that it accounts, schematically but simply, for a number of facts, such as the possibility of man applying his mathematics to observed phenomena.

What has previously been stated with regard to beauty can also be said about the sacred. To be sure, the sacred can be given a purely sociological explanation, just as the impression of beauty can be given a purely biological explanation. But this does not imply that either of these notions is thereby fully accounted for. If such were the case, we would not be far from the assertion that sociological explanations of scientific discoveries *fully* account for the latter. Obviously this is not the case. With regard to the sacred, we must therefore consider reasonable the idea that it might not be altogether vain to strive to reach Being beyond things this way. But, of course, such an idea is valid only if what is at stake is Being itself, not empirical reality. The idea of the sacred is thus partly opposed to history, which centers on concepts from everyday life. If it ever makes use of history, this can be valid only in the manner in which the physicists make use of models: in order to sketch—using our everyday language—some truths that are not literally expressible in that language. From this point of view, the fact that within our modern culture most of the servants of the sacred have made concessions to the fashion of the philosophies of history is particularly unfortunate. This might well be the present cause of the flight of many young people towards other spiritualities. But, beyond such ups and downs, we must focus on what is essential. The opening that the sacred conceivably gives towards Being is admittedly a conjecture. But so, in such a field, is any idea. Hence a moderate and nonliteral fidelity to the religion of their younger years is presumably, for those people who had one, the attitude of mind with which the risk is smallest of barring valid perspectives.

Finally, other facts might also conceivably open rather vague vistas towards Being. In particular, those related to care (Heidegger) should be mentioned, and also those such as mysticism, for example, that are associated with a weakening of the subject–object separation (Jaspers). But here we enter a dim field which many thinkers have tried to explore and about which physicists can add nothing to what philosophers have already said.

In conclusion, with regard to the question of the apprehension of Being—or of "reality," to use a more ambiguous and therefore, as we shall see, more inspiring word—the ultimate wisdom that physics can teach us is perhaps that we must focus our gaze, so to speak, on two planes at once, which just correspond to the two meanings the philosophers give to the word "reality." On the one hand, we must contemplate independent reality, Spinoza's *substance* or, more precisely (since actually our mind cannot behold that reality as it is), we must ponder the idea of reality. We must admire the source of phenomena, of beauty, and of values, and must aspire to join it, while knowing at the same time that reality is as inaccessible as the horizon. And, on the other hand, we must not fail to focus on the plane of empirical reality as well, while knowing that it *is* only empirical. In other words, we must always remember that its true nature is to be relative to the subject–object separation. The plane of empirical reality is that of things, of life, of evolution, and even of the universe. To attribute to it its true importance, its genuine "quality of existence," without at the same time identifying it with the ultimate horizon, is what constitutes the entire subtlety of this wisdom.

CHAPTER 14

Conclusions

The contribution of physics to the general system of knowledge is an essential one. Covering chemistry, on the one side, and cosmology, on the other, physics today is genuinely the science of all natural phenomena apart from life and consciousness. And, what is more, the exception concerning life may well be merely temporary. To all these phenomena physics gives, at least in principle, a unified description. Not that it can claim the ability to calculate all of them directly and in detail, starting solely from the most fundamental principles; but it has relays, so to speak, at its disposal, which are constituted by the macroscopic physical constants. Deduced, with the help of quantum theory, from four or five "universal constants"—not more—these macroscopic constants serve for calculating the detailed laws of macroscopic phenomena, by means of classical physics. With the help of this, and of some other stratagems, contemporary physics encompasses within a closely woven descriptive tissue the bulk of the phenomena that we observe and whose diversity is so striking. By means of its theories and equations, it establishes their mutual consistency and gives us methods for predicting almost all of them, statistically at least. Hence, it is doubtful that any thinker can validly construct a nonsuperficial and nonarbitrary conception of the world—and of the relationship of mankind with the world—if he knows nothing about physics or if he chooses to ignore it.

But is it enough merely to note the preceding, that is, the very general fact that the science in question can be said to account for all natural phenomena? This, if it were true, would entitle the thinker to quickly turn over a new leaf, in the same way as an individual who aims at forming nonsuperficial ideas about the architecture of a building can be content with quickly registering the fact that the *security* of the latter has been checked by competent authorities, a fact which, here, would correspond to disregarding any information bearing on the *foundations* of physics.

Such an assumption is simplistic, as we have seen. In fact, when the statement has been made that physics accounts for almost all phenomena, the main contribution of this science to basic knowledge has *not yet* been formulated. Indeed such a statement gives us only an oversimple view of the actual state of affairs. According to the thesis we uphold in this book, the truly basic contribution of contemporary physics is essentially contained in the dichotomy that this science, through its very foundations, seems to establish between Being and objects or between reality and phenomena. Being does not identify itself with the set of all objects. This truth, glimpsed by Descartes and by many other philosophers, can now, in light of quantum mechanics or of experiments bearing upon nonseparability, hardly be questioned anymore, even by the individuals who philosophically favor realism. It shows that the rationalists of the past were basically right on one point: the human senses, the experimental method, cannot, even when aided by theory, enlighten us with certainty with regard to *what really is*. What the rationalists had not foreseen—and could hardly foresee!—is that, in spite of this, the information that our senses provide, once suitably refined, scanned, and sifted by means of the scientific method, would prove to constitute a stable mathematically describable and almost entirely coherent set, the very set that we call "physics" and which enables us to obtain useful significant answers to all our operational questions.

But, indeed, this is precisely the situation now. The sensory data of various individuals generally converge in such a way that they can be described all together by means of a model which is realistic on the macroscopic scale and which is based on the notion of separable macroscopic objects. Presumably this circumstance constitutes the reason why mankind has elaborated a language essentially based on the concept of such objects. Again, constructed in this way, empirical reality is obviously not identifiable with Being, since the idea on which it rests, that of macroscopic objects, is a vague one and is itself definable only with reference to the community of human beings. Moreover, as soon as man's thinking leaves the domain of the macroscopic, he can no longer rely on the notion of separable objects and he can *only* predict the results of observations (even though he still does this wonderfully well).

If somebody cared to ask for the "why?" of these circumstances, we should not try to let him think that the answer is elementary. As in other similar cases, we should first of all remind him of the fact that cautious investigators generally reject those questions that are based on "why" instead of "how." If he nevertheless insists, we shall have to grant that a situation in which the entities introduced by the theory could be assumed to exist *by themselves,* quite independent of man (and to be just *observed* by him), would be a highly more satisfactory one from the point of view of intersubjective agreement. To try to return to the conditions of such a situation is to try to construct a realistic theory. And many physicists have embarked upon such a search with the results that have been noted. The results exist, but they are ambiguous. Several solutions are available which deeply differ from one another, and experiment—competent exclusively with regard to *empirical* reality—obviously cannot decide between them. All of them, however, share the common feature that they require Being itself to be nonseparable, and, again, this forbids us to identify.

it with the set of observed objects. More generally, the circumstances just recalled prevent any identification of intrinsic reality with the set of the mathematical entities of contemporary physics, since these possess the locality property (one-point functions). Still more generally, they throw unquestionable discredit upon all the conceptions of (intrinsic) reality that are based on *near* realism, that is, that aim at describing Being with the help of concepts borrowed from everyday life. This excludes the animists and the naively naturalistic descriptions just as much as those based on scientism.

Things being so, the solution put forward here is that of *far* and even *nonphysical* realism, a thesis according to which Being—the intrinsic reality—still remains the ultimate explanation of the existence of regularities within the observed phenomena, but in which the "elements" of the reality in question can be related neither to notions borrowed from everyday life (such as the idea of "horse," the idea of "small body," the idea of "father," or the idea of "life") nor to localized mathematical entities. It is not claimed that the thesis thus summarized has any scientific usefulness whatsoever. Quite the contrary, it is surmised, as we have seen, that a consequence of the very nature of science is that its domain is limited to *empirical* reality. Thus the thesis in question merely aims—but that objective is quite important—at forming an explicit explanation of the very *existence* of the regularities observed in ordinary life and so well summarized by science.

Once the certainty that Object is not identical to Being is acquired, it becomes possible to formulate the assumption according to which the concepts of object and of subject correspond to entities of comparable ontological status (and hence according to which it is meaningful to speak of an object–subject separation). If we remember the ever-increasing role intersubjectivity plays in the investigations aimed at increasing the strictness of the formulation of physics, we are even led to believe that such an assumption is, after all, a very reasonable one, in spite of the fact that it is vague and not easily formulated in a fully adequate way. But, of course, these deficiencies of the assumption in question are of less importance than would be the case if we proposed using it in some scientific context. We therefore proposed to take it up. The extensions of such a view were schematically studied, both at the philosophical and at the cultural level, and also at the level of the way in which each individual accepts the world, which is a more familiar matter, but one that is more important.

There is no disguising the fact that, according to these views, some mystery enfolds—and will continue to enfold—the notion of Being. This may look frustrating to some acute intelligences. But the frustration decreases when it is observed that the opposite assumption would have even more frustrating implications. For example, for twenty years physicists were quite excited by the beta-decay riddle, which was extremely difficult to solve. And then, suddenly, it *was* solved, and in a fully satisfactory way. All of a sudden this subject became uninteresting and dull, for there simply was no more to say about it. Fortunately, other problems arose. Metaphorically, we can thus put forth the idea that in choosing to remain far beyond our reach, Being is perhaps kind to mankind—and kind to each individual!

The thoughts contained in this book do not aim to convince anybody that without a detailed knowledge of physics it is impossible to form a valid world view. Fortunately, this is not the case. What, however, still seems true is that a total ignorance of the problems connected with the foundations of this science is a considerable disadvantage, at least if it extends so far as to encompass the very *nature* of the problems in question. For indeed such an ignorance leads to a choice of either one of two directions of research, both of which lead to dead ends. The first one consists of implicitly identifying ultimate reality with the set of all objects: this is the path followed by scientism. The other is a view of the world as an arena in which more or less magical forces oppose each other: this points to the path—still much more popular than the first—marked out by horoscopes and taken by naive naturalism. The fortunately quite widespread intuition that such descriptions of Being are childish too often generates either a generalized skepticism or a tendency to fritter away one's efforts in fragmentary fields of knowledge, the significance of which is inflated abusively. Or, again, it can lead to some *unreasoned* flight into one or another of the few established doctrines. While gaining a suitable knowledge of philosophy can sometimes help set things straight, it must be granted that, presently, what is available in that field makes such a solution quite hazardous indeed. The risk of being led astray is great.

The conclusion is that, after all, there seems to be no better path to truth than that which involves some—be it succinct—information about the problems concerning the foundations of physics. With account being taken of the considerable range of application of this science, both with regard to the description of phenomena and the construction of technologies, such a study—which also discloses, as we have seen, the ontological limits of this knowledge—is also one of those that provide the best opportunities for soundly appraising—without vainglory, but also without any misplaced contempt—the limits and the strength of serious thinking enhanced by action and factual observations.

Explicit Proof of the Theorem in the Case of Bar-Magnet Pairs

Let A and B be the measurement devices, the directions of which are labelled by the vectors **a** and **b**, respectively. Let us call *responses* the individual results noted by the experimenter in the manner explained in the text. When the angle between vector **a** and the north–south direction of a given bar magnet is acute (obtuse), let us conventionally say that the *projection* of this magnet along **a** is positive (negative). Finally, let $E_{ab}(++)$, $E_{ab}(+-)$, $E_{ab}(-+)$, and $E_{ab}(--)$ be the sets of all the magnets that are members of pairs undergoing measurements by means of A and B and the projections of which are, respectively, positive along both **a** and **b**, positive along **a** and negative along **b**, negative along **a** and positive along **b**, and negative along both **a** and **b**. Since the direction ("to the left" or "to the right") along which each magnet travels is independent of the direction of the axis of this magnet in space, each one of the magnets composing, say, $E_{ab}(+-)$ has a 50% change of traversing A and a 50% chance of traversing B. The number of magnets in $E_{ab}(+-)$ that traverse A is therefore (to within statistical fluctuations that can be made negligible) half the total number of magnets composing $E_{ab}(+-)$. (The same holds true with regard to the other three sets.) Such a magnet obviously "gives" a positive response. Its partner (the magnet initially associated with it within the same pair) traverses device B. Since, within any given pair, the projections along any direction of the two magnets composing it are opposite, this partner is an element of $E_{ab}(-+)$. Hence, it also gives a positive answer. The pair in question thus gives a doubly positive answer. It is then quite easily seen that to within statistical fluctuations the total number of pairs that give a doubly positive response is equal to half. the number of elements of $E_{ab}(+-)$ or, what amounts to the same, to half the number of elements of $E_{ab}(-+)$, since these two numbers are obviously equal.

The foregoing concerns the magnet pairs submitted to measurements by means of the A and B devices, but it can, of course, be repeated with regard to the pairs (in equal numbers) submitted to measurements by means of devices A and C and B and C. If these three samples of pairs are unbiased, the number of elements of, say, $E_{ab}(+-)$ is proportional to the numbers of magnets having positive and negative projections along **a** and

b, respectively, *in the total set of magnets.* Each of the latter has, along **c**, either a positive or negative projection. The argument developed in the text then shows that their number is smaller than, or at most equal to, the sum of the number of magnets in the total set that have positive and negative projections along **a** and **c**, respectively, and of the number of magnets in the total set that have negative and positive projections along **b** and **c**, respectively. It follows from this that the number of elements of $E_{ab}(+-)$ is smaller than, or at most equal to, the sum of the number of elements of $E_{ac}(+-)$ and the number of elements of $E_{bc}(-+)$. Now the latter is itself equal to the number of elements of $E_{bc}(+-)$ for the same reason as above ("head to tail" structure of the pairs). From the first part of the argument, it then follows that the number of doubly positive responses in the first series of measurements is necessarily smaller than, or at most equal to, the sum of the numbers of doubly positive responses in the two others. This is what was to be proved. Of course, in the case of the spins, the proof is valid only if the separability assumption is made, since the latter—or some equivalent one—turns out to be necessary for establishing the simultaneous existence of the components along **a**, **b**, and **c**.[1]

---

[1] In contradistinction to this, note that the supplementary assumption concerning the *direction of travel* (which is also used above) can easily be eliminated simply by substituting the "number of doubly positive answers" by "the number of doubly positive *and* doubly negative answers" everywhere.

APPENDIX II

The first model briefly sketched on page 86 bears the name of "Everett–Wheeler theory." [H. Everett, Rev. Mod. Phys. **29,** 454 (1967), J. A. Wheeler, Rev. Mod. Phys. **29,** 463 (1957)]. H. Everett, its main author, stressed the fact that his model is based on a real multiplication such as the one described in the text. (The universe actually *does,* when an appropriate measurement is made, split into two universes, one in which I am living and another in which I am dead.) He and other authors indeed considered this to be the key idea of the model. But other physicists rightly felt that such a thesis is somewhat ambiguous. For indeed the multiplication in question can obviously either occur or not occur. No intermediate case is conceivable. Hence, the model should specify in which cases it actually takes place. Now, it asserts that the multiplication takes place "in measurementlike phenomena." Therefore the model must specify which of the interaction phenomena are measurementlike phenomena. If it does this by referring to the observer—considered (because he is conscious) to be a physical system qualitatively differing from all other systems with which the measured system could have interacted—then nothing is gained in comparison with, for example, the conception subsequently mentioned in the text (Wigner's conception), which, moreover, has the advantage of being simpler. The model should therefore, in some other way, define the term "measurementlike phenomenon." *A priori,* some possibilities seem to exist (see Chapter 11, "the macroscopic diversion"). But to apply them to the present problem is difficult, and the conceptual hypotheses that would be necessary to accomplish this in a fully consistent way were never totally clarified.

A number of the physicists who perceived, at least to some extent, these difficulties nevertheless did not abandon this model. More precisely, they tried to retain what *in their eyes* was its main idea, namely, not actually the multiplication of Worlds, but the fact that the wave function never collapses. Therefore they insisted on speaking no longer of the multiplications of Worlds, but "simply" of multiplications of branches of the universe.

It is quite true that the (multidimensional) domain in which the wave function of a system has an appreciable amplitude can split, when time elapses, in two or more regions. Actually, this is admittedly what takes place in measurementlike phenomena and in a great many other cases as well, and, by itself, this does not give rise to any conceptual problem. Moreover, the splitting can be gradual and partial: no "yes or no logic" is implied here. But, on the other hand, if we want the model to have at least *some* relationship with experiment, we must grant that to the states of at least some of these systems or parts of systems, there correspond experimental data, hence, sensory impressions as well. Then let us assume that the measurement under study consists of looking at the signal light of some instrument, which is *on* in some branches of the universe and *off* in others. It is an experimental fact that, under such conditions, our sensory impression in the case of a measument is either that of a light totally *on* or of a light totally *off*. We then have two choices: *either* to the "I" who sees the light *on* there corresponds another "I" who sees it *off* and then a real multiplication of the "I"'s *does* actually take place, regardless of the language we use; *or* this is not the case. *A priori* both theses can be maintained. But they are not compatible. Between them a choice must be made. If, for the reasons stated above, we reject the real multiplication of the "I's," we must then grant that if, for example, my "I" sees the light *on,* this differentiates the branch or branches of the universe—or of the "wave function"—in which the light *is* actually turned *on* from those in which it is not. If the various "branches" of the wave function exist simultaneously (which is the initial thesis), it then seems that, after all, the clearest way of describing the version of the theory to which we have just been led entails abandoning (as too ambiguous and ill defined) the expression "branches of the universe." More precisely, it seems that this "clearest way" of speaking is to assert, on the one hand, that the wave function—with all its components—corresponds to physical truly existing "quantum" fields and, on the other hand, that, in addition to it, there exist other physical parameters, namely the states of consciousness of the observers or some physical variables that determine the states in question. As pointed out in the text, the version of the Everett–Wheeler model proposed here is ultimately more closely related to the supplementary variable models than to the basic idea of Everett and other authors who believe in a real multiplication of worlds.

It is somewhat regrettable that two models that are, after all, very different from one another should bear the same name ("Everett–Wheeler model") in the specialized literature. Apparently this arises from the fact that both of them are based on the same mathematical formalism and also from the fact that physicists have a natural tendency to attribute more importance to formal analogies than to differences bearing upon concepts. At any rate, this circumstance quite clearly shows the difficulty in trying to penetrate to the core of such views of the world. Philosophers are not qualified for such a task, for they lack the appropriate training. And physicists are not quite up to it either, for they are well trained in handling equations, but not so well trained in the analysis of ideas. This is why we must finally grant that this is a field in which obscure points still remain.

Glossary

Influence

This notion generalizes the notion of cause, and its definition meets with the same difficulties. Schematically, it can be said that the type of definition that tries to reduce these notions to that of regularity (in the sequences of events) ultimately turns out to be insufficiently specific for expressing what these two notions are actually supposed to mean. It is therefore necessary to resort to some other type of definition. Thus, if A and B are two repeatable events, A taking place before B, and if A is an event of such a type that can be initiated at will, it is possible to take the following statement as a definition: "It is said that event A causes event B if and only if B takes place in all cases in which A is initiated and only in these cases." The meaning of the expression "A influences B" (or, better, "A *appreciably* influences B") is then obtained by changing the strict correlations to statistical ones. It should therefore be stated that "*events A and B being of the types specified above, the event A (appreciably) influences the event B if and only if the frequency with which the event B takes place is (appreciably) different according to whether or not the event A is initiated.*" (The meaning of the word "appreciably" should be specified according to the specific situation being studied.)

One of the advantages of such a definition over the one based exclusively on regularity observations is that, concerning two series of events, with a definition of the other type, it is extremely difficult to express a distinction that, nevertheless, is a specific part of the concept of cause. This is the distinction—which obviously *must* be made—between correlations due to the fact that, individually, the events in one series cause those in the other series, on the one hand, and correlations due to the fact that the two correlated events are due to one and the same cause, on the other hand.

Strictly speaking it is, of course, in the sense specified by the definition italicized above that the word "influence" is to be understood in the present book. Correlatively, the notion of *event* must then be understood as including the creations of *definite—known or unknown—values* of physical quantities (in the sense specified in section 12.3). For more details, see Reference 13.

Intersubjectivity

See Objectivity (Weak).

Nonlocality

See Nonseparability.

Nonseparability (of a Complex Extended System)

(a) Impossibility of considering that a description of the complex system in question is literally true if this description represents the system as being composed of two (or several) subsystems all of which are localized in distinct regions of space and free from instantaneous or faster-than-light interactions with one another. Though such descriptions can quite often be indispensable, they must nevertheless be considered to be merely attractive images. (Thus, in general, two particles that have interacted in the past and that have not interacted since with any other system must, strictly speaking, be considered to be a "nonseparable" system, regardless of the distance between the locations where they will eventually be detected. In quantum mechanics, this corresponds to the fact that, in general, it is not possible under these conditions to associate a wave function with each particle individually. A wave function can be attributed only to the composite system.)

(b) Existence of interactions that allow for instantaneous or faster-than-light "influences" between localized parts of an extended system.

(a') and (b'): Same definitions as (a) and (b), respectively, but without the phrase "instantaneous or faster than light."

N.B. These four definitions are obviously not equivalent. For specifying, in some context, that it is one of the first two [(a) or (b)] that is meant, it is sometimes said that *Einsteinian* separability is violated. As far as basic principles are concerned, this violation is the one that raises the most arduous conceptual problem. It does so because of the fact that, within a realistic philosophy, this violation resembles a violation of a basic principle of relativity theory (often called the "principle of causality") according to which no *signal* can travel faster than light. With regard to this, however, it is essential to note (as has already been done in the text) that the faster-than-light influences mentioned here cannot be used to send any utilizable signal. Consequently, the existence of these "influences" does not invalidate relativity theory as long as this theory is understood along the lines of the *operationalist* philosophy. On the other hand, it must also be noted that even when nonseparability is defined by means of the less stringent (a') or (b') formulations, it still raises a serious difficulty concerning the *picture* we can form of the world. This, at least, holds true if, as indicated both by theory and by experiment, the strength of these "influences" does not decrease when distance increases; for obviously it then makes it impossible to raise to the level of strictly true statements the description of the universe made in terms of space-localized parts that can be conceived to be at least approximately isolated from one another.

Finally, it is another problem to know whether or not definitions (a) and (b) should be considered equivalent. It is a fact that they differ quite appreciably with regard to the language in which they are stated, since definition (b) implicitly assumes that it is meaningful to speak of the localized parts of the extended system under study, which is exactly what definition (a) denies. For this reason, some authors incline to call the two definitions (a) and (b) by different names. The choice of the word "non-separability" for designating definition (a) and of the word "nonlocality" for designating definition (b) may then appear to be the most convenient one, and indeed this choice is sometimes made (with various shades of meaning, depending on the authors) in the specialized literature. Non-separability would then somehow appear to be a property of independent reality and nonlocality would appear to be a reflection of nonseparability in the description made in terms of empirical reality, that is, in terms of localized events. Linked as it is with the notion of "influence" (see the glossary entry), nonlocality is thereby linked to the concept of events that can be initiated *at will,* and specifically, in fact, to that of measurement. Thereby, nonlocality turns out to be linked to the notion of the collapse of the wave function. Thus it may be difficult to define in some of the theories (see Appendix II) in which no such collapse is supposed to take place.

On the other hand, it should also be noted that at present no experimental criterion is available that enables us to distinguish between a "non-separable" and a "nonlocal" complex system in the senses just specified. Rightly or wrongly, some people may therefore doubt that the distinction between these notions is actually a meaningful one. It is to avoid taking sides in a semantic debate, whose importance does not equal its difficulty, that only one of these two terms has been used in the text.

Object

(a) Synonym of thing, pp. 13, 14, 21, 166. The object is here considered to be localized.

(b) A term opposed to that of subject (p. 167). Its meaning is more general here.

Objectivity (Weak) (Synonymous with Intersubjectivity)

Of a statement: A statement is weakly objective if it is supposed to be valid for *any* observer (see details on p. 58). A statement that is objective merely in the weak sense generally takes the form of a calculation rule.

Of a theory: If it contains statements that are objective but in the weak sense.

Objectivity (Strong)

Of a statement: A statement is strongly objective if it contains no essential reference whatsoever to the community of human beings (with regard to the meaning of the word "essential" in this context, see footnote p. 58).

Property (Synonymous with Attribute)

This notion is defined (see Chapter 12) either by means of the partial definitions method or by means of the method that makes use of the notion of *counterfactuality*. For the reasons stated in Chapter 12, it is in the sense defined by means of the second method that this word should be understood in this book. For more details, see Ref. 13.

Realism

This is the conception according to which the notion of "independent reality" (i.e., of a reality that would exist even if there were no human observers) is meaningful, and according to which such a reality does indeed exist. Realism opposes, in particular, the standpoint of the positivists of the Vienna Circle, according to whom only operational definitions are meaningful, and who conclude from this that neither the proposition according to which independent (they say, "external") reality exists nor that according to which it does not has a meaning.

Realism (Far)

This is the conception according to which not all the elements of reality are describable by means of concepts extrapolated from our everyday experience. Far realism can be *physical* (this is the case of Pythagorism and, in particular, of the philosophical standpoint within which classical general relativity is usually implicitly described) or nonphysical (this is the view ultimately taken in the present book, following a systematic analysis of the facts and of the theories of microphysics).

Realism (Near)

All the basic elements of reality are assumed to be adequately describable by means of concepts that are familiar to mankind or that can easily be extrapolated from such concepts. (Example: Democritian atomism.)

Realism (Nonphysical) (Synonymous with the Theory of Veiled Reality)

A conception according to which it is intrinsically impossible to describe independent reality as it really is, even by making use of nonfamiliar concepts such as concepts derived from mathematical algorithms.

Realism (Physical)

A conception according to which independent reality *can* be described as it really is, specifically by means of physics.

Reality (Synonymous with Independent Reality, Intrinsic Reality, Strong Reality, Reality in Itself, Being)

Quite obviously it is not possible to define *all* the terms of a language. Here, the notion to which the words *Being* or *existence* refer should be considered as primitive. Even a diehard idealist can hardly deny the fact that, at least at the moment when he considers the question, he himself somehow *exists*. And any attempt to define existence exclusively by referring to observation would constitute a vicious circle since the very notion of observation implies that an observer exists. On the other hand, it is of course quite another problem to know whether or not a certain concept we have formed corresponds to something that actually exists. It is still another problem to know whether or not it is meaningful to speak of something that would exist even if no human observer existed, and so on. The notion of independent reality is meaningful only if it is assumed that something would exist even if no observer existed. And it then labels the whole of the "something."

Reality (Empirical) (Synonymous with Weak Reality)

This is the set of all phenomena. This set is structured by means of a few simple laws which, under specified conditions, would in principle make it possible to predict phenomena, statistically at least. The analysis of the principles of modern physics shows, however, that these laws cannot all be stated using strongly objective formulations. We must therefore grant that empirical reality does not coincide with independent reality and that, quite the contrary, it is in fact in part a set of appearances or, in other words, that its structures depend in part on those of our own minds.

Reality (Physical)

An expression used mainly by Einstein and other upholders of physical realism (or by physicists who discuss the analyses of the latter). Definition: p. 130.

Veiled Reality (See Realism (Nonphysical))

References

1. J. S. Bell, Physics *1*, 195 (1964).
2. J. F. Clauser, M. A. Horne, A. Shimony and R. A. Holt, Phys. Rev. Letters *23*, 880 (1969).
3. *Foundations of Quantum Mechanics, Proc. Int. School of Physics Enrico Fermi*, Varenna, Italy, Course 49, Summer 1970, edited by B. d'Espagnat, Academic, New York 1971.
4. S. J. Freedman and J. F. Clauser, Phys. Rev. Letters *28*, 938 (1972).
5. J. F. Clauser and M. A. Horne, Phys. Rev. *D10*, 526 (1974).
6. G. Faraci, S. Gutkowski, S. Notarrigo and A. R. Pennisi, Lett. Nuovo Cimento *9*, 607 (1974).
7. J. F. Clauser, Phys. Rev. Letters *36*, 1223 (1976).
8. E. S. Fry and R. C. Thompson, Phys. Rev. Letters *37*, 465 (1976).
9. M. Lamehi-Rachti and W. Mittig, Phys. Rev. *D14*, 2543 (1976).
10. H. Stapp, Phys. Rev. *3D*, 1303 (1971); Nuovo Cimento *40B*, 191 (1977). E. Wigner, Am. J. Phys. *38*, 1005 (1970).
11. J. F. Clauser and A. Shimony, Report on Progress in Physics, *41*, 1881 (1978).
12. B. d'Espagnat, Phys. Rev. *D11*, 1424 (1975); Phys. Rev. *D18*, 349 (1978); *Quantum Logic and Nonseparability* in *The Physicist's Conception of Nature*, Reidel Dordrecht 1973; Scientific American, *241*, 158 (1979).
13. B. d'Espagnat, Foundations of Physics, *11*, 205 (1981).
14. A. Aspect, P. Grangier and G. Roger, Phys. Rev. Letters *49*, 91 (1982); A. Aspect, J. Dalibard and G. Roger, Phys. Rev. Letters *49*, 1804 (1982).

NOTE: This is a schematic bibliographical survey of the works concerning nonseparability and related topics. An extensive list of references on these topics may be found in Ref. 11. A few references concerning other problems appear as footnotes in the text.

Index*

---

* Italicized page numbers refer to footnotes.